Comics and the Senses

Attempts to define what comics are and explain how they work have not always been successful because they are premised upon the idea that comic strips, comic books and graphic novels are inherently and almost exclusively visual. This book challenges that premise, and asserts that comics is not just a visual medium. The book outlines the multisensory aspects of comics: the visual, audible, tactile, olfactory and gustatory elements of the medium. It rejects a synaesthetic approach (by which all the senses are engaged through visual stimuli) and instead argues for a truly multisensory model by which the direct stimulation of the reader's physical senses can be understood. A wide range of examples demonstrates how multisensory communication systems work in both commercial and more experimental contexts. The book concludes with a case study that looks at the works of Alan Moore and indicates areas of interest that multisensory analysis can draw out, but which are overlooked by more conventional approaches.

Dr. Ian Hague holds a BA in English from the University of Hull, an MA in Cultural Studies from the University of Leeds, and a PhD from the University of Chichester. He is the director of Comics Forum (http://comicsforum.org).

Routledge Research in Cultural and Media Studies

For a full list of titles in this series, please visit www.routledge.com

25 **International Journalism and Democracy**
Civic Engagement Models from Around the World
Edited by Angela Romano

26 **Aesthetic Practices and Politics in Media, Music, and Art**
Performing Migration
Edited by Rocío G. Davis, Dorothea Fischer-Hornung and Johanna C. Kardux

27 **Violence, Visual Culture, and the Black Male Body**
Cassandra Jackson

28 **Cognitive Poetics and Cultural Memory**
Russian Literary Mnemonics
Mikhail Gronas

29 **Landscapes of Holocaust Postmemory**
Brett Ashley Kaplan

30 **Emotion, Genre, and Justice in Film and Television**
Detecting Feeling
E. Deidre Pribram

31 **Audiobooks, Literature, and Sound Studies**
Edited by Matthew Rubery

32 **The Adaptation Industry**
The Cultural Economy of Contemporary Literary Adaptation
Simone Murray

33 **Branding Post-Communist Nations**
Marketizing National Identities in the "New" Europe
Edited by Nadia Kaneva

34 **Science Fiction Film, Television, and Adaptation**
Across the Screens
Edited by J. P. Telotte and Gerald Duchovnay

35 **Art Platforms and Cultural Production on the Internet**
Olga Goriunova

36 **Queer Representation, Visibility, and Race in American Film and Television**
Melanie E. S. Kohnen

37 **Artificial Culture**
Identity, Technology, and Bodies
Tama Leaver

38 **Global Perspectives on Tarzan**
From King of the Jungle to International Icon
Edited by Annette Wannamaker and Michelle Ann Abate

39 **Studying Mobile Media**
Cultural Technologies, Mobile Communication, and the iPhone
Edited by Larissa Hjorth, Jean Burgess, and Ingrid Richardson

40 **Sport Beyond Television**
The Internet, Digital Media and the Rise of Networked Media Sport
Brett Hutchins and David Rowe

41 **Cultural Technologies**
The Shaping of Culture in Media and Society
Edited by Göran Bolin

42 **Violence and the Pornographic Imaginary**
The Politics of Sex, Gender, and Aggression in Hardcore Pornography
Natalie Purcell

43 **Ambiguities of Activism**
Alter-Globalism and the Imperatives of Speed
Ingrid M. Hoofd

44 **Generation X Goes Global**
Mapping a Youth Culture in Motion
Christine Henseler

45 **Forensic Science in Contemporary American Popular Culture**
Gender, Crime, and Science
Lindsay Steenberg

46 **Moral Panics, Social Fears, and the Media**
Historical Perspectives
Edited by Siân Nicholas and Tom O'Malley

47 **De-convergence in Global Media Industries**
Dal Yong Jin

48 **Performing Memory in Art and Popular Culture**
Edited by Liedeke Plate and Anneke Smelik

49 **Reading Beyond the Book**
The Social Practices of Contemporary Literary Culture
Danielle Fuller and DeNel Rehberg Sedo

50 **A Social History of Contemporary Democratic Media**
Jesse Drew

51 **Digital Media Sport**
Technology, Power and Culture in the Network Society
Edited by Brett Hutchins and David Rowe

52 **Barthes' *Mythologies* Today**
Readings of Contemporary Culture
Edited by Pete Bennett and Julian McDougall

53 **Beauty, Violence, Representation**
Edited by Lisa Dickson and Maryna Romanets

54 **Public Media Management for the Twenty-First Century**
Creativity, Innovation, and Interaction
Edited by Michał Głowacki and Lizzie Jackson

55 **Transnational Horror Across Visual Media**
Fragmented Bodies
Edited by Dana Och and Kirsten Strayer

56 **International Perspectives on Chicana/o Studies**
"This World Is My Place"
Edited by Catherine Leen and Niamh Thornton

57 **Comics and the Senses**
A Multisensory Approach to Comics and Graphic Novels
Ian Hague

Comics and the Senses

A Multisensory Approach to Comics and Graphic Novels

Ian Hague

Routledge
Taylor & Francis Group
LONDON AND NEW YORK

First published 2014
by Routledge

2 Park Square, Milton Park, Abingdon, Oxfordshire OX14 4RN
711 Third Avenue, New York, NY 10017

Routledge is an imprint of the Taylor & Francis Group, an informa business

First issued in paperback 2018

Library of Congress Cataloging-in-Publication Data

Hague, Ian, 1986–
Comics and the senses : a multisensory approach to comics and graphic novels / Ian Hague.
pages cm. — (Routledge Research in Cultural and Media Studies ; 57)
Includes bibliographical references and index.
1. Comic books, strips, etc.—History and criticism. 2. Graphic novels—History and criticism. 3. Senses and sensation in literature.
I. Title.
PN6710.H27 2013
741.5′9—dc23
2013020354

ISBN: 978-0-415-71397-9 (hbk)
ISBN: 978-1-138-54839-8 (pbk)

Typeset in Sabon
by Apex CoVantage, LLC

Contents

Illustrations

Note

Sections of this book have appeared, in a different form, in the following publications:

Hague, Ian. 2010. 'Beyond the Visual—The Roles of the Senses in Contemporary Comics'. Edited by Ralf Kauranen, Erin La Cour, Rikke Platz Cortsen and Fredrik Strömberg. *Scandinavian Journal of Comic Art* 1 (1): 96–110.

Hague, Ian. 2013. 'A Defining Problem'. In *Comics & Politik—Comics & Politics*, edited by Stephan Packard. Bochum, Germany: Christian Bachman.

Acknowledgements

Since beginning work on this book I have been immensely lucky to have been supported by a wonderful group of people and institutions.

My former PhD supervisor, Dr Hugo Frey, has been endlessly patient and helpful, and offered guidance but not interference, something for which I am very grateful. The University of Chichester provided me with a bursary for three years and additional funding to attend conferences, without which I would not have been able to undertake the research presented here. I must also thank the staff of Chichester's history department for their continuing support of my research and the new perspectives they encouraged me to take. A huge thank-you also to: Carolene Ayaka, Helen Hester, Chris Jannides, Soozi Mead, Bethany Simmonds and Steve Smith.

Over the course of writing I have also been privileged to encounter numerous individuals whose assistance in developing my ideas has been critical to the success of this project. Many thanks to, among others: Bart Beaty, Robert Duggan, Randy Duncan, Mel Gibson, William Grady, Paul Gravett, Kirstie Gregory, Simon Grennan, David Huxley, Fabrice Leroy, Chris Murray, Ernesto Priego, Julia Round, Roger Sabin, Joe Sutliff Sanders and Lisa Wood.

I must also thank a brilliant group of friends, without whom I would certainly not have completed this book. For all the help you gave, thank you: Dave Bentley, Laura Corbett, Alex Crisp, Julia Marsh, Hannah Mattacks, Richard Matthews, Hayleigh Nash, Megan Parsons, Nicki Bailey, Helen Graham, Claire Smith, Ollie Suckling, Chris Todd, Richard Tomlinson and Michelle Welbourn.

I am very grateful to my parents, Alan and Katharine, and my sister Jill, all of whom have been a constant source of support throughout my education and have given me the capabilities I needed to pursue my dreams, however challenging.

Finally, a huge thank you to Hannah Wadle; you are my blue sky.

Introduction

In recent years there has been a considerable surge of English language scholarship on the medium of comics. Where academic attention to comics was once confined to a sporadic output of journal articles and occasional special issues, along with a small number of books (often, but not always, written by fan-scholars or creators as opposed to institutionally situated academics), we now have a significantly more well-developed field.[1] This is not to belittle the contributions of those early writers, many of whom are rightly considered among the pioneers of the field, but rather to point out that in its earliest incarnations comics scholarship was far from being a coherent and structured entity. While Roger Sabin has persuasively argued that British scholarship on the medium goes back at least as far as Elizabeth Pennell's 1886 article 'The Modern Comic Newspaper', and Thierry Groensteen has noted that Rodolphe Töpffer's 1845 *Essai de physiognomonie* 'initiated the theorization of this new form of storytelling', it is only more recently that the field of comics scholarship has begun to take on a more organised feel.[2] In fact, it was perhaps not until the publication of the first issue of *The International Journal of Comic Art* (*IJOCA*) in 1999 (or possibly *Inks: Cartoon and Comic Art Studies*, which ran 1994–1997) that the idea of comics scholarship *as* a field came into being. Although publications such as *The Comics Journal,* founded in 1977, had gestured towards a higher level of research and engagement than had been presented by the fanzines that preceded it, *IJOCA*'s more definite focus on scholarly research gestured beyond the limits of highbrow criticism and into the realm of formal academic study. *IJOCA* set important precedents and offered a sense of longevity and community to comics scholars (rather than fans *per se*) that was unparalleled at the time of its launch.

The International Journal of Comic Art has not remained the lone voice of comics scholarship. The year 2000 saw the launch of the online journal *Image [&] Narrative*, with *ImageText* (also online) following in 2004, *Mechademia* in 2006, *European Comic Art* in 2009, *Studies in Comics* and *The Journal of Graphic Novels and Comics* in 2010 (the last four titles in that list are available in print and online), *The Comics Grid* (online) and *The Scandinavian Journal of Comic Art* (online) in 2012. There has also been a shift towards establishing more rigorous scrutiny, with all the journals listed here operating some form of peer or expert editorial review (blind or otherwise). While quality is of course preferable to quantity, the plethora of titles being published, and the variety of subjects they cover, is an encouraging sign of both the growing strength of the field of comics scholarship and its sustainability. Rather than being a transitional moment that is likely to pass, the launch and continuation of ongoing, high-quality journals is indicative of an increasingly established area of study that is beginning to develop a stable infrastructure. The substantial comics-related output of the University Press of Mississippi, which has published a number of major works on the medium, and translated into English what is probably the most important and influential book on comics of the last ten years, Thierry Groensteen's *The System of Comics* (*Système de la bande dessinée*) further contributes to the sense of stability within the field. Outside the publishing arena, regular conferences on the subject around the world, and the launch of academic courses on comics that approach the medium from a variety of angles, are further signs that the subject is beginning to develop a level of maturity within the academy that exceeds what it had in the past.[3]

Of course it is wise to be wary of overstating the matter. As Chris Murray, the leader of the UK's first MLitt in Comics Studies, which was launched at the University of Dundee in 2011, told me in an interview: 'I don't know if there's going to be a great rush in the next couple of years to bring forth an undergraduate comics degree, but I hope there is and I think that will come in time'.[4] Nevertheless, it is clear that both comics *scholarship* as a general field taking in all scholarly works on comics and Comics Studies as a more defined discipline with a specific focus on the medium and its own operational principles are coming into clearer focus than has previously been the case. If the first 154 years of its existence were comics scholarship's childhood, then the launch of *IJOCA* perhaps marks the beginning of its adolescence. With that adolescence come the questions that confront everyone as they make the difficult transition from infancy to maturity. Questions of identity and purpose now confront the field more directly than ever before. As the self-indulgent concerns of fan scholars give way to more academic research, the subject of comics scholarship must also shift away from personal interests elaborated into scholarly discourse, and towards a consideration of what is genuinely important, even necessary, in the field. This type of shift is likely to be driven, at least in part, by political concerns, as Roger Sabin noted in an interview in 2011:

> […] in the future, I think we're going to see many more political battles, and also, possibly, a shift in the kind of comics research being pursued. I'm not saying textual analysis will die, or anything as dramatic as that, but merely that things like the study of comics' use in schools, in the military, in hospitals, etc. will move more to the centre as the impact agenda takes hold.[5]

While Sabin's remarks are very specific to the context in which they were being made, and relate strongly to the growing significance of impact as a measure for the value of research in the UK higher education sector prior to the 2014 Research Excellence Framework exercise, they do indicate some of the influences that are at work upon the field of comics scholarship. Thinking more broadly, though, the maturation of the field will necessitate a period of self-examination and self-reflection that seeks to understand what Comics Studies does. This is not to say that all comics scholarship will or even should endeavour towards "functional" research that fits neatly into administrative definitions of impact; rather that it must determine what it can do well, what its most potent and valuable contributions are, and how these can best be communicated. Although this may not be an easy process, it is far from an impossible one, and as the most significant works in the field so far demonstrate, the study of comics *can* make major contributions to our understandings of culture, media and society. Texts such as Ariel Dorfman and Armand Mattelart's *How to Read Donald Duck: Imperialist Ideology in the Disney Comic* and Martin Barker's *Comics: Ideology, Power and the Critics*, both of which made significant contributions to cultural theory in a general sense, are two particularly obvious examples of this type of work, but they are far from the only ones.

Over the course of this book, I will seek to contribute to this process of examination and reflection by presenting an argument for a reconsideration of the *object* of comics scholarship. Following the lead of thinkers such as Roger Sabin, Mel Gibson, Charles Hatfield and Ernesto Priego, I will emphasise that materiality matters. I will also go further, and challenge the idea that comics are a purely visual medium, arguing that they are in fact possessed of a wide variety of properties that address themselves to readers' senses of hearing, touch, smell and in some instances taste as well. The context for and premises of this argument are laid down in a broad sense in chapter 1, in which I draw a distinction between two major 'projects' in comics scholarship: the definitional project and the mechanical project. The former, which aims to answer the question, 'What is a comic?', has to a large extent conditioned the latter, whose intention is to understand how comics work. I suggest that this has resulted in the essentialist qualities found in definitions being transferred into the mechanical project, and consequently to an understanding of the mechanics of comics that incorrectly assumes the fundamental components of comics to be the only relevant ones in determining how the medium works. As sociological studies and the published remarks of comics readers and creators have demonstrated, however, this is not the case, and there is a variety of factors that are actively engaged in the making of meaning in the medium. I argue that the notion that comics are inherently and/or exclusively visual (and therefore that only their visual elements are meaningful) is unsatisfactory because it does not account for the myriad multisensory aspects of comics.

Chapters 2–5 seek to consider these aspects through a discussion of comics in terms of the five Aristotelian senses: sight, hearing, touch, smell and taste. Each chapter takes one of these senses (with the exception of chapter 5, which discusses both smell and taste) and elaborates a range of techniques and technologies that allow the medium to communicate in what is truly a multisensory fashion. Nevertheless it is worth acknowledging that the model employed here is in some senses very limited, as David Howes makes clear: 'A conservative estimate would put the number of senses at 10, but it is generally accepted that our senses number 21, and radical estimates put the number as high as 33'.[6] There are two major reasons why I have elected to stick to the classical model throughout this text. The first is that many of the models that propose a larger number of senses derive their notions of what these additional senses are from breaking down one of the classical five senses into smaller and more limited systems. For example, the sense of sight might be broken down into two senses: light and colour (this is a generally accepted idea) or even into four: light, red, green and blue senses (this is more radical).[7] There are also arguments for some senses that are not subsets of the five classical concepts, such as chronoception (the sense of time) and equilibrioception (the sense of balance). While I do find this more precise differentiation between the senses useful, I have not opted to employ it here because (a) the alternative models of the senses are still somewhat contentious and shifting, so to commit to one larger set of senses may not turn out to be any more useful than committing to a small one in the longer term given that the boundaries of the senses I selected may well shift again, and (b) talking about the senses as five broader categories does not eliminate the possibility of discussing more specific aspects of those senses, and some of the more refined versions of the senses are discussed here. In chapter 2, for example, I talk about light (section 2.2) and colour (section 2.3) but do so under the broader category of sight. Similarly in chapter 4, I discuss temperature (thermoreception), but subsume it under the broader category of touch rather than affording it a chapter of its own. While this bundling together of the senses may not be to everyone's satisfaction, I believe it is a sensible approach to keep the discussion manageable. The second reason I have not engaged so explicitly with the broader sensory spectrum is that this book is intended as a foundational text that serves to set sensory theory in a dialogue with comics scholarship. It is not supposed (and does not pretend) to be the last word on multisensory elements of comics. There is plenty of scope for further additions to be made to the observations presented here, and it is not difficult to see that one of the ways in which multisensory theories of comics may develop is through a further refinement of the senses under discussion. Here, though, I offer a general introduction to the subject.

In chapter 2, the first of the four chapters devoted to the five Aristotelian senses, I further develop the discussion of ocularcentrism that I undertook in chapter 1 through an outline of the concept of the ideal perspective.[8]

I argue that this mode of understanding, which treats the comic's page as an idea rather than a material object, is implicit in most criticism and scholarship on the medium. For this reason it can be argued that it is not only sight but a particular mode of "seeing" that is the prevalent means of understanding and analysing comics. The remainder of chapter 2 engages sight as a physical, rather than conceptual, process and outlines the ways in which comics work to stimulate that sense. I present a number of visual phenomena and processes (glossiness, accommodation) as well as visually affective techniques (bleeding, puzzle pages, colouring, anaglyphs). Rather than simply seeking to attack the ideal perspective, what I intend in presenting such a selection is to suggest productive possibilities by which the sense of sight might be incorporated into comics scholarship in a more holistic fashion through a better understanding of it and a greater emphasis upon the temporal nature of the experience of comics reading. In particular, I seek to indicate through the processes discussed here that comics are not simply static objects that can be considered from an atemporal perspective. They change and are changed over time, modifying the space they occupy as they are being read. The reading of a comic, I argue, constitutes a performance (a term which has previously been applied to comics by Bart Beaty, Annalisa Di Liddo and Jennifer Worth, albeit in different ways to how I use it here).

Chapter 3 provides a detailed discussion of existing approaches to sound in comics and establishes a distinction between imagined and perceived sounds. The former, I would argue, are the primary focus of existing writing on the medium, but the latter (which is the only one of the two to actually stimulate the ears) has much to offer as well. They can work to involve the reader with the comic as an object, and to constitute a complex diegetic environment that addresses the reader in a multiplicity of registers. They embed temporality within the comic in a way that no other sensory stimulus could, and they generate powerful emotions and connections that go beyond what is possible through visual elements. Over the course of the chapter I consider the role of hearing in comics by outlining the sounds of, in, with, as and around comics.

Chapter 4 moves on to consider the sense of touch, and endeavours to present a more nuanced discussion of touch in relation to comics than has previously been put forward. I begin by outlining the dualistic mode of understanding that is currently applied to the sense, which treats touch either as a taboo or as a fetish. Neither approach, I would suggest, is particularly desirable in the long term given the increasingly complex tactile experiences we are being presented with in comics of both printed and digital varieties. I subsequently break the discussion down into two major parts, which I see as the constitutive elements of the tactile experiences of comics. The first of these derives from the physical properties of the comic itself, and the conditions in which those properties exist. These are the aspects that we can look for in most if not all comics, and which regulate what it is possible for us to feel when we touch a comic: the materials of its composition, their textures, hardness, flexibility, weight and temperature. The second section of the chapter considers the ways in which these aspects are brought into play through the act of reading the comic and the modification of the object over time.

Chapter 5 discusses the two remaining senses: smell and taste. Although these senses are difficult to study due to their strong links to emotion and memory, there are certain elements that are amenable to scholarly discussion. Like hearing, smell and taste are strongly connected to time, but where hearing has a tendency to enforce duration in a work (sounds must be played at certain speeds), smell and taste subvert duration and linearity. They deny us the possibility for a clear, logical path forward because they pull us backwards into our memories. In some instances, comics creators have become aware of these elements, and use them very effectively to challenge or intervene in our memories. Like sounds, the smells and tastes involved in comics can come from a variety of sources, and in some cases creators implicate the reader very strongly in the production of this multisensory experience. Recipes, adverts and even scratch and sniff systems all involve the reader in producing, in *performing*, the comic to a greater degree than we might otherwise expect, and all emphasise that the reader is more than a passive receiver of information.

Finally chapter 6 takes the works of one particular comics creator, Alan Moore, and considers the ways in which Moore makes use of materiality to express stories that engage a number of the reader's senses at the same time. Among other examples, I consider his employment of sound and hearing in *V for Vendetta*, the ways in which he plays with the material form of the comic book in *Promethea* and his manipulation of the reader's sense of sight using 3D glasses in *The League of Extraordinary Gentlemen: The Black Dossier*. The overall aim of this chapter is not to provide a complete multisensory analysis of Moore's *oeuvre*, but rather to suggest the new areas that multisensory analysis is capable of opening up and to demonstrate the value of repositioning comics as a medium that engages more than the reader's sense of sight in communicating ideas. Additionally, I aim to emphasise here that the multisensory understanding I am arguing for can be applied to any comic; it is not restricted to special or experimental works. Although some of Moore's comics do use unusual physical formats or devices (e.g., *The League of Extraordinary Gentlemen: The Black Dossier*) others make use of standardised comic book formats to generate powerful material effects (e.g. *Promethea*). This is something I aim to make clear throughout chapters 2–5 as well by drawing on a wide range of examples from a variety of artistic and commercial traditions. Materiality and the sensory elements of comics are not the sole purview of a select number of fringe texts; they sit firmly within the realm of "normal" comics as well, although they may be more noticeable in works that exploit them overtly. In this writing I have tried to focus on those comics and creators whose works bring the greatest value to an explanation of multisensory analysis, and which enable me to most fully explore the strengths and weaknesses of this approach.

Ultimately the intention of this book is not to undermine existing scholarship on comics but to expand it; to indicate that there is more to the medium than words and pictures, that our objects of study are more numerous than we might initially assume. In this regard it is an assertion that as Comics Studies becomes more stable and formalised, it is unwise to narrow our vision too far (or indeed to rely solely on vision at all), because to do so underestimates the creativity of creators and readers and understates the sheer variety of processes that go into the production and reception of comics. Rather, we ought to retain a view on the whole experience of comics reading, and an awareness of the reader as a physical being, not just a theoretical concept. Readers do not interact with comics through their eyes alone; their whole bodies are involved in the *performance* of the work. The physicality of comics, their embodiment, is a crucial element of what they are and what they can be; how they do work, and how they could work. Given the awareness of the physicality of comics that is frequently demonstrated by their producers and consumers, this is something we cannot afford to forget. The question now is not so much *whether* these factors will be incorporated into comics scholarship, but *how*.

A secondary aim of this text is to bring comics scholarship into a productive dialogue with the field of sensory theory, which has experienced substantial growth in disciplines including History, Anthropology and Media Studies in recent years as scholars become increasingly conscious of the significance of the senses (although it should not be inferred from this that sensory theory is a totally new field). Key recent works in the area would include Berg's Sensory Formations Series, which includes titles such as *Visual Sense: A Cultural Reader* (2008, eds. Elizabeth Edwards and Kaushik Bhaumik) *The Auditory Culture Reader* (2003, eds. Michael Bull and Les Back), *The Book of Touch* (2005, ed. Constance Classen), *The Smell Culture Reader* (2006, ed. Jim Drobnick) and *The Taste Culture Reader: Experiencing Food and Drink* (2005, ed. Carolyn Korsmeyer) among others. Thinking more specifically of approaches to media and the senses, particular progress has been made in developing sensory theories of film, with scholars such as Vivian Sobchack, Laura U. Marks, Tarja Laine and Thomas Elsaesser and Malte Hagener producing important works in the field, some of which I cite in this study. As I have discussed elsewhere, however, while there are some similarities between comics and film, they are far from interchangeable media and there are substantial differences between them as well.[9] Thus, while a multisensory theory of comics may draw some ideas from sensory approaches to film (and indeed contribute ideas to the study of film as well) it must necessarily develop along its own path, drawing upon the theoretical bases of comics scholarship in doing so. It is this path that I endeavour to chart in the chapters that follow.

NOTES

1. For more on early comics scholarship see the collection of articles under the title 'There at the Beginning: Early Days of Comics Scholarship' in *The International Journal of Comic Art* 4.1 and the 'Pioneers of Comic Art Scholarship Series' in numbers 5.1, 5.2 and 7.1 of the same journal. Martin Barker's article, 'Kicked into the Gutters: or, "My Dad Doesn't Read Comics, He Studies Them"' is likely to be of particular interest to readers of this book. 'In Focus: Comics Studies: Fifty Years After Film Studies' (ed. Bart Beaty) in *Cinema Journal* 50.3 is also an excellent introduction to the history and debates surrounding the study of comics.
2. Sabin, Roger. 2009. "Mavericks and Zinesters: Comics Scholarship in the UK before 'Comics Scholarship.'" *Possibilities and Perspectives: A Conference on Comics*. Leeds, UK; Groensteen, Thierry. 2007. *The System of Comics*. Translated by Bart Beaty and Nick Nguyen. Jackson, MS: University Press of Mississippi. 1.
3. For more on the changing situation in the United Kingdom see: Huxley, David. 2011. *A Dazzling Lack of Respectability: Comics and Academia in the UK: 1971–2011*. Edited by Ian Hague. July 29. Accessed October 4, 2011. http://comicsforum.org/2011/07/29/a-dazzling-lack-of-respectability-comics-and-academia-in-the-uk-1971—2011-by-david-huxley/. On the United States see: Witek, Joseph. 1999. "Comics Criticism in the United States: A Brief Historical Survey." Edited by John A. Lent. *International Journal of Comic Art* 1 (1): 4–16. See also Hatfield, Charles. 2009. *The State of Comics Studies, and What to Do about It*. September 9. Accessed September 18, 2009. http://www.thoughtballoonists.com/2009/09/the-state-of-comics-studies.html. For an international perspective see: Lent, John A. 2010. "The Winding, Pot-Holed Road of Comic Art Scholarship." Edited by Julia Round and Chris Murray. *Studies in Comics* (Intellect Ltd.) 1 (1): 7–33.
4. Hague, Ian. 2012. *The Nimble Scholar: An Interview with Chris Murray*. March 20. Accessed March 20, 2012. http://comicsforum.org/2012/03/20/the-nimble-scholar-an-interview-with-chris-murray-by-ian-hague/.
5. Priego, Ernesto. 2011. *Interview with Roger Sabin*. December 5. Accessed March 16, 2012. http://www.comicsgrid.com/2011/12/roger-sabin-interview/.
6. Howes, David, ed. 2009. *The Sixth Sense Reader*. Oxford: Berg. 23.
7. Ibid., 24.
8. The term 'ocularcentric', meaning '"dominated" by vision' (Jay, *Downcast*, 3) is a neologism whose spelling varies between texts. Throughout this book I follow the spelling used in: Jay, Martin. 1994. *Downcast Eyes: The Denigration of Vision in Twentieth Century French Thought*. Berkeley, CA: University of California Press. See p. 3 and footnote 7 (also p. 3) in that text for more on this term.
9. See: Hague, Ian. 2012. "Adapting *Watchmen*" In *Framing Film: Cinema and the Visual Arts*, edited by Steven Allen and Laura Hubner, 37–55. Bristol, UK: Intellect.

1 Eye Like Comics, or, Ocularcentrism in Comics Scholarship

1.0 APPROACHES TO COMICS

Writing in the inaugural edition of the seminal *International Journal of Comic Art*, Matthew Lombard, John Lent, Linda Greenwood, and Asli Tunç identify seven perspectives on the medium (sociological, psychological, art and aesthetics, business and economics, historical, philosophical and health/medical) and ten techniques for applying those perspectives (semiotic analysis, discourse analysis, literary analysis, rhetorical analysis, content analysis, historical analysis, case study, surveys, interviews and the experiment).[1] While they acknowledge that this listing is 'certainly not exhaustive' it does provide a good overview of many of the common means by which comics have been approached.[2] Nearly ten years later, some of the perspectives identified by Lombard and colleagues were also picked up on by Thierry Groensteen in his assertion that '[s]emiotics, history and sociology' are 'the three major academic disciplines brought into play by the study of comics'.[3] As both of these accounts imply, approaches to comics are many and varied, and we should not assume that these broadly disciplinary categories are fully representative of the sheer diversity of routes into the study of comics, given that within each discipline there are ranges of methodological and perspectival foci to choose from as well. Furthermore, since 'multidisciplinarity is a working fact of comics studies', it is certainly worth considering the ways in which various disciplines treat comics and how their coexistence and/or interaction contribute to the broader field of comics scholarship.[4] Yet in addition to these more specific concerns surrounding disciplinary and perspectival approaches, it is important to note the existence of broader areas of consideration that transcend the limitations of any one particular discipline and in some cases serve to underpin substantial swathes of scholarship on the medium.

One such area of common focus is what we might call the formal or aesthetic approach to comics, which is the primary subject of this book. In his book *Artworld Metaphysics*, Robert Kraut writes:

> The task of the philosopher of art is to provide an accurate systematic picture of the artworld, making explicit the norms sustained therein: norms that govern recognition, evaluation, and interpretation of artistic objects and events.[5]

In this description of the project of aesthetics as an academic and philosophical discipline, Kraut concisely enunciates the work I seek to undertake in relation to comics over the course of this book. Note particularly the three processes Kraut identifies as pertinent: recognition, evaluation and interpretation. Each of these processes is common in formal approaches to comics. The first, recognition, has largely been the domain of what Aaron Meskin and Joseph Witek have labelled the definitional project or projects, which seek(s) to produce a definition of comics that allows us to determine what is a comic and what is not.[6] Put simply, the definitional project can be summed up as that body of literature that tries to answer the question: 'What is a comic?' The second and third processes, evaluation and interpretation, have formed what we might call the mechanical project, which is more concerned with how the elements identified as the components of comics interrelate. The mechanical project then (and I am here using the term 'project' loosely, as Meskin and Witek do), aims to respond to the question: 'How do comics work?' Taken together, these two questions comprise the aesthetic/formal approach to comics.

It is primarily to the latter question that this book addresses itself. This is not to say, however, that the definitional project can be forgotten altogether. Although its value has been called into question by some thinkers, others have asserted that they find it to be inescapable.[7] Definitions of comics are particularly common in works on the mechanics of comics, as many (e.g., Will Eisner's *Comics and Sequential Art,* Scott McCloud's *Understanding Comics: The Invisible Art* and Thierry Groensteen's *The System of Comics*) seek to delimit their field before explaining how it works, though some prefer to take up an existing definition and apply it to a new set of works instead (e.g., Nielsen and Wichmann). While this book does not aim to present a new definition of comics per se, it does seek to present an alternative mode of understanding comics, 'making explicit [some] of the norms sustained' in existing approaches as it does so. In order to do this, it is important to begin by considering definitions in order to investigate the ways in which we recognise comics. It is only then that we can move on to develop the modes of evaluation and interpretation that may be involved in understanding the medium, because how we define comics determines what it is that we evaluate and interpret, and the ways in which we are able to do so.

Over the course of this chapter, I will outline the nature of the definitional project not by placing a strong focus on specific definitions and pulling them apart in great detail, but rather by describing three *types* of definition, which we can use to classify existing definitions and understand their functionality more satisfactorily. Undertaking this task, then, is an attempt at understand the mechanisms of recognition more fully. It is not a response to the question 'What is a comic?', rather, it is an answer to the question 'How do we recognise comics?' It is in that sense an interrogation of comics scholarship more than of comics per se. As we will see, considering the field in this way yields interesting insights into the treatment of comics by scholars (and in the cultural sphere more generally) because it exposes elements of the medium that are taken as a priori but which are actually far less certain than they appear. The most significant of these for this study is the notion that comics are a visual art form. Although this may seem to be a very basic assertion, one that is not worth questioning, there is substantial evidence to suggest that it is not sufficient for the development of a comprehensive understanding of comics (though it certainly is not incorrect as such). If we are to continue moving forward in our understanding of the information, messages and narratives communicated by comics, I will argue, we must go beyond the visual, and consider the medium more holistically. Doing so will require a greater breadth of understanding that can take in elements of comics that address all five of the senses; it is the development of this breadth that I will lay the groundwork for in this chapter, before moving on to discuss the senses more specifically over the remainder of the book. For now, though, let us turn our attention more concertedly to the definitional project and consider the various ways in which it has sought to identify comics.

1.1 THE DEFINITIONAL PROJECT

While the notion of defining words such as 'comic(s)' and related terms such as 'graphic novel' has been a significant concern of comics scholarship for many years, in recent times it has come in for some criticism. The reasons for such attacks range from simple boredom with discussions of terminology or the methodological and theoretical difficulty or impossibility of developing a satisfactory definition to more holistic and sustained denials of the value of the definitional project as a whole.[8] Perhaps the most substantial single critique of attempts at defining comics comes from Aaron Meskin in his essay 'Defining Comics?' Therein, Meskin challenges the idea that explicitly defining comics is of benefit to scholars. In seeking to determine the potential value of the definitional project, Meskin moots three possibilities: the identification of comics, their evaluation and interpretation, and the determination of their standard and contra-standard features. Echoes of Robert Kraut's discussion (see above) are clear here, and somewhat expected since both men are working within the sphere of the philosophy of art. Meskin dismisses all three of the characteristics listed as validating factors, finally asserting that comics scholarship must 'get beyond the definitional project'.[9] Problematically, in doing so Meskin overlooks the consequences of acts such as the identification of comics. On this subject he argues: 'There are challenging cases, and we may have an interest in categorizing correctly', going on to point out that in such instances we could turn to alternative modes of identification that do not require a definition.[10] In this, Meskin is correct. If we are aiming solely to clarify whether something is or is not a comic, then a comprehensive definition is not, strictly speaking, necessary, for a fairly minimal set of characteristics will suffice. We need not fully define an elephant to determine that a large grey creature with four legs and a trunk is one. Yet Meskin overlooks the more substantial philosophical implications of identification. In defining a comic, the definer specifies the boundaries of the object of study and thereby indicates the ways in which it is possible for her/him to interact with that object. As David Carrier has pointed out: '[t]he answer to [the question 'What is a comic?'] determines the shape of analysis and so also its starting point', and '[o]nce we know what kind of a thing the artwork is, we are prepared to explain its history'.[11] It is perhaps for this reason that scholars such as Catherine Labio have stated that they find the question of definition to be inescapable when considering comics.[12]

Conventionally, attempts to define comics involve either selecting a set of existing definitions and critiquing them before offering an alternative that remedies their faults, or simply presenting a new definition without reference to previous ones. While I do not think it wise to attempt to present a new definition without context, nor do I think it particularly helpful to return to existing definitions and critique them in detail here because the major points of contention are likely to have been covered elsewhere already. Debating and unpicking individual definitions of comics will not yield many new insights at this point. Instead of considering the *terms* of particular definitions, then, I would like to spend some time here discussing how definitions of comics tend to work in a more general sense, because this is what will ultimately allow us to understand how the definitional project shapes our analyses of the medium.

1.1.1 Elemental Definitions

Broadly speaking we can identify three categories of definitions of comics, which I will call elemental, knowingly incomplete, and social. In the elemental category, we can place those definitions that seek to identify comics on the basis of specific, observable characteristics, or elements. Examples would include David Kunzle's 1973 definition, which outlines the object of his historical study into the early comic strip:

> For our present work, I would propose a definition in which a "comic strip" of any period, in any country, fulfills [sic] the following conditions: 1) There must be a sequence of separate images; 2) There must be a preponderance of image over text; 3) The medium in which the strip appears and for which it was originally intended must be reproductive, that is, in printed form, a mass medium; 4) The sequence must tell a story which is both moral and topical.[13]

Bill Blackbeard's 1974 definition, offered as a direct response to Kunzle's, also falls into this category:

> *Comic Strip: A serially published, episodic, open-ended dramatic narrative or series of linked anecdotes about recurrent identified characters,*

> *told in successive drawings regularly enclosing ballooned dialogue or its equivalent and generally minimal narrative text.*[14]

One final example of an elemental definition (and perhaps the most famous definition of comics) comes from Scott McCloud (1993), who describes comics as: '[j]uxtaposed pictorial and other images in deliberate sequence, intended to convey information and/or produce an aesthetic response in the viewer'.[15] He subsequently goes on to outline his own understanding of the mechanics of comics. In each of these examples of definitions we see two key things that demonstrate the operation of the elemental definition quite clearly. The first is the presence of particular, observable qualities that are taken to constitute the comic as object. In all three of the definitions presented here there is a focus on images in sequence as a critical component. Some of the definitions also include publishing conditions and other elements, but what is important is that all the qualities presented here can be identified within the comic itself; they are observable. The second important point to note is that these definitions all endeavour to define a whole term, that is, they each state what a comic (or comic strip) is, and by implication what it is not. Anything that possesses the qualities laid out in the definition is a comic; anything with different properties is not a comic. Because they are so clear-cut, these definitions are relatively easy to apply; although we may quibble with the validity of the terms employed, it is simple enough to compare an object to the definition to determine whether it does or does not count as a comic.

Yet such definitions have come in for criticism from scholars in the past, particularly on the basis of their inclusive/exclusive nature. In the first instance the approach is seen as problematic from a practical standpoint, since 'essentialist definitional projects often devolve into analytical cul-de-sacs and hair splitting debates over an apparently endless profusion of disputed boundary cases and contradictory counterexamples'.[16] Definitions of this type can seem too restrictive or too wide-ranging, including or excluding objects that common sense might suggest should be classified otherwise. Scott McCloud's definition in particular has come under criticism for the way it expands the field to include huge numbers of objects that would not otherwise have been integrated as comics per se (e.g., the Bayeux tapestry).[17] Thierry Groensteen, writing in *The System of Comics,* implies a second strand of critical consideration in his argument that David Kunzle's definition is 'made to measure in order to support an arbitrary slice of history' for it 'only serves to justify the fact that he chose the invention of printing as a starting point for *The Early Comic Strip*'.[18] As Groensteen makes clear here, the elemental mode of definition is particularly vulnerable to political and/or personal bias since it can be employed to bracket off a body of works just as much as it can serve to expand one. Its easy applicability and in/out nature makes it very amenable to canon-formation, which can of course be extremely problematic.

1.1.2 Knowingly Incomplete Definitions

Some of these concerns are addressed by the second category of definitional paradigm: knowingly incomplete definitions. In this category we can locate definitions that do specify some observable quality that forms the basis of all comics, but explicitly maintain that this quality is not sufficient in and of itself to *be* a comic; other factors, from social elements to printing methods, can also play roles. Examples of this type of definition include Will Eisner's 1985 approach, presented in the introduction to *Comics and Sequential Art:*

> This work is intended to consider and examine the unique aesthetics of Sequential Art as a means of creative expression, a distinct discipline, an art and literary form that deals with the arrangement of pictures or images and words to narrate a story or dramatize an idea. It is studied here within the framework of its application to comic books and comic strips, where it is universally employed.[19]

Interestingly, although Thierry Groensteen declares the definition of comics 'impossible' in *The System of Comics,* he does provide the following basis for his discussion[20]:

> If one wishes to provide the basis of a reasonable definition for the totality of the historical manifestations of the medium, and also for all other productions unrealized at this time but theoretically conceivable, one must recognise the relational play of a plurality of interdependent images as the unique ontological foundation of comics.[21]

He gives this 'relational play of a plurality of interdependent images' a name: 'iconic solidarity', going on to specify the meaning of this term more fully as well:

> I define [iconic solidarity] as interdependent images that, participating in a series, present the double characteristic of being separated—this specification dismisses unique enclosed images within a profusion of patterns or anecdotes—and which are plastically and semantically over-determined by the fact of their coexistence *in praesentia.*[22]

Later still, Groensteen remarks that: '[t]he necessary, if not sufficient, condition required to speak of comics is that the images will be multiple and correlated in some fashion'.[23] In so doing, he effectively enunciates the basic properties of the knowingly incomplete definition, and marks up how his definition is comparable to Will Eisner's (although Groensteen has more explicitly aligned himself with Scott McCloud's approach).[24] What both Eisner's and Groensteen's definitions do is establish a very minimal empirically observable condition that is necessary for something to be a comic, and then indicate that other factors will also contribute to its constitution. In both these examples the observable condition is the series of images, which Eisner calls 'sequential art' and Groensteen labels 'iconic solidarity'. Central to understanding this type of definition is the distinction between these 'necessary, if not sufficient' *components* of comics and the comic itself. The sequential art/iconic solidarity is only a part (a critical part perhaps, but only a part) of what constitutes the comic as a whole. The nuances of this mode of definition have at times been lost by writers who conflate the original terms. Eisner's distinction between 'comics' and 'sequential art', for example, is often missed by scholars whose discussions are rendered less precise by their implications that comics *are* sequential art, when it would be more accurate to say that comics *are partly comprised of* sequential art, or perhaps that comics *use* sequential art.[25]

The knowingly incomplete definition is capable of overcoming some of the problems with the elemental approach. It is more flexible, yet it allows for a degree of consistency through its anchoring of the discussion around a set of definite properties. It also enables us to draw a wider array of elements into our considerations. Where the elemental definition has a tendency towards a very limited focus of study, the knowingly incomplete method enables us to take aspects such as the material forms of the comic and its paratextual elements into account more easily; we are not tied to a specific physical form by the knowingly incomplete definitions provided above, but they do enable us to consider physicality. For this reason they allow us to consider the ways in which similar ideas might be presented in different ways as formats, technology and transmission media change over time, enabling discussions of how "a comic" has changed in various presentations, rather than necessarily suggesting that one version of a comic is fundamentally different to another (as would be required if the comic and its medium of transmission were held to be wholly integrated). Such considerations were critical to Thierry Groensteen in developing his definition, which is preceded in *The System of Comics* by the following consideration of the work of Roger Odin:

> [. . .] Roger Odin shows clearly that it is almost impossible to express a definition of cinema that also applies to animated films and to all the forms of experimental or 'widened' cinema. The aporia that the semiotician necessarily unblocks is thus described:
>
>> By what right do we exclude from cinema these productions when their authors present them explicitly as "films"? The fact that these productions do not enter into our definition of the "cinema," is that a sufficient justification for this exclusion? If not, must we revise our definition of cinema in a more generalizable [sic] manner in order to integrate these counter-examples? But if so, where do we stop this generalization: at the absence of film? At the absence of the screen? At the absence of the projector? Won't we arrive at a sort of definition that tells us nothing about its object?

> Roger Odin suggests that it is necessary to surpass this immanent approach to cinema in order to take into account its social uses. No longer considering the 'cinematic object' but the 'cinematic field,' he concludes (p. 57) that 'cinematic objects are definable objects, but variable objects in space and time.'[26]

Groensteen's identification of iconic solidarity, then, is an attempt to grasp the object of comics scholarship in such a way that it can be both '"definable"' and '"variable [. . .] in space and time"'. The 'relational play of a plurality of interdependent images' is a generic and ahistorical condition but it is also empirically determinable. Coupling it with an acknowledgment that it is '[t]he necessary, *if not sufficient,* condition required to speak of comics' (my emphasis), however, allows that elemental unit to retain its spatial and temporal variability. Yet it is important to note that there remains a sense of constraint about knowingly incomplete definitions because while they do enable some flexibility, they also tend towards emphasising a very specific element and considering the various ways in which that element (and often only that element) works. Knowingly incomplete definitions lead to knowingly incomplete studies. This is evident in both *The System of Comics* and *Comics and Sequential Art,* both of which emphasise the ways in which the image-narrative components of the comics work, rather than considering, for example, the way in which the comic is printed and bound (although Will Eisner did later revise his book to include some wider elements such as printing). It is also worth noting that when knowingly incomplete definitions are predicated upon a particular formal element like an image sequence, they are not necessarily any more flexible than elemental approaches in dealing with the 'disputed boundary cases and contradictory counterexamples'.[27] They could not, for example, account for Dave Sim and Gerhard's *Cerebus: Reads* (1993–1994) or Grant Morrison and John Van Fleet's *Batman* #663 (2007), both of which incorporate lengthy prose pieces into the standard numbering and formats of existing comics series, but nevertheless arguably become comics through their association with an existing corpus in the minds of their readers and producers.

1.1.3 Social Definitions

Predictably, it is social factors such as these that contribute to the third category of definitions. In the social definition, the determination of what is or is not a comic lies with the producers and consumers of the medium rather than in any particular observable element. Martin Barker approached this type of understanding as early as 1989 when he wrote in *Comics: Ideology, Power and the Critics:*

> [As well as] internal characteristics that define what a comic is, something else is involved in their definition. It is hard to state without sounding

> tautological: *a comic is what has been produced under the definition of a 'comic'*. There has been a historical process whereby public arguments about comics, and what is acceptable under that name, have become in their turn powerful determinants of what is produced.[28]

More recently Joseph Witek (2009) has made a similar observation, albeit from the other side of the reader/producer divide, asserting:

> [. . .] "comicness" might usefully be reconceptualized from being an immutable attribute of texts to being considered as a historically contingent and evolving set of reading protocols that are applied to texts, that to be a comic means to be *read* as a comic.[29]

He goes on to look at two devices that aided in the development of such reading protocols: the numbering of panels within the grid upon the page, and the use of arrows to direct the reader's gaze across the page. These, he argues, served to establish the "correct" ways to read comics, though they may seem largely obsolete today. Herein we see the benefit of the social mode of definition. Where elemental and even knowingly incomplete definitions seek to identify an unchanging element that is constant across a large body of work (and across time), Witek's employment of reading protocols in the definitional project allows him to build variation into his definition. The comic is transformed from a fixed object or a set of either/or conditions into an active, mutable object that can change over both space and time. As Witek's discussion of the arrow and the grid serves to emphasise, there are *some* elements that persist across *some* comics, but there need not be any elements that are evident in *all* comics.[30] There is no 'unique ontological foundation of comics' as a whole medium.[31] While this type of definition is somewhat susceptible to claims of arbitrariness, it is important to remember Martin Barker's mention of the 'historical process' involved in the determination of comics. The traditions from which comics derive will to a large extent determine what is included or excluded in the term, so the vast majority of works contained therein will not present a substantial challenge to common sense thinking. Where the other types of definition risk falling prey to particular disputes, however, as in the case of *Cerebus: Reads* and *Batman* #663, the social definition could unproblematically include disputed items as a result of not just their physical similarities to other objects produced and consumed as comics, but also the social contexts in which that production and consumption takes place.[32]

Most explicitly stated definitions of comics fall into the elemental or knowingly incomplete categories, and it is fairly common in English language scholarship to see Will Eisner's and Scott McCloud's definitions being cited as the foundation of a study. They certainly represent foundational texts for the broader mechanical project, which, as I have already observed, is heavily intertwined with the definitional project. In many cases, definitions form part of a discussion of the mechanics of comics, and even where a mechanical study does not provide a unique definition, considerations of how comics work tend to establish the context of their discussion before they go on to consider a particular element of comics' functionality. Prior to Joseph Witek's work, the social definition tended to be employed in more sociological and/or historical texts. Martin Barker's work in *Comics: Ideology, Power and the Critics* represents an early foray into the social contexts of comics consumption (Barker was one of the first thinkers to work with comics using sociological research methods), and it is referenced in Roger Sabin's *Adult Comics: An Introduction,* which is itself very aware of the social aspects of comics.[33] Both these studies are cited by Mark Rogers as part of a brief flirtation between comics as a subject and British cultural studies as a discipline that took place 'in a relatively short period from the late 1970s to the early 1990s'.[34] Yet in Witek's application of a social definition in this later period, we see an important reinvigoration of the social mode of understanding that emphasises its ability to approach form as well as sociocultural contexts. The value of this connection between the social and the formal should not be underestimated, and it has significant implications for the mechanical project.[35]

1.2 THE MECHANICAL PROJECT

The derivation of the formal principles of comics from formally oriented elemental and knowingly incomplete definitions has led to a very advanced understanding of the interrelations between images, and in some cases the principles of image-text relations. In *The System of Comics,* for example, we find a compelling and persuasive theory of the functionality of these components; so significant is this work that it has been described as 'the culmination of both Groensteen's own work on comics form and larger debates within semiological comics theory'.[36] Yet as Thierry Groensteen himself makes clear within that text, it is to some degree incomplete because of its focus upon the principles of iconic solidarity:

> Many other conditions can be legitimately debated, which would touch in priority, initially the "nature" of these images (their substance, their mode of production, their formal characteristics), followed by their mode(s) of articulation, eventually even the published form that they take, their distribution and the conditions of their reception—in short, everything that inscribes them in the specific process of communication.[37]

In eliminating these elements from his work, Groensteen removes a huge number of potentially confusing factors, but he also restricts the study's focus substantially. Thus, while the discussion of iconic solidarity within *The System of Comics* is exemplary, it is also limited, and subjects comics as whole objects to a process of distortion. '[. . .] *not having a full sensation of the Object, we must be very lame and imperfect in our conceptions about it, and in all the proportions which we build upon it;*' wrote the polymath Robert Hooke in *Micrographia:*

> *hence, we often take the* shadow *of things for the* substance, *small* appearances *for good* similitudes, similitudes *for* definitions; *and even many of those, which we think, to be the most solid definitions, are rather expressions of our own misguided apprehensions then* [sic] *of the true nature of the things themselves.*[38]

Of course, it should not be inferred from this critique that Groensteen is alone in his restricted focus. In fact, the reason that I selected his work here over that of Will Eisner or Scott McCloud (or others) is that it demonstrates an unusually high level of awareness of the issue of completeness. What I hope to have demonstrated, however, is that when elemental or knowingly incomplete definitions are employed, much is left aside in the study of comics. Though these omissions are perhaps not inherently problematic, the works of scholars such as Martin Barker and Joseph Witek compel us to avoid leaving behind the context in favour of the form as an (artificially) isolated element of comics.[39]

Ultimately, the risk of narrowing the study of comics' mechanics to the realm of iconic solidarity, sequential art or any of the similar areas that might be addressed is that we narrow the focus of comics scholarship as a whole and overlook numerous relevant factors in favour of a relative few elements that are deemed to be unique to the medium. As Georg Lukács wrote in his seminal *History and Class Consciousness:*

> [. . .] the more intricate a modern science becomes and the better it understands itself methodologically, the more resolutely it will turn its back on the ontological problems of its own sphere of influence and eliminate them from the realm where it has achieved some insight. The more highly developed it becomes and the more scientific, the more it will become a formally closed system of partial laws. It will then find that the world lying beyond its confines, and in particular the material base which it is its task to understand, *its own concrete underlying reality* lies, methodologically and in principle, *beyond its grasp.*[40]

The implications of such developments are far-reaching, and contribute to scholarship in significant ways. This is particularly the case because both the definitional and the mechanical projects underpin much of comics scholarship, determining not only *what* we are speaking of when we discuss comics, but even how we are able to speak. The objects of study are to a large extent established by our answers to the question 'What is a comic?', whether these answers are made explicit within a text or not. The language in which that study takes place and is expressed is also conditioned by our answer to that question, since, as Walter Benjamin and others have observed, 'What the speakers of a language think it worthwhile to say depends on their opportunities for expression, what modes of discourse are generally available to them'.[41] In establishing the modes of discourse employed in comics scholarship around terms such as 'iconic solidarity', 'sequential art' and '[j]uxtaposed pictorial and other images in deliberate sequence' we build a discipline upon the notion of information and narrative conveyed by images. In so doing we 'turn [our] back[s] on the ontological problems of [our] own sphere of influence', because the notion that comics are a medium of images is itself underpinned by certain ideological positions, although these are rarely made explicit.[42]

1.2.1 Comics as a Visual Medium

One such position is the idea that comics is a visual medium, which I would argue represents one of the largest and most substantial foundation stones of comics scholarship, and a common understanding of the medium in the wider public sphere. Certainly, the conception of the medium as one of stories told through a series of images and often words adheres to and maintains this notion as an a priori component of thought. Where a definition of the medium is as clear-cut as Scott McCloud's, and posits *only* the series of images as the defining characteristic of comics, this understanding is particularly obvious and exclusive (and as we will see, McCloud is one of the thinkers who is most explicit in his assertions that comics is a visual medium). Yet even in those knowingly incomplete definitions proffered by Will Eisner and Thierry Groensteen we find an emphasis upon the visual, because the specific units offered as the basis of an incomplete definition (sequential art and iconic solidarity respectively) are visual in nature. Thus comics are essentially visual, even if they do have other, nonvisual elements. Since the mechanical project has thus far tended to stem most strongly from elemental and knowingly incomplete definitions, it should come as little surprise that the workings of comics are also generally taken to be visual. The visible components, particularly the words and images upon the page, are taken to constitute the critical elements of comics as a medium. These components and the principles of their interactions form the language of comics, that is, the mode by which comics communicate and are able to communicate.[43]

In some cases, the idea that comics are a visual medium is expounded very strongly. Scott McCloud is perhaps the best example of this, asserting in *Understanding Comics* that: 'Comics is a *mono-sensory* medium. It relies on only *one* of the senses to convey a *world* of experience. But what of the other four?'[44] We will come back to the question McCloud poses here shortly, but for now let us stay with his initial assertion that comics is a monosensory medium. When we know a little more of McCloud's background, it is perhaps unsurprising that he is so assertive in the idea that comics are visual in nature: 'Of the five senses, vision is the one that I appreciate the most and it's the one I can least take for granted,' he has remarked; 'I think this is partially due to my father who was blind'.[45] This appreciation of sight permeates McCloud's writings on comics, which he very consciously situates in the realm of formalism.[46] As the quotation from *Understanding Comics* above makes clear, McCloud's definition of comics is not only exclusive in the sense that it defines the word as a whole term (i.e., everything that complies with McCloud's definition is a comic, everything that doesn't is not), it is also exclusive in its emphasis upon sight as the conveyor of information. For McCloud, what is not visual is not comics; or to put it another way, all comics are exclusively visual in nature. In approaching comics in this way, McCloud explicitly rejects the notion that comics are able to communicate information in nonvisual ways (for example through audio content).[47]

In answering the question posed in the quotation above, McCloud goes still further in his assertion that comics is a visual medium, arguing that comics do access the senses other than sight, but only through the eye and the process of synaesthesia. Synaesthesia, or the stimulation of one sense by way of another (this can occur physiologically, psychologically or rhetorically), is an extremely important concept for comics scholarship. It appears, whether named as such or not, in numerous studies on the medium and it is particularly common in those that consider the nature of sound effects as visual devices.[48] As a means for understanding comics within the terms of a visually oriented definition it is a valuable theoretical tool, one that helps us to understand the structuring and conceptualisation of the senses in comics in a clear and effective way. What it does not enable us to do, however, is go beyond the visual and consider the object of our studies in a more holistic and truly multisensory fashion. All sensory content within comics, it would seem, is filtered through the lens of the eye.

1.3 MATERIALITY MATTERS

The overall effect of the ocularcentric and synaesthetic approach to comics is to render the comic as an object immaterial and transparent. This latter term is an important one, and it was invoked by Charles Hatfield in a discussion of the materiality of comics that drew on concepts first outlined in his book *Alternative Comics: An Emerging Literature*[49]:

> Analyzing the self-effacing, disembodied text (which we never encounter in reality, but imagine as we mentally reconstruct what we've read) requires assuming that the medium of delivery is transparent. When we presume to be indifferent to the material packaging of a text—when we think about that text as a sequence of words only—we assume the transparency or unimportance of its material medium. On the other hand,

> when we find ourselves turning a book over and over in our hands, feeling it and gazing at it, remarking its tactile and visual feel—in other words, when our reading becomes re-embodied—then we consider the opacity of the material medium. We no longer look *through* that medium but instead look *at* it. Our eyes stop—that's where the reading of the marked text starts. That's where the reading of comics starts. The text is not merely a string of symbols that winds its way through the book's text block, but rather a constellation of things that must be given *sites*, given spaces, on the page. In this view the book becomes a material enfoldment or nesting of spaces: we think of the book in an architectonic way, as a navigable or habitable environment, materially realized.[50]

In this description we find a relatively recent approach towards the materiality of the comic and an emphasis upon the comic as an object. Although Hatfield's remarks are largely oriented around a visual conception of materiality, a page that is literally seen by a real human eye rather than an ideological mind's eye (see my discussion of the ideal perspective in section 2.0 for more on this aspect of sight in comics scholarship specifically), he does also pick up on another element: touch. In remarking on both the physicality of sight and the existence of tactility as a means for accessing comics, Hatfield begins to move beyond the formalist abstraction of McCloud and acknowledges the significance of the physical form that comics take. Note also his assertion that a focus upon the materiality of a comic results in different kinds of understanding; we move from reading a text to 'feeling' and 'gazing at' an object. Yet, as we will see throughout this book, these processes are not as linear or separable as Hatfield's remarks imply; we can both read and feel (and hear and smell) the work simultaneously, and comics as a multisensory medium must therefore also be understood as a multimodal one; they communicate information and meaning in many ways at once. Comics are polysemic not just in their visual content, but in their physicality as a whole.

Hatfield is not alone in considering the materiality of comics. Remaining with more general elements of materiality for the moment (we will go on to consider the more specific field of the senses shortly) we can note that Ernesto Priego has outlined a model of comics scholarship that emphasised materiality as a core component of study.[51] Rather than seeing it as a primarily immanent element of a comic as an object, though, Priego asserts that four elements are brought into play by the term 'materiality', as depicted in figure 1.1.

What we see here is an emphasis on broadening the context of the discussions surrounding comics. The text is only one part of a larger field of enquiry that also takes account of the physicality of the comic as object (physical interface), the surroundings in which the act of reading takes place (space, habitat) and the physical capabilities of the reader (human body). As will likely have occurred to the reader, each of these conditions is fairly generic; there is nothing here that distinguishes comics from any other medium per se. Yet as Tim Dant has observed, 'The meaningfulness of objects unfolds

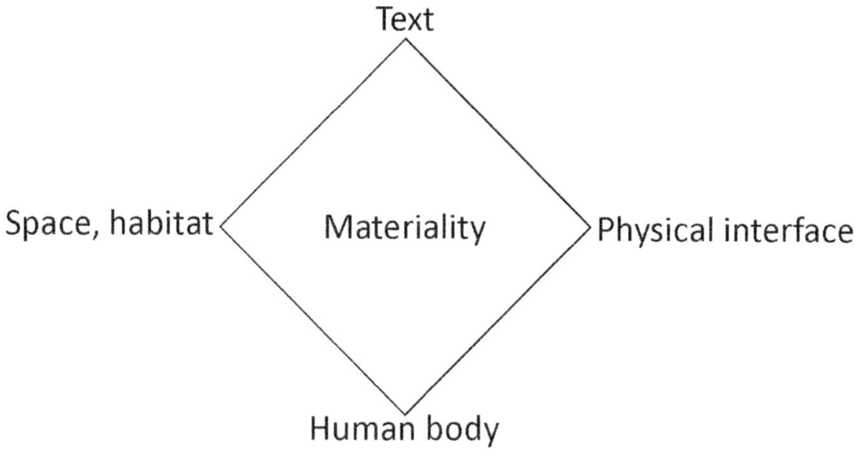

Figure 1.1 Ernesto Priego's concept of materiality (adapted for this publication). Image used with the kind permission of the creator.

through interaction', and it is by considering Priego's categories in discussions of comics that they become specific to the medium.[52] When we speak of the interactions between the four elements Priego identifies *with reference to a comic*, they begin to function as means for understanding the meaningfulness of that comic. Like Hatfield's comments above, this model provides us with a means for making comics "opaque"; it enables us to deal with the comic in a manner that takes account of its physical form. In addition to this though, it marks up the fact that a multiplicity of elements, including the text, are meaningful at the same time. Materiality is not on/off in terms of its significance, it is always on, although certain elements of it may be more or less prominent depending on the situation, both spatial and temporal. Thus one may at certain times focus more heavily upon the text, while at others concentrate more on its physical form, but each element is present continuously; the four elements identified by Priego are codeterminative.

Although some of the elements Priego picks up on have been investigated in some detail by scholars, materiality as a whole remains a relatively neglected area of comics scholarship. Of primary importance to scholarship thus far has, as the preceding discussion should have made clear, been the text, and this is discussed in numerous ways and by far too many scholars to list here. In fact, almost all scholarship on comics focuses upon the text, in many cases to the exclusion of all other aspects. The space/habitat has also received a fair amount of attention from scholars in a broad sense; the social contexts in which reading takes place are important in various ways, and considerations of comics spaces such as comic book shops, gallery spaces, libraries and other contexts of consumption have also been forthcoming.[53] The physical interfaces employed by comics have received some attention in recent years as well, with Pascal Lefèvre, Chris Couch and Gary Spencer

Millidge all producing important, if relatively brief, studies of the material forms and formats that comics take.[54] It is worth noting, however, that this aspect is significantly less well developed as an area of study than the text and space/habitat areas. By far the least heavily investigated aspect of Priego's four areas is the human body, though this is not to say that it has been entirely unappreciated by scholars.

In addition to Charles Hatfield, we can count Roger Sabin among those scholars who has drawn attention to the reader's physical experiences of interacting with comics. Writing on the differences between printed and digital comics, he observes:

> It's easy to forget that we read—or rather 'use'—comics in a very physical way (we tend to think of them as being two-dimensional, but in fact they exist in three dimensions). They can be bent, rolled-up, roughly opened or whatever. They can be held in different ways: cradled in your hand or gripped at the edges. We know how far into a comic we've read because we can feel how many pages are left. There are also smells: of dust, glue and paper. Compared to this very sensual experience, clicking a mouse just isn't the same.[55]

While we will return to the specifics of Sabin's comments later in the book, what is notable in the first instance is the very clear focus not simply on how comics tell stories through visual formations, but on the sensuality of comics; the ways in which they physically affect the reader's body, and the ways in which the reader takes information from the comic using a variety of senses ('We know how far into a comic we've read because we can feel how many pages are left'). Although the senses of sight and hearing have tended to be viewed as more 'epistemologically and ethically respectable' than touch, smell or taste, it would certainly be true to say that the other senses have much to offer in terms of knowledge acquisition.[56] The less specific, more personal elements of Sabin's discussion also point towards the ways in which the various nonvisual elements of comics can contribute to the formation of memories and readers' impressions. This was further developed by a 2002 study conducted by Mel Gibson, which involved interviews with comics readers. She noted (my italics):

> Patterns emerged in interview regarding memories of comics [. . . .] readers often wanted to check details, testing memory against outside sources. Further discussion included titles and narratives *alongside physical aspects of the texts, including paper quality, feel, scent and size.*[57]

What both Sabin's and Gibson's accounts indicate is the disparity between the rationalised, visually oriented approach to the mechanics of comics, and the experiences readers actually have while they are engaging with the medium. While explications of the principles of iconic solidarity and so forth can give us a tremendous insight into how comics work as a 'formally closed system of partial laws', they do not tell us how readers encounter a work or explain the various ways in which they take meaning from it.[58] What we find in the works of Sabin and Gibson (along with Hatfield and others) is a set of clues that indicate some of the elements that may be in play, but go beyond the exclusively visual notion of comics.[59]

At the same time, it is clear that the producers of comics are keenly aware of the ways in which comics' physicality affects both readers and the status of the object. In 2009, the first issue of the British small press anthology *Solipsistic Pop* included a manifesto entitled 'Declaration of The New Vague', which made this awareness very clear:

> **We reject the notion print is dead.**
>
> True, the screen promises endless possibilities but we vow to create beautiful work you can hold, and beautiful work you cannot. We are committed to producing gorgeous, tactile Comics [sic] that readers will cherish.[60]

In addition to the comics' tactile qualities, editor Tom Humberstone has also remarked that the smell of the comic was a major concern for him (see section 5.2 for more on this). Yet the work of Humberstone and the team on *Solipsistic Pop* is only one of the more blatant announcements of a concern with the physical qualities of comics. One need only look to an example such as Chris Ware's *Acme Novelty Library* (whose every issue is published in a different format) or *Building Stories* (a single work comprising a set of texts in various formats contained within a single box), DC Comics' Absolute Editions line (which republishes comics deemed to be major titles by the publisher in a very high-quality print format) or Robot Comics' experiments with digital comics on handheld platforms to realise that materiality matters for creators too, and matters greatly for a variety of reasons. Artistic innovation, financial concerns, canon formation and technological development are only some of the many motivations for thinking about materiality, and over the course of this book we will encounter all these and more. What all these elements demonstrate, however, is that just as readers take meaning from the physicality of comics, so too do creators recognise that the power of comics lies not just in their '[j]uxtaposed pictorial and other images in deliberate sequence' but also in their tactile, olfactory and even auditory and gustatory qualities. Reading comics is not just a visual process, it is a multisensory *experience*.

This multisensory experience is not limited to printed comics. Although it is tempting to understand digital formats as transparent mediums of transmission, windows onto a media landscape, and indeed some critics have lamented the loss of comics' sensorial elements in the move towards the digital image (see section 4.0 for more on this), digital manifestations of images do have a physicality to them. As Heidi Rae Cooley makes clear, this physicality is no more separable from the image than the page of a book is separable from the images that *it* presents:

> Whereas a window distances viewers from what they are looking at, the screen draws them toward the images that are displayed on the screen (not beyond it). In which case, window-ed seeing institutes a detached engagement, while screenic seeing encourages an experience of encounter. Vision, no longer a property of the window and its frame, becomes an extension of the screen. Likewise, that which is being viewed (and perhaps recorded) no longer exists separate from that which is framing it.[61]

There is no image other than an image that is manifested physically, whether this physicality is printed or digital. Nevertheless, there are some stark differences between the types of physicality that the two formats are able to access. Over the course of this book, I will begin to address some of those differences, and consider both printed and digital comics as material objects that are capable of using physical properties other than images to convey information. That said, I should also emphasise that I will not present a comprehensive survey of digital systems in this work, and while I will discuss some digital comics they are not my primary focus here. There are a number of reasons for this, not the least of which is the extensive history of printed comics, which itself merits investigation through a multisensory lens and offers a wealth of information and ideas. To add digital comics and concepts to this history in anything like a comprehensive way would simply extend the length of this study too far for it to be considered reasonable. As a consequence of this, I have elected to draw some comparisons between printed and digital comics where it is illuminating to do so, but to refrain from trying to cover digital more completely and ending up impoverishing both sides of the discussion. More significantly, while digital comics have certainly become much more visible in recent years, at the time of this writing in 2013 there is relatively little stability in the field. A few formats and systems are beginning to become prominent but there is no clear idea of what the general boundaries and conventions are yet, and there is much experimentation being done and remaining to be done. Mapping the digital comics landscape is certainly a valuable project, and doing so would allow us to determine more effectively the nature of digital comics' physicality, but this is a large project that goes beyond the remit of this book. For this reason I have chosen instead to consider a few relevant examples (see sections 3.2.2, 3.3, 4.2.1, 4.2.4 and 4.3), but not to make digital the primary focus of my work here.

1.4 TOWARDS A MULTISENSORY APPROACH

Over the course of this book, I will begin to develop ways in which the multisensory experience of comics may be approached. The central notion around which the work is organised can be stated concisely as: Comics is not just a visual medium. To avoid confusion, some words of clarification and specification on this notion may be helpful. Firstly, note the presence of the word 'just', which I have included to emphasise that the work presented here is *not* intended as a wholesale attack on existing scholarship or on the notion that comics are visual in nature. Indeed, such a statement would be an extremely foolish one to make since most comics are visual to some degree (though there are arguably some exceptions, as we will discover in section 3.3.). I am not suggesting that comics are nonvisual, but rather that they are only *partly* visual, and that they also possess a wide variety of other sensation-stimulating components. When I speak of the senses, I am speaking of the actual senses as we experience them, and when I speak of the sensation-stimulating elements of comics I am speaking of those components that *stimulate* our actual senses, not those that *simulate* sensation through processes such as synaesthesia. In my discussion of hearing in chapter 3, for example, I will talk about the actual, audible sounds that comics make and/or employ, as opposed to the visually represented sounds upon the page.

The definition of comics that underpins the book will, perhaps predictably, be social in nature. Drawing on the works of both Martin Barker and Joseph Witek, I will work on the basis that a comic is what is produced or consumed as a comic.[62] In most instances the examples I discuss are not likely to be particularly contentious, although where there may be some obvious dispute as to whether something is or is not a comic I will provide some explanation on why I deem it a valid example of the medium (see my discussion of Ben Katchor and David Isay's 'audio cartoons' in section 3.3, for example). The breadth of study that is enabled by a social definition is, I would suggest, far more useful for this kind of research than a selection determined by whether or not the examples feature sequential art (although again, most of the examples I discuss do). Note particularly that in drawing on both Barker and Witek, I emphasise both sides of the production/reception coin, and I will refer to both over the course of the book. In speaking of producers, I am of course referring to the conventionally recognised creators: the writer, the penciller, the inker, the letterer, the colourist and so forth, but I am also indicating all the other individuals and processes involved in the production of a comic. This may include (but is not limited to) editors, book designers and printers, since all of these groups will contribute to the *production* of the comic as a whole object. While I will be discussing the visual artwork in comics, it should be understood that this artwork is here taken to be manifested physically (whether this physical form is printed or digital), and to be inextricable from this physical manifestation. To recall Ernesto Priego's terminology, the text is inseparable from the physical interface. In speaking of receivers I am speaking of readers, but again, I am also speaking more broadly of purchasers, collectors and others (as Gérard Genette has made clear, the addressee and the reader of a text are not the same thing).[63] I am not implying any of the roles mentioned to be mutually exclusive, either internally or externally. A reader may also be a collector; a receiver may also be a producer.

In emphasising both aspects of this relationship, I lean heavily on the notion of a 'contract' between producers and receivers. In his second book on the form, *Graphic Storytelling and Visual Narrative,* Will Eisner speaks on this idea in the following way:

> At the outset of the telling of a story, whether oral, written, or graphic, there is an understanding between the teller and the listener, or reader. The teller expects that the audience will comprehend, while the audience expects the author will deliver something that is comprehensible. In this agreement, the burden is on the teller. This is a basic rule of communication.[64]

Although Eisner's basic premise here is sound, the idea that 'the burden is on the teller' has been disputed both in wider spheres of cultural production and reception and in relation to comics more specifically.[65] While the teller may be responsible for creating an object, the reader is also heavily involved in the production of meaning from that object. Reading is not simply an act of reception, it is an extension of the reader into metaphysical space; a cognitive process through which meaning is *pressed onto* sensory information according to the codes by which that reading is taking place. 'By the nature of sequential art, the reader's mind is filling in what happens between the images that I present,' asserts David Mack, '[t]he readers are bringing their own past experience and perspective. The artwork, the story, happens inside the readers' mind when they read the book'.[66] In this regard the producer/receiver divide is to some extent destabilised as it becomes clear that each embodies the other, making necessary a more complex notion of comics reading. Nevertheless it is clear that what is read, and how it is read, is partly determined by the input of the producers. Thus, Eisner's notion of a contract is a useful one because it allows us to understand the act of reading comics as a negotiation between producer-intent and receiver-input. While neither of these elements will be entirely dominant at any point, it is certainly true that there are ways in which authors can seek to control the way in which a text is read, or indeed relinquish control. A creator may use audio content to modulate the speed at which a comic is read (see section 3.2.2), for example, or employ smells and tastes to place the burden of meaning more firmly on the shoulders of the reader (see section 5.4). Over the course of this book I will discuss comics in terms of both readers and producers, paying attention to the ways in which the produced physical forms of comics affect readers' bodies, but also noting the physical presence of the reader in the act of reading and the ways in which the reader modifies the physical object. In this sense the physicality of the comic becomes the meeting point for the two elements; it is the site at which the relationships between producer and receiver are negotiated.

In this early stage of development for multisensory research it is logical that the discussion be based around existing literature, reported experiences and case studies. Participant observation, interview and experiment based research will certainly comprise a significant part of the future development of multisensory comics research (see conclusion for more on this), but at this point the primary goal is establishing a working foundation from currently available material. In some ways, the next four chapters could therefore be understood as an extended literature review, which seeks not to comprehensively undermine existing approaches to the mechanics of comics, but rather to expand upon them and demonstrate the broader possibilities for meaning that already exist within the medium. I will seek to offer a foundational "catalogue" of the existing multisensory elements of comics, as well as providing some means for understanding how these elements work and their strengths and weaknesses as communications systems. This catalogue and the ideas behind it will then be employed and expanded through a case study in chapter 6. Striving to move beyond the limits of existing ocularcentric, synaesthetic approaches to the medium, this study will show the richness and complexity of the physical and contextual relationships involved in reading comics, and the value of studying them. In coming to consider all five of the senses, this book will endeavour towards not only a broader understanding, but also a means by which we might more satisfactorily answer the fundamental question that lies at the heart of the mechanical project: How do comics work?

NOTES

1. Lombard, Matthew, John A. Lent, Linda Greenwood, and Asli Tunç. 1999. "A Framework for Studying Comic Art." Edited by John A. Lent. *International Journal of Comic Art* 1 (1): 17–32. 18-26.
2. Ibid., 28.
3. Groensteen, Thierry. 2008. "A Few Words about The System of Comics and More . . ." Edited by Laurence Grove, Mark McKinney, and Ann Miller. *European Comic Art* 1 (1): 87–93. 91.
4. Hatfield, Charles. 2010. "Indiscipline, or, The Condition of Comics Studies." *Transatlantica* 1–15. 2. For the sake of accuracy it is worth noting that Hatfield is speaking specifically of North American comics studies in the quotation cited here, however, the remark certainly applies elsewhere as well.
5. Kraut, Robert. 2007. *Artworld Metaphysics*. Oxford: Oxford University Press. 3.
6. Meskin, Aaron. 2007. "Defining Comics?" *The Journal of Aesthetics and Art Criticism* 65 (4): 369–379. 369; Witek, Joseph. 2009. "The Arrow and the Grid." In *A Comics Studies Reader*, edited by Jeet Heer and Kent Worcester, 149–156. Jackson, MS: University Press of Mississippi. 149.
7. Meskin, 'Defining'; Labio, Catherine. 2009. "Turning to Art: Comic Books and Artists' Books." *International Bande Dessinée Society Sixth Bi-Annual Conference*. London.
8. Berlatsky, Eric L. 2010. "Review of Annalisa Di Liddo's Alan Moore: Comics as Performance, Fiction as Scalpel." *ImageText* 5 (4). Accessed September 22, 2011. http://www.english.ufl.edu/imagetext/archives/v5_4/berlatsky/; Witek, 'Arrow', 149; Groensteen, Thierry. 2007. *The System of*

Comics. Translated by Bart Beaty and Nick Nguyen. Jackson, MS: University Press of Mississippi. 12–17. Meskin, 'Defining'.
9. Meskin, 'Defining', 376.
10. Ibid., 375.
11. Carrier, David. 2000. *The Aesthetics of Comics*. University Park, PA: Pennsylvania State University Press. 3, 7.
12. Labio, 'Turning'.
13. Kunzle, David. 1973. *The Early Comic Strip: Narrative Strips and Picture Stories in the European Broadsheet from c.1450 to 1825*. Berkeley, CA: University of California Press. 2.
14. Blackbeard, Bill. 1974–1975. "Mislabeled Books." *Funnyworld* (16): 40–41. 41. Italics in original.
15. McCloud, Scott. 1993. *Understanding Comics: The Invisible Art*. New York, NY: HarperPerennial. 9.
16. Witek, 'Arrow', 149.
17. For a rigorous and lucid exploration of McCloud's approach, see: Horrocks, Dylan. 2001. "Inventing Comics: Scott McCloud's Definition of Comics." *The Comics Journal* (234): 29–39.
18. Groensteen, *System*, 13.
19. Eisner, Will. 2006. *Comics and Sequential Art*. Paramus, NJ: Poorhouse Press. 5.
20. Groensteen, *System*, 12–17.
21. Groensteen, *System*, 17.
22. Ibid., 18.
23. Ibid., 19.
24. Groensteen, Thierry. 2012. "The Current State of French Comics Theory." *Scandinavian Journal of Comic Art* 1 (1): 111–122. 111.
25. Meskin, 'Defining', 270. Nielsen, Jesper, and Søren Wichmann. 2000. "America's First Comics? Techniques, Contents, and Functions of Sequential Text-Image Pairing in the Classical Maya Period." In *Comics and Culture: Analytical and Theoretical Approaches to Reading Comics*, 59–77. Copenhagen, Denmark: Museum Tusculanum Press and University of Copenhagen. 61; Witek, Joseph. 1989. *Comic Books as History: The Narrative Art of Jack Jackson, Art Spiegelman, and Harvey Pekar*. Jackson, MS: University Press of Mississippi. 34, but cf. also 5–6.
26. Groensteen, *System*, 17.
27. Witek, 'Arrow', 149.
28. Barker, Martin. 1989. *Comics: Ideology, Power and the Critics*. Manchester, UK: Manchester University Press. 8. Italics in original.
29. Witek, 'Arrow', 149.
30. See also: Groensteen, 'Current', 112–114.
31. Groensteen, *System*, 17.
32. cf. Frahm, Ole. 2000. "Weird Signs. Comics as Means of Parody." In *Comics and Culture: Analytical and Theoretical Approaches to Reading Comics*, edited by Anne Magnussen and Hans-Christian Christiansen, translated by Michael Hein, 177–191. Copenhagen, Denmark: Museum Tusculanum Press and University of Copenhagen. 178.
33. Sabin, Roger. 1993. *Adult Comics: An Introduction*. London: Routledge. 35. See also: Barker, Martin. 1992. *A Haunt of Fears: The Strange History of the British Horror Comics Campaign*. Jackson, MS: University Press of Mississippi.
34. Rogers, Mark C. 2001. "Ideology in Four Colours: British Cultural Studies Do Comics." Edited by John A. Lent. *International Journal of Comic Art* 3 (1): 93–108. 93.

35. For a similar (but not identical) approach to the definitional question, which suggests that an institutional approach to the comics world is more useful than essentialist definitions, see chapter 2 of: Beaty, Bart. 2012. *Comics versus Art.* Toronto, Canada: University of Toronto Press.
36. Fischer, Craig, and Charles Hatfield. 2011. "Teeth, Sticks, and Bricks: Calligraphy, Graphic Focalization and Narrative Braiding in Eddie Campbell's Alec." Edited by Jared Gardner and David Herman. *SubStance* 40 (1 (#124)): 70–93. 81. For more on these debates and the contexts they grew out of, see: Fresnault-Deruelle, Pierre. 1989 (1990). "Semiotic Approaches to Figurative Narration." In *The Semiotic Web*, 587–603. Berlin, Germany: Mouton de Gruyter. See also Thierry Groensteen's, 'The Current State of French Comics Theory'. Semiotic/semiological approaches to comics in the English language are not huge in number, but there are some important texts besides Groensteen's *The System of Comics*, perhaps the most notable of which come from Umberto Eco, particularly 'A Reading of Steve Canyon', 'The Myth of Superman' and 'On Chinese Comic Strips: Counter-Information and Alternative Information' (this last piece is included, along with Eco's introduction to a collection of *Peanuts* comics, in *Apocalypse Postponed*). Eco, Umberto. 1994. *Apocalypse Postponed.* Edited by Robert Lumley. Bloomington, IN: Indiana University Press and British Film Institute. Eco, Umberto. 1972. "The Myth of Superman." *Diacritics* (Johns Hopkins University Press) 2 (1): 14–22. Eco, Umberto. 1987. "A Reading of Steve Canyon." In *Comic Iconoclasm Exhibition Catalogue*, edited by Sheena Wagstaff, translated by Bruce Merry, 20–25. London: Institute of Contemporary Arts.
37. Groensteen, *System*, 18.
38. Hooke, Robert. 2005. "Micrographia: Some Physiological Descriptions of Minute Bodies Made by Magnifying Glasses with Observations and Inquiries Thereupon." Vers. EPUB. *Project Gutenberg.* March 29. Accessed March 5, 2012. http://www.gutenberg.org/ebooks/15491.epub.images. 4. Italics in original.
39. See also: Brienza, Casey. 2010. "Producing Comics Culture: A Sociological Approach to the Study of Comics." Edited by David Huxley and Joan Ormrod. *Journal of Graphic Novels and Comics* 1 (2): 105–119; Woo, Benjamin. 2011. "The Android's Dungeon: Comic-Bookstores, Cultural Spaces, and the Social Practices of Audiences." Edited by David Huxley and Joan Ormrod. *Journal of Graphic Novels and Comics* 2 (2): 125–136; Dines, Gail. 1995. "Toward a Critical Sociological Analysis of Cartoons." *Humor* 8 (3): 237–255; Pustz, Matthew J. 1999. *Comic Book Culture: Fanboys and True Believers.* Jackson, MS: University Press of Mississippi. These studies have similar implications to Barker's and Witek's works.
40. Lukács, Georg. 1968 (1971). *History and Class Consciousness: Studies in Marxist Dialectics.* Translated by Rodney Livingstone. London: Merlin Press. 104. Italics in original.
41. Benjamin, Walter. 2005. "A State Monopoly on Pornography." In *Walter Benjamin: Selected Writings.* Vol. 2, Part 1, *1927–1930*, by Walter Benjamin, edited by Michael W. Jennings, Howard Eiland and Gary Smith, translated by Rodney Livingstone, 72–74. Cambridge, MA: The Belknap Press of Harvard University Press. 72–73. See also: Havelock, Eric A. 1963. *Preface to Plato.* Cambridge, MA: The Belknap Press of Harvard University Press. 149.
42. Lukács, *History*, 104.
43. Varnum, Robin, and Christina T. Gibbons. 2001. *The Language of Comics: Word and Image.* Jackson, MS: University of Mississippi Press. Saraceni, Mario. 2003. *The Language of Comics.* London: Routledge. Versaci, Rocco. 2007. *This Book Contains Graphic Language: Comics as Literature.*

New York, NY: Continuum International; Cohn, Neil. 2005. "Un-Defining 'Comics': Separating the Cultural from the Structural in Comics." Edited by John A. Lent. *International Journal of Comic Art* 7 (2): 236–248.
44. McCloud, *Understanding*, 89.
45. McCloud, Scott. 2009. *Scott McCloud on Comics*. Online video. Produced by TED. Performed by Scott McCloud. Accessed September 25, 2011. http://www.ted.com/talks/scott_mccloud_on_comics.html.
46. Swanson, Gunnar. 2005. "The Four Tribes of Comics: [Interview with] Scott McCloud." In *The Education of a Comics Artist*, edited by Michael Dooley and Steven Heller, 204–209. New York, NY: Allworth Press. 207.
47. It is worth noting that McCloud does briefly discuss the sensual properties of comics as objects in *Reinventing Comics*, although this is more from the perspective of attempting to understand the medium of transmission of (still visual) comics, than it is an assertion that those physical properties carry meaning as part of the comic, and he suggests that ultimately the context and physical manifestation of a comic do not affect its underlying meaning. McCloud, Scott. 2000. *Reinventing Comics*. New York, NY: Paradox Press. 177–179.
48. See especially: Covey, Suzanne. 2006. "Beyond the Balloon: Sound Effects and Background Text in Lynn Johnson's For Better or For Worse." *ImageText: Interdisciplinary Comics Studies* 2 (2). Accessed January 18, 2012. http://www.english.ufl.edu/imagetext/archives/v2_2/covey/. Khordoc, Catherine. 2001. "The Comic Book's Soundtrack: Visual Sound Effects in Asterix." In *The Language of Comics: Word and Image*, edited by Robin Varnum and Christina T. Gibbons, 156–173. Jackson, MS: University Press of Mississippi; Kunzle, David. 2001. "The Voices of Silence: Willette, Steinlen and the Introduction of the Silent Strip in the Chat Noir, with a German Coda." In *The Language of Comics: Word and Image*, edited by Robin Varnum and Christina T. Gibbons, 3–18. Jackson, MS: University Press of Mississippi. Lefèvre, Pascal. 1999. "Recovering Sensuality in Comic Theory." Edited by John A. Lent. *International Journal of Comic Art* 1 (1): 140–149. Pollmann, Joost. 1999. "An Art of the Real: About the Adulthood of Contemporary Comics." Edited by John A. Lent. *International Journal of Comic Art* 1 (2): 107–126. Pollmann, Joost. 2001. "Shaping Sounds in Comics." Edited by John A. Lent. *International Journal of Comic Art* 3 (1): 9–21.
49. Hatfield, Charles. 2005. *Alternative Comics: An Emerging Literature*. Jackson, MS: University Press of Mississippi. 58–65.
50. Hatfield, Charles, and Jared Gardner. 2011. *Charles & Jared Talk Comics and Narrative Theory*. April 19. Accessed January 27, 2012. http://thepanelists.org/2011/04/charles-jared-talk-comics-and-narrative-theory/.
51. Priego, Ernesto. 2010. "Floppy Things with Staples: Comics and Materiality in the Digital Age." *Graphic Novels and Comics Conference*. Manchester.
52. Dant, Tim. 2007. "The 'Pragmatics' of Material Interaction." *Journal of Consumer Culture* 8 (1): 11–33. 13.
53. See: Pustz, *Comic*. Woo, 'Android's'. Beaty, Bart. 2007. *Unpopular Culture: Transforming the European Comic Book in the 1990s*. Toronto, Canada: University of Toronto Press; Barker, Keith, ed. 1993. *Graphic Account: The Selection and Promotion of Graphic Novels in Libraries for Young People*. Newcastle-under-Lyme, UK: Youth Libraries Group.
54. Lefèvre, Pascal. 2000. "The Importance of Being 'Published'. A Comparative Study of Different Comics Formats." In *Comics and Culture: Analytical and Theoretical Approaches to Reading Comics*, edited by Anne Magnussen and Hans-Christian Christiansen, 91–105. Copenhagen, Denmark: Museum Tusculanum Press and University of Copenhagen; Lefèvre, Pascal.

2010. "Intertwining Verbal and Visual Elements in Printed Narratives for Adults." *Studies in Comics* 1 (1): 35–52. Couch, Chris. 2000. "The Publication Formats of Comics, Graphic Novels and Tankobon." *Image and Narrative: Online Magazine of the Visual Narrative* 1 (1). Accessed December 14, 2009. http://www.imageandnarrative.be/inarchive/narratology/chriscouch.htm; Millidge, Gary Spencer. 2009. *Comic Book Design*. Lewes: ILEX. See also: Gibson, Mel. 2011. "'I Do Have the Annuals but Somehow They Are Just Not the Same as the Weeklies Printed on that Dreadfully Poor Quality Paper': British Girls' Comics, Publication Formats and Perceptions of Class." *Materiality and Virtuality: A Conference on Comics*. Leeds, UK.

55. Sabin, Roger. 2000. "The Crisis in Modern American and British Comics, and the Possibilities of the Internet as a Solution." In *Comics and Culture: Analytical and Theoretical Approaches to Reading Comics*, edited by Anne Magnussen and Hans-Christian Christiansen, 43–57. Copenhagen, Denmark: Museum Tusculanum Press and University of Copenhagen. 52.
56. Rée, Jonathan. 1999. *I See a Voice: Language, Deafness and the Senses—A Philosophical History*. London: Harper Collins. 34. See also: Jay, Martin. 1994. *Downcast Eyes: The Denigration of Vision in Twentieth Century French Thought*. Berkeley, CA: University of California Press.
57. Gibson, Mel. 2008. "What You Read and Where You Read It, How You Get It, How You Keep It: Children, Comics and Historical Cultural Practice." *Popular Narrative Media* 1 (2): 151–167. 151–152.
58. Lukács, *History*, 104.
59. See also: Walton, Saige. 2009. "Baroque Mutants in the 21st Century? Rethinking Genre through the Superhero." In *The Contemporary Comic Book Superhero*, edited by Angela Ndalianis, 86–106. New York, NY: Routledge. 101–102.
60. Humberstone, Tom, ed. 2009–2012. *Solipsistic Pop*. 4 vols. London: Solipsistic Pop Books. Vol. 1, n.p.
61. Cooley, Heidi Rae. 2004. "It's All about the Fit: The Hand, the Mobile Screenic Device and Tactile Vision." *Journal of Visual Culture* 3 (2): 133–155. 143.
62. See particularly: M. Barker, *Comics*, 8, and Witek, 'Arrow', 149.
63. Genette, Gérard. 1987 (1998). *Paratexts: Thresholds of Interpretation*. Translated by Jane E. Lewin. Cambridge, UK: Cambridge University Press. 75.
64. Eisner, Will. 2006. *Graphic Storytelling and Visual Narrative*. Paramus, NJ: Poorhouse Press. 49.
65. Barthes, Roland. 1977. *Image, Music, Text*. Edited by Steven Heath. London: Fontana Press. 142–148. Baetens, Jan. 2001. "Revealing Traces: A New Theory of Graphic Enunciation." In *The Language of Comics: Word and Image*, edited by Robin Varnum and Christina T. Gibbons, 145–155. Jackson, MS: University Press of Mississippi.
66. Mack, David. 2005. "The Whole-Brained Approach." In *The Education of a Comics Artist: Visual Narrative in Cartoons, Graphic Novels, and Beyond*, edited by Michael Dooley and Steven Heller, 86–90. New York, NY: Allworth Press. 89.

2 Sight, or, the Ideal Perspective and the Physicality of Seeing

2.0 THE IDEAL PERSPECTIVE

In chapter 1, I sought to demonstrate the ocularcentrism of comics scholarship. This done, it now becomes necessary to complicate this notion through an examination of the nature of sight as it is employed in the field. While it is true that comics scholarship displays a visual primacy, it would be inaccurate to suggest that this is a simple matter of one sense dominating (or negating) the other four. Rather, and in keeping with the rational (and rationalised) deployment of sight since at least the time of the Enlightenment, only relatively restricted modes of sight and seeing have been taken up. To explicate this notion more fully, let us now return to those remarks made by Roger Sabin in his essay on the differences between printed and electronic comics, and add some emphasis (my italics):

> It's easy to forget that we read—or rather 'use'—comics in a very physical way (*we tend to think of them as being two-dimensional, but in fact they exist in three dimensions*).[1]

Here, Sabin concisely enunciates one of the key characteristics of comics scholarship in the broadest sense. Scholars tend to see the page from what we might call an ideal perspective. While this is not quite a view from nowhere, it does confer upon the critic a similar level of power over the limited example of the comic.[2] In comics scholarship the notion of vision tends to be simplified to the point where the viewer is able to see an absolutely flat image in its entirety, and with perfect clarity. Light does not bounce off the surface of a comic's page; the comic *is* light, or at the very least is similarly intangible. Whichever formulation one prefers, the end result is the same: the viewer is able to see the comic (not the light it reflects) as a clean, flat manifestation of images that are consistent from one copy to the next, and can discuss it as such. The effect of this is to place the emphasis of that scholarship resolutely upon the *seen* (which is assumed to be the comic), rather than the *seeing*. The assumption is made that what is seen is seen unproblematically. As Heidi Rae Cooley puts it:

> Much of the time the practice of seeing is divorced from the experience of seeing, insofar as people tend to focus on and value *what* they see, not *how* they see, which means that people engage seeing in a manner similar to viewing snapshots, as a succession of discrete images. They become distanced observers, whose vision is objectified and quantifiable and, therefore, manageable.[3]

This is not to say that the *seer* is absent; scholars have considered the ways in which the composition of images can serve to generate and modify relationships between the reader and the comic. To give one example: at the first Women in Comics conference in 2009, Catriona MacLeod approached two *bandes dessinées*, *Barbarella* (Jean-Claude Forest) and *La Femme Piège* (Enki Bilal), using Laura Mulvey's concept of the Male Gaze.[4] She clearly and effectively demonstrated the ways in which images presented in those works serve to structure power relations along the lines of sex/gender, and thereby indicated the ways in which the reader is positioned relative to the texts under discussion. Approaching comics in this way is not uncommon, but it is slightly limited (or limiting) because it steps directly to the level of the reader's interaction with the image/text and skips over her/his interaction with the comic as a physical object, that is, it negates the *act* of seeing in favour of a more cognitive approach, which we might describe as the *idea* of seeing. This approach does represent a relationship between seer and seen, but this relationship is not quite the same as seeing because the seeing is a subordinate of the other two terms. Seeing is only the (assumedly transparent) process/means by which a power relationship is entered into by the seer and the seen. It is incapable of agency in and of itself.

Of course there are some good reasons for the ideal perspective to exist. Perhaps the most obvious (and significant) is the requirement for consistency. If we are to make arguments that can be expanded beyond specific examples and applied to the field of comics as a whole (which is particularly important for the development of a mechanics of comics), it is necessary for us to be able to speak in a manner which is consistent from one example to the next, and from one reader to the next. Therefore, we tend to assume that each instance of a particular comic is the same, and also that each reader sees that comic in the same way. When Charles Hatfield talks about *American Splendor* in *Alternative Comics: An Emerging Literature*, we must assume that this is the same *American Splendor* to which Joseph Witek is referring in *Comic Books as History*. We write not about a comic, but about the idea of a comic, or to put it another way, we speak about the text ('a methodological field') but not the work ('a fragment of substance').[5] This is hardly surprising because if 'the work can be held in the hand [while] the text is held in language', then to write about the work would require each reader (of the scholarly text) to have access to a single object in a single point in time and space.[6] The comic would effectively be understood as an *event* as Einstein, following Minkowski, uses the term (i.e., as a four-dimensional coordinate, a specific point in space and time).[7] This is clearly not practical; even attempting to take into account all the environmental factors that could affect a single comic's reading would be a Sisyphean task. Not only are they far too numerous to catalogue, they are also continuously changing over time (think, for example, of how the changing position of the sun relative to the Earth over the course of the day affects ambient light). We can also add social, historical and cultural factors to these physical ones. Each individual's ability to process the visual information with which they are presented will depend upon all these elements and more. The ideal perspective represents one solution to this problem: an assumption that the viewing environment does not affect how the comic is seen or how it produces meaning. We speak of comics' texts, discussing them in a manner that assumes all instances are identical or at least very similar (differences between editions are occasionally taken into account). This means that the critic's ability to *see* the comic is of no import, but her/his ability to *read* it is crucial.

Nevertheless in a study such as this one, which asserts the importance of materiality and the physical interactions between the reader and the comic, it is necessary to move beyond the ideological reader-text relationship and towards a more nuanced understanding. We are therefore required to discover some other means of conceptualising comics, a means by which we might include environmental elements without being overwhelmed by them. While contemplating the comic as an *event* is not practical for the reasons outlined above, one way in which we might be able to understand the function of comics in relation to their environment is by thinking about them in terms of *performance*. This idea is not entirely new, but it is only fairly recently that it has begun to permeate comics scholarship, with thinkers such as Bart Beaty, Annalisa Di Liddo and Jennifer Worth explicitly positing comics as a performative medium, although each goes about doing so in very different ways.[8] Without speaking about a specific comic for the moment, we might begin to think about some of the ways in which this approach may function. For me, conceptualising the act of "reading" comics as a performance means explicitly taking up the concept of materiality in reading, but also understanding that that materiality changes over time. While Ernesto Priego's four fairly generic categories of materiality (text, physical interface, space/habitat and human body) are useful, they are not sufficient, I would argue, to allow us to fully understand the act of performing comics. Each of these categories is important in allowing us to identify what, where and who is involved in reading, and so provides us with vital data, but it is only by emphasising temporality that we can begin to work on the relationships *between* the various elements.

At its most superficial level, emphasising temporality in concert with materiality means thinking about the time in which a comic is read, both in broad and narrower terms. In the broad sense, an individual reading an edition of *Ally Sloper's Half Holiday* in 1884 would have a very different experience (both physically and mentally) to one in 2014, because of course the material and cultural contexts of that reading will have changed significantly over 130 years.[9] Thinking more narrowly, the individual reading a comic at four o'clock in the afternoon will have a different experience to one reading at eleven o'clock at night. Even if there are few major changes to that reader's sense of history over that time, seemingly minor alterations to lighting, temperature, clothing and geographical location (among other things) will affect the physical bodies of the reader and the comic, and the location in which that comic is read, thereby effecting a substantively different experience. 'One can never [read] the same [comic] twice' to borrow a turn of phrase from film scholar Giuliana Bruno.[10] The comic is not performed in the same way all the time. While it would clearly be impossible to talk about every context in which a comic could be read, we can nevertheless consider elements such as lighting, temperature and the comic's physical composition because these elements are present in all comics reading experiences. The specific variables of these conditions may differ, but there are certain observations we can make about the conditions in general that can tell us important things about experiences of comics. Yet these two modes of temporal contextualisation are only the most obvious means by which time might be incorporated into an understanding of comics, and when considering how comics work to stimulate all five senses it becomes necessary to think about more subtle elements as well.

While some senses, like hearing, may be more obviously temporal in nature (see chapter 3), each is operable only over the course of time. From the time taken by photons to bounce off a comic's page and enter the eye, to the duration of a nerve impulse's journey from fingertip to brain stem, sensation is an inescapably temporal phenomenon. Thus, it is impossible to talk about how we experience comics without discussing time simultaneously. This is not to say that we will continually speak explicitly of the temporal aspects of the senses over the course of this study. Rather, it should be understood that each of the senses presented here is taken to comprise a number of necessarily temporal processes. In discussing, for example, motion on the part of the reader or the comic, I am assuming a certain level of temporality that is built in. The experience of the comic changes over time, as both object and experiencer move relative to each other. Yet while I will discuss the concept of motion in some detail, I will not repeatedly emphasise that motion is a temporal phenomenon; I will assume that this is self-evident from this point onwards. Where temporal concerns are more pressing or different senses specifically engage temporality in important ways (again, see chapter 3, as well as chapters 5 and 6) I will discuss them more explicitly, but by endeavouring to get closer to the realities of sensation, I am automatically incorporating time more comprehensively, in contrast to the abstract and atemporal formalism of the ideal perspective. This is not to say that we are going as far as considering the comic as an event, however, because while many of the processes I will discuss here take place *over* time, they are not unique *to* a particular time. Thus, as I mentioned above, we can draw some generalisations from the observation and analysis of these replicable phenomena. As we will see, there are some areas where this notion becomes problematic and the complexity of elements such as the reading environment presents a challenge to our understanding (see particularly sections 2.3 and 3.4). Nevertheless, I would argue that this approach does offer us a more comprehensive means of assessing the comic that goes some way towards negating the neutrality of the ideal perspective's reader-text relationship.

To develop these ideas further, let us now turn to some more specific concepts and examples, and consider the comic's visual performance as it is communicated to us through the eye as a physical (rather than conceptual) body.

2.1 A BRIEF INTRODUCTION TO SIGHT AND THE EYE

As Martin Jay notes, 'the optical mechanism of vision has been well understood since the time of Kepler', and it is a basic component of school science courses, so I will not bore the reader with too detailed a recounting of the process of sight, though a brief refresher might be of value.[11] We see things because the light that they emit or reflect passes into our eyes through the cornea and the pupil, travelling through focusing lenses and the aqueous and vitreous humours to the retina, which is a light-sensitive membrane composed of photoreceptive cells and nerve endings (see figure 2.1 for an indication of the structure of the eye).[12] These photoreceptors are of two types: rods and cones. The former allow us to detect shades of grey, shape and movement, while the latter detect colour.[13] We see three-dimensional images because the input from our two eyes is integrated to provide depth perception. The process by which this occurs is something of a mystery but the idea that binocular vision provides us with depth perception is not contentious.[14]

The nature of vision presents us with a philosophically interesting proposition: 'Vision and hearing [. . .] are indirect and abstract, since they connect us not with physical things, but only with the light and sound they emit or reflect'.[15] We will return to this aspect of hearing in section 3.0, but for now let us consider the implications of this notion for sight and the reading of comics. To put the matter simply: we never see the comic we read. Therefore the rather loose classification of seer and seen that I used earlier is not, strictly speaking, valid. In fact, the seen is composed of the light that enters our eye when we read a comic, not the comic itself. The nature of this light is of course affected significantly by the composition of the comic but

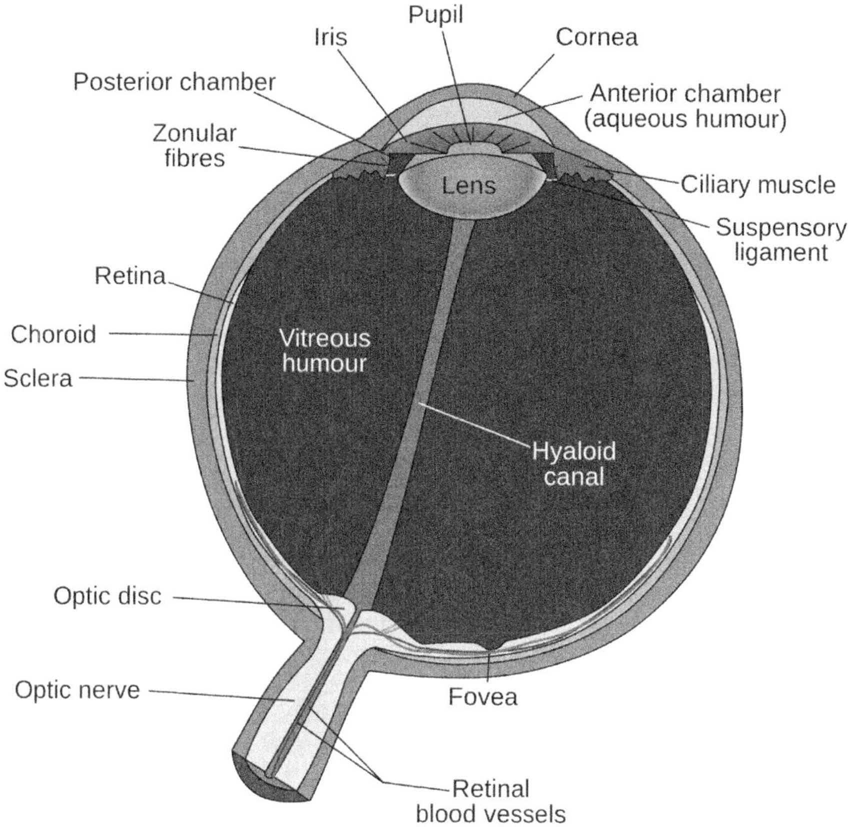

Figure 2.1 The structure of the human eye. Anonymous, public domain.

the environment also plays a major role, because aspects such as lighting and visibility will inevitably condition what we see and how we see it. The condition of the reader's eyes and the orientation of the reader's body to the work will also be important in determining how the seen is configured by the time it passes from the retina into the brain proper. While it would clearly be impossible to cover *all* the factors that affect our visual perception of comics, we can consider a selection of aspects.

2.2 GLOSS

The quantity of light a printed comic reflects is significantly affected by two primary factors. The first is the strength and position of the light source(s). These are extremely difficult to specify in terms of reading, because of course everyone reads in different environments. Nevertheless, we can confidently assert that viewers are always aware of at least a part of their surroundings when they are reading the comic, because whereas films are actively and intentionally isolated within the field of vision by the darkness of the cinema, the comic book must be apprehended in an environment where the lighting is sufficient for the reader to perceive it.[16] As we will see in sections 2.3 and 2.5, this awareness of the reading environment can play a significant role in the reader's understanding of the comic, but for now let us leave it as a passive element of the reading experience.

The second factor affecting the page's reflectivity is the composition of the page itself. The physical composition of the page affects light in two ways. Firstly, the colours of the page and the inks upon it affect the amount of light that is absorbed into or reflected by it, modulating the light and giving us the sensation of colour. This will be our primary focus in section 2.3, however, so I will not dwell upon it here. Secondly, the material the page is made of contributes significantly to the quantity of light it reflects. Where paper or cardboard are the compositing materials, the most obvious quality of note is the level of glossiness of the page. Though this may appear to be a relatively minor aspect of the comic, the glossiness (or lack thereof) of a comic book page can have considerable cultural import. Consider, for example, the differences in paper stock between the original publications of *Sandman* (Neil Gaiman et al. 1988–2000) in the late 1980s and early 1990s, and its republication in *The Absolute Sandman* editions in the 2000s. In the former, the paper stock used is rough and dull. Although it clearly reflects light (given that we can see the pages), it is not shiny or glossy, and there are no points of whiteout (i.e., spots where the light reflected from the surface is so bright as to obscure the reader's view of the images) even in very bright light. Conversely, in the later republications, each of these series was printed on thick, glossy paper that has a definite reflective sheen. Although this type of change is not unique to the Absolute Editions format and is evident to some degree in most graphic novels (see section 6.2 for more on the graphic novel as a format) the contrast is particularly stark here. In this case, the glossiness serves (along with other elements that I will discuss later) to confer a level of cultural prestige upon the comics. It suggests that they are important and worthy of preservation and republication, or perhaps that they have a nostalgic value, thereby reflecting and contributing to their canonisation as classics of the medium.

Here, the prestige afforded by the glossiness of the page comes from the contrast between it and the original publications' rough paper stock. We see a mutual reinforcement as the glossiness contributes to the prestige of the books, while the prestige of the books validates the use of glossy paper. It is possible, however, to manipulate this relationship so that it becomes less bidirectional, through the use of particular physical formats to confer prestige upon works that might not otherwise have achieved such presence. This can have significant economic benefits given the additional cost of glossy paper over the cheaper newsprint (or similar) paper stock of many original comics. Without wishing to appear too cynical, I suspect few would argue that *Superman: For Tomorrow* (Brian Azzarello and Jim Lee), *Green Lantern: Rebirth* (Geoff Johns and Ethan Van Sciver) or the first seven issues of *Danger Girl* (Andy Hartnell and J. Scott Campbell) are of historical or narrative significance equal to *Sandman*, but their inclusion in the same (very limited) publishing format does afford them a cultural cache through physical substantiality.[17] The glossiness of the pages here serves a validating function for the books, but the books themselves do not necessarily justify the use of glossy paper.

As Gary Spencer Millidge has observed, publishers and comic book designers are acutely aware of the changes that even such an ostensibly minor component as paper stock can make to the reader's perception of a comic, and are working to take advantage of these elements. He writes:

> Rather than designing to the standard "comic book size," we are now seeing rectangular publications of all sizes as well as square and landscape-shaped formats. Hardcover volumes with embossing and debossing, innovative dust jackets, softcovers with French-style end flaps, gloss and matt lamination, spot, varnishing, and die-cuts are all becoming more common. Particular paper stocks are often specified and bespoke color printing in any number of spot colors is no longer unusual.[18]

We will consider some of the other elements Millidge mentions here later in the book, but remaining with paper for the moment, it becomes important to ask *why* gloss is considered to be prestigious. There are, I think, two major reasons for this. Firstly, in the majority of areas where comics production is now on a scale that can be called industrial (e.g., America, France and Japan (this is not a comprehensive list)), comics have tended to be printed in a low-quality paper stock first and then upgraded to a more durable (and often glossier) stock when they are collected. While paper quality has improved since the early days of newsprint publishing, a time when Sterling North described American comics as 'pulp-paper nightmares', it is still the case that serialised publication formats tend to employ lower-quality paper than later collected editions (particularly in America and Japan, less so in France due to the prominence of the album format since the 1980s).[19] Gloss is one component of this format upgrade and where it is employed it suggests value in a way that, as I have indicated, goes beyond the narratives presented by the words and images upon the page. So widely has this convention permeated that even those works that have never been published in a nonglossy format, like Bryan Talbot's *Alice in Sunderland* and *Grandville*, are able to draw upon this broad tradition in their composition. Yet there is another possible reason why gloss is such a strong indicator of the cultural value of a comic (whether "inherent" or assigned).

Edging towards Marxism, it is quite possible to argue that the veneer of smoothness that accompanies gloss tends towards concealing the labour involved in the production of the page. It emphasises the mechanical processes involved in the manufacture of the book, and implies a level of consistency that is rarely possible in artisanal production.[20] The marks of the comic's artists and writers are erased by the smooth continuity of the gloss. Thus gloss makes an active contribution to the commoditisation of the page and the negation of the text. Such contributions and transformations have been lamented by critics, who feel that the proper use of comics is to be read, rather than prized for commercial value.[21] Nevertheless, it is fair to say that an increase in economic value does tend to be attended by a magnified cultural cache within a capitalist economic system. This, I think, is how most would understand gloss, and they would therefore see it as a primarily economic element of the composition of comics. If we follow this logic further we might also infer the converse, namely that matte surfaces, which do not implicitly smooth the producer's labour out of the page (or at least not as much as gloss), are more textual and less commoditised. This perhaps explains the regular employment of matte or near-matte pages in what are ostensibly artistic and/or independent books (e.g., *Asterios Polyp* (David Mazzucchelli), *Kramer's Ergot* (Sammy Harkham, ed.), *Solipsistic Pop* (Tom Humberstone, ed.)), where the role of the author is often viewed as more important than in commercial books (by which I mean that in commercial books, the property (e.g., Spider-Man) is more important than the authors (e.g., Stan Lee and Steve Ditko)). It should be noted, however, that commercial books did not always have glossy pages (and there are still a number that do not), and for this reason it is risky to assign too much significance to matte surfaces. Nevertheless, in combination with other elements, such as paper thickness (which we will consider in more detail in chapters 3 and 4) it can aid us in situating the work within a sociocultural context.

Yet there is an alternative understanding of the gloss upon the page that is diametrically opposed to this one, which I would like to consider here. Essentially, when we see that a page is glossy we are not seeing the images and writing upon that page. Rather, the cognisance of a glossy page is an awareness of the *surface* of the page; it is a moment when seeing the page becomes difficult; when the act of seeing becomes visible. This directs the attention not towards opening up the text but to grappling with the physicality of the form, and the reader's mind is, even if only momentarily, directed towards the comic as a physical object and the reader's interaction with it. Awareness of the physical object prevents the page from '[changing] into a thing which transcends sensuousness', a possessor of 'grotesque ideas'; it *denies* the commoditisation of the page, keeping it firmly entrenched in the realm of the real, the thing.[22] The gloss upon a page reminds the reader of the specificity of the moment and the space in which (s)he encounters that page; it connects her/him to a particular performance of that comic because (s)he is reminded not just of *what* (s)he is experiencing in that work, but *how* (s)he is experiencing it. This latter reading is, I think, just as valid as the former, but perhaps a little more offbeat. When considered closely, we can see that where the former is more resolutely and conventionally Marxist in its understanding of the comics page, the latter slightly repositions the argument to make the reader its primary focus. The reader is here presented as an active participant in the production of meaning within the text, and some of the acts of labour are thereby conferred upon the reader. The reader is not a passive audience member in front of whom the performance takes place; (s)he is a part of that performance.

Of course, gloss is not the only element of comics that emphasises their physicality to the reader and makes explicit the act of seeing. As we progress through the chapter, and indeed the book as a whole, we will see that in fact, there are many other ways in which comics' objecthood is made more obvious (see particularly section 2.3 and section 2.5). In many instances, this objecthood goes beyond emphasising what I have here loosely termed 'cultural value' and affects the narrative and form of comics themselves. Gloss is a very important example, but it is fairly basic and is not indicative of the heights comics are capable of reaching when considered as a performative medium.

2.3 COLOUR

As I have already implied, the materials of which comics are composed, and the sizes and shapes into which these materials are arranged, are all extremely important in determining the comic's visual character. In the case of printed comics, the selection of paper (and other materials), inks and paratextual elements such as attached bookmarks all contribute to a complete package which modulates the light transmitted to the reader's eye. The paper stock selected for the comic is particularly important to the overall look of the finished object, and can determine the content of the text to a large degree. Colour provides us with an excellent example of this, which also neatly demonstrates the importance of the reading environment to the reading itself.

Newsprint paper stock tends to have a dulling effect on colour, which is why early American superhero comics present characters and environments that are bright and colourful to the point of being garish; colourists were driven to overcompensate in order that their books would be attractive to the eye rather than dull and lifeless.[23] Though this is no longer a necessity given improvements in printing techniques and the availability of higher-quality paper types, it is worth noting that modern reprints of early works do tend to retain or reproduce the bright colours of the original printings, giving images a sense of historical specificity that is determined not only by line but by colour. It can also be observed that the brightness of the colours employed in these books makes them physically easier to see and read, given that the eye's colour-detecting cones are more effective in bright conditions, and brighter colours will reflect more light into the eye than dark ones. This may contribute to the comics' attractiveness to readers, but it also implies a simplicity and even vulgarity that was a cause for concern at least as early as 1940, when Sterling North famously wrote of comics:

> Badly drawn, badly written and badly printed—a strain on young eyes and nervous systems—the effect of these pulp-paper nightmares is that of a violent stimulant. Their crude blacks and reds spoil the child's natural sense of color; their hypodermic injection of sex and murder makes the child impatient with better, though quieter, stories.[24]

Here, the boldness and simplicity of the comics' colour scheme serve to incite a strong polemic against the medium, and although we may not agree with North's assertions per se, it is not difficult to hear echoes of this argument in the remarks of those who denounce comics, particularly those in colour, as visually simplistic, or see colour as an element of '"bad" comic books' as opposed to '"good" [black and white] graphic novels'.[25]

Even from relatively early in the history of art theory, the roles and value of colour have been contentious issues for thinkers. In 1671, Louis Gabriel Blanchard launched a spirited defence of colour, asserting that '[. . .] masterfully applied colour always represents the truth, whereas design represents only a reasonable possibility'.[26] Blanchard's ideas were swiftly rebutted by Charles Le Brun thus:

> [. . .] the role of colour is exclusively to satisfy the eye, unlike design, which satisfies the intellect. Since paintings aim to please both the senses and the intellect, colour has its own part to play [. . .] in the perfection of the work. Therefore we should not neglect it, nor should we hold it in low esteem. On the contrary, we should apply ourselves to its study with care. We should, however, let design be our guide, leading and directing our study like a compass so that we do not become submerged in the ocean of colour in which many drown who seek refuge there.[27]

What is interesting in these two (admittedly very old) arguments is the directness and power that each man ascribes to colour. In both, we see an acceptance of the idea that while design appeals to the mind, colour has a clear connection to the sensual aspects of human beings. Yet as Pascal Lefèvre reminds us, it is unwise to assume that the function of colour is wholly nonrational given that 'the experience of colors [sic] is [. . .] culturally determined'.[28] 'Nevertheless', he goes on to assert, 'colors also have a certain a-cultural potential to arouse', and while it is difficult to quietly accept the notion of an acultural condition, it is certainly true that colours are particularly capable of generating powerful, nonrational (e.g., emotional, sensual, etc.) responses.[29] Yet the power of colour is one of the elements of comics that is particularly vulnerable to environmental change. Because the colour-detecting cones in the eye are less capable of functioning in low light conditions, reading comics in such conditions can have a substantial impact upon the reader's ability to detect chromatic variation.[30] While this will not affect the reader of *Maus* (Art Spiegelman) or *From Hell* (Alan Moore and Eddie Campbell), and will arguably have only a minimal impact upon the reader of comics where colour is (in theory at least) incidental (see note), where colour is an integral and inextricable element of the work (for example, in David Mazzucchelli's *Asterios Polyp*), it is important to give it the best chance of being seen properly.[31]

Here we stumble upon something of a paradox for comics scholarship, which reaffirms the problematic nature of the ideal perspective. On the one hand, colour is a prime example of the importance of the reading environment to the meaning contained within the comic. The signifying functions of colour that have been marked up by Scott McCloud and Pascal Lefèvre are in some works extremely important, and can play fundamental roles in the understanding of them.[32] But because colour is *so* vulnerable to change, it represents a very unstable component of the comic's composition; the meaning conveyed by a patch of colour upon a comic's page is entirely subject to the vagaries of light within the reading environment. Thus, it behooves us to consider this environment if we are to understand how comics actually express meaning. Yet what colour also demonstrates is the complexity, if not impossibility, of actually doing so. One solution to this problem, as we have already observed, is the ideal perspective: an assumption that the viewing environment does not affect how the comic is seen or how it produces meaning. But there are problems with this approach because, as mentioned above, it promotes reading at the expense of seeing. We strive to 'produce the text, open it out, *set it going*', yet colour denies us the possibility to consider the text in abstraction because it is too firmly entrenched in the realm of the work, which is limited, individual and changeable (by environmental conditions).[33] The same is true of the other elements of vision that I have mentioned here, though it is perhaps in colour that the most explicit emphasis upon the effects of spatial and temporal change can be found. Even a model of comics as performance can only begin to approach an answer to this query by suggesting a selection of relevant elements for consideration in order to generate a *more* holistic understanding, but we will never achieve an entirely event-specific reading unless we move to a very particular model of scholarship predicated upon a gallery type approach whereby all the conditions of viewing are strictly controlled. This is hardly practical. This being the case, it makes sense to return to our discussion of relevant categories of expansion somewhat chastened but not altogether deterred by colour.

2.4 FOCUS AND EYE-MOTION

The function of the eye's lens is to bend the rays of light passing through the eye, directing them towards the photoreceptive cells on the retina. The lens is held in place by the suspensory ligaments and its shape is regulated by the ciliary muscles. The shape of the lens is critical for our ability to focus. When focusing on nearby objects, the ciliary muscles contract and cause the lens to become thicker and increase its curvature. Conversely, when we focus on more distant objects the muscles relax and the lens becomes flatter. This process is called accommodation, and it is shared with some reptiles, birds and other mammals.[34] It has even featured in comics. In *Action Comics* #8, a small information box offers readers tips on 'Acquiring Super-Strength' and 'Super-Vision', suggesting that if readers 'first glance at a distant object' and 'then glance at a close object' for 'a few minutes every day' they will soon 'be able to peer more distantly than any of [their] friends!'[35] The means by which the child is to acquire 'super sight' here presumably involve training the ciliary muscles so that they are able to carry out the process of accommodation more quickly and effectively.

Yet accommodation plays other roles in comics besides providing an interesting activity for children seeking superpowers. In fact, it is a partial analogue for one of the most important aspects of comics theory, which we can describe, borrowing terminology from Charles Hatfield, as the distinction between sequence and surface. In *Alternative Comics: An Emerging Literature,* Hatfield identifies comics as 'an art of tensions'.[36] He distinguishes four specific types of tension evident within the medium, one of which is 'sequence vs. surface'.[37] 'The page,' he argues, 'functions both as sequence and object, to be seen and read in both linear and nonlinear, holistic fashion'.[38] The sequence is comprised of the individual panels (or other units) understood as single images apprehended in their reading order, while the surface is the page in its entirety; the former is what we read; the latter is what we see. While this concept did not originate with Hatfield, his presentation of the idea does have the benefits of coherence, eloquence and concision, and while his approach has been criticised for '[feeling] oppressively schematic', the distinction between sequence and surface is fairly useful in understanding how narratives are deployed in comics, particularly in formally experimental ones such as *Watchmen.*[39] On the first page of chapter/issue #4, for example, we see the tension between sequence and surface masterfully manipulated by Alan Moore and Dave Gibbons to give the reader the same power over the page as the nearly omniscient character of Doctor Manhattan has over time itself.[40] The reader, like Manhattan, can see the past, present and future simultaneously in the page's surface, while at the same time being aware of the linear progression of the narrative through those temporal phases in the sequence.[41]

Understood in terms of the comic as a discrete physical object (ignoring the reader and/or reading environment), the sequence/surface conceptualisation is quite satisfactory because it accurately outlines the deployment of information within the boundaries of that object. But when we come to integrate these missing elements we encounter problems because they do not necessarily fit with the highly abstracted sequence/surface model Hatfield proposes. That said, he does also acknowledge the practical difficulty of applying his approach wholesale to the comic as an object, asserting:

> Despite the codification of techniques designed to ease [the negotiation among various possible meanings . . .] there is no one "right" way to read the comics page, nor any stable, Platonic conception of that page. There is simply no consistent formula for resolving the tensions intrinsic to the experience. In fact awareness of these tensions, an awareness expected of the prepared or "sophisticated" reader, may multiply the number of choices available to the reader and can result in an even more intensive questioning of the page [. . .] The foregoing analysis, then, cannot tell us How to Read Comics [sic]; it can only suggest certain heretofore neglected aspects of the experience.[42]

Although Hatfield's model is not oriented *around* the senses, and he makes little reference to the functions of the reader or the reading environment, it is possible to adapt it so that it can work *with* the senses, though this may not be immediately obvious.

When we first encounter a page in a comic, it is usually the case that the surface will have the most powerful impact. We naturally take in the whole page (or spread) before moving on to consider the sequential elements that convey the narrative.[43] When we do move on, accommodation takes us from focusing on the broader spread to the tighter focus on the more specific details (panels, word balloons, etc.) adjusting the curvature of the eye to ensure that we are able to see each element clearly as required. We could therefore argue that the reality of sight negates Hatfield's notion of comics as an *art* of tensions because the need to focus differently at different levels means we are unable to hold the sequence and the surface in *physiological* tension. Of course, we can hold them in mental tension, but the realities of sight would seem to undermine Hatfield's conception of comics in the strictest terms.

The wide/narrow focus shift is not unique to comics; the process of accommodation is also involved in other art forms. Cinema is one obvious example, with the IMAX format in particular presenting an image type that requires the viewer to shift between wide and narrow focus in order to take in both the entirety of the massive image with which (s)he is presented, and study the more minute details of that image. This effect is even more obvious in the IMAX Dome format, where the screen stretches over the viewer's head, making it extremely difficult (if not impossible) for her/him to take in the whole of the screen at once; requiring the viewer to move from one mode of focusing to the other repeatedly in her/his reception of the images. Turning to other art forms, it is difficult to see how either wide or narrow focus in isolation could allow the viewer to understand something like the works of Hieronymus Bosch, which teem with complex chaos in their representations of a multitude of tortures on a grand scale. Neither the wide view of the whole nor the narrow view of the seemingly endless details will give the viewer a good understanding of the image, but when worked together they provide a complete visual package. Thus, it would be rather foolish to suggest that accommodation is somehow unique to comics, though it is of course fair to assert that it is present in the act of reading comics.

Yet there is another type of musculature involved in the act of seeing, one that is worth discussing before we consign the notion of tensions entirely to the theoretical/mental realm. The extrinsic ocular or extraocular muscles surround the eye (and are therefore not a part of it as the ciliary muscles are) and serve to direct the eyeball in whatever direction the individual wishes to look. As Will Eisner has made clear, the conventional mode of reading in Western comics will require a top-left to bottom-right motion of the eyes.[44] The direction of movement is different in manga (top-right to bottom-left), but the principle of the eyeball's motion is essentially the same. As the reader will doubtless have realised, this type of movement is no more unique to comics than is accommodation; with the exception of concrete poetry and some other forms (e.g., advertising), the majority of written texts in Romance languages follow this ocular path.

We do enter the territory of comics more specifically, I would suggest, when we consider the combination of accommodation and eyeball motion together, and use both processes as the bases for our understanding, rather than accommodation by itself. Of course, the art forms I have just mentioned do use a combination of each element to some degree, but they do so in a slightly different way to comics. If we consider a conventional prose book, it can be observed that although the reader's eyes do move over the page linearly through the use of the extraocular muscles, the employment of the process of accommodation is relatively minimal. All the words tend to be the same size, and are arranged in such a way that their visual position upon the page relative to each other is largely irrelevant (again, examples such as concrete poetry are exceptions to this general rule); in most written works the sequence is what matters, not the surface. Conversely, while we may look at an IMAX film or a Hieronymus Bosch painting using wide or narrow focus (or a combination of the two) our eyes do not tend to be driven across the screen in a linear fashion as they are in books. This is not to say that there is *no* direction of the eyes, but it is fair to say that cinema does not direct the motion of the eyes in as rigidly linear a fashion as prose.

Comics, however, *do* employ a combination of the two elements, and in a largely consistent fashion. Our eyes tend to move over the page of a comic in a particular way and following a generally linear path. This path may follow a reading convention like top-left to bottom-right, or it may be directed by other visual cues upon the page (e.g., arrows, numbers etc.) but it is characterised by a directed motion.[45] As Joseph Witek puts it: 'We experience panels in comics at once and in any order, but as narrative elements they presuppose a left-to-right and top-to-bottom (that is, a reading) order'.[46] Additionally, the eyes shift between the different levels of focusing through the process of accommodation while they are being directed.[47] It is here, in the combination between accommodation and ocular motion, that we find a physical analogue for Hatfield's sequence/surface tension. While I am reluctant to suggest that this form of what I will call FocusMotion is a defining characteristic of comics, it is certainly worth considering if we extend Joseph Witek's assertion that 'to be a comic means to be *read* as a comic' to include elements of the physical act of reading.[48] The directed, multilevel focusing required of the comics reader sets comics apart from other media, and although it is not enough in and of itself to underpin a complete theory of comics, it is a piece of the larger puzzle. As we move through the other sections of the book we will uncover more such pieces, which help us not only to view the comic as a performance, but to situate the comic's reader as a critical element of the comic itself.

2.5 SIZE, SHAPE AND MOVEMENT

As I noted earlier (see section 2.2), the comic reader is always aware of at least a part of his surroundings when reading a comic, because it must be experienced in an environment where the lighting allows the reader to perceive it. Though it could be argued that viewers could move the comics close enough to their eyes that they could not perceive anything else, the fact that they rely upon light to see the comic disproves this notion. The viewer is incapable of direct visual contact with the comic: (s)he is reliant upon light bouncing off its surface and into her/his eyes to see it. The viewer never sees the comic; (s)he only sees its reflected or emitted light. The reader's awareness of the comic's size and shape always arises in the context of a larger environment, and this contextualisation also applies to the images and text within the comic. Comics narratives are not viewed from the ideal perspective's isolated position, rather they are continually situated and resituated within a changing reading environment: '[. . .] there is no such thing as an independently existing [comics narrative], but only a [comics narrative] relative to a particular body of reference', to repurpose a phrase from Albert Einstein.[49] While this reference may seem flippant, it is worth pointing out that the shift from analysis undertaken from the ideal perspective to the more complex form of analysis that incorporates the environment, the object and the reader as they change over time is not wholly dissimilar to the move from classical to relativistic physics that Einstein advocated. In highlighting the importance of these components, we seek to destabilise the idea of a fixed body of reference in favour of a continually moving one in which objects and environments both affect and are affected by each other. A natural consequence of employing this mode of analysis is that we come to emphasise the size, shape and motion of the comic as relevant components of its overall composition, because all three categories influence the relational play between the comic and the context in which it is read.

The size and shape of a comic are not specific to the visual field. They also serve to modify the sound and the feel of the object, and we will return to these considerations when we discuss the senses of hearing and touch in chapter 3 and chapter 4 respectively. For now, though, let us remain focused upon the roles that size plays in our visual understanding. In his 'Notes on Sculpture', Robert Morris makes a number of important statements about the significance of size. Though his remarks are directed towards the field of sculpture, I do not think it inappropriate to employ them in the study of comics given that comics tend just as much towards sculpture as they do literature and ostensibly visual arts like painting and cartooning. Both comics and sculpture tend to involve the manipulation of physical substances to modify space in a particular way. In this sense they can be understood as similar entities and it is quite surprising that the analogies between the two media have not yet been investigated rigorously by scholars, though this situation is beginning to change.[50]

Morris observes that '[t]he size range of useless three-dimensional things is a continuum between monument and the ornament'.[51] In the case of comics, we might argue that this continuum stretches from the postage stamp to the Sunday broadsheet if we wish to remain within a fairly conventional categorisation.[52] With increasing size comes an increasing presence in the viewers' field of vision, but more than that, the development of an emphasis upon size itself as the subject of the work. To return to Morris:

> While specific size is a condition that structures one's response in terms of the more or less public or intimate, enormous objects in the class of monuments elicit a far more specific response to size *qua* size. That is, besides providing the condition for a set of responses, large-sized objects exhibit size more specifically as an element. It is the more conscious appraisal of size in monuments that makes for the quality of 'scale'. The awareness of scale is a function of the comparison made between that constant, one's body size, and the object.[53]

Similarly, where a comic is very large and occupies a substantial portion of the viewer's field of vision, this property of size is imbued with a significance that can be culturally suggestive. I have already discussed the added prestige that DC Comics' Absolute Editions impart to their reprinted comics through the use of gloss upon their pages, and it is surely also true that the sizes of the works (here taken in comparison not only with the reader's body but also with the original publication format) play major roles in according these works a form of cultural prestige of the type I mentioned earlier. Without wishing to repeat myself, it is worth noting that the Absolute Editions can give a literal, physical largeness to those (culturally or narratively) "big" comics that they re-present to the readership. This largeness can also have an impact upon the way in which the comics' details are understood by the reader. To return once again to Robert Morris: 'Properties that are not read as detail in large works become detail in small works' (although note that Morris's position on this is not universally upheld).[54] Thus, paradoxically, as a work gains in cultural prestige by increasing in size from one publication format to the next, it loses intricacy as details of the artwork shed their complexity and become more visually simplistic thanks to the increased space afforded to them. This process, of course, will contribute to the uptake of the work into the broader sociocultural mythological sphere because the simplification of the image will make it easier to understand as a 'total term' by removing the necessity to 'ask [. . .] questions about the composition of the language-object' or to focus upon 'the details of the linguistic schema'.[55] A large size can therefore serve to increase the ease with which a work is understood and its messages are conveyed, giving it great transmissibility at the expense of its (apparent) complexity. Conversely, a small work can seem extremely dense and complex, even when its content is actually relatively simplistic.

But the role of size does not end with the composition of the comic itself, because it also has a significant impact upon the ways in which that comic interacts with the environment in which it is read. To draw a final quotation from Robert Morris: 'The better new work takes relationships out of the work and makes them a function of space, light, and the viewer's field of vision. The object is but one of the terms in the newer aesthetic'.[56] Just as Ernesto Priego emphasised the need to consider the multiple terms of space/habitat, physical interface, text and the human body as interrelated elements of the reading experience, Morris here points out that the meaning-producing relationships involved in the understanding of art do not lie solely in the discrete and delimited field of the artwork as an object, but rather in the totality of experiences that involve that object. Further than that though, he observes that the best work is that which displays a conscious awareness of the importance of these relationships. I would now like to consider some works that do display such awareness, and a selection of techniques that work to emphasise or minimise it through the manipulation of size and shape.

Perhaps the most basic means by which a comic interacts with both its environment and the reader's physical body is through its visibility. Visibility affects the reader's ability to see the comic and to situate it in the reading environment, and there are a number of techniques open to the creator that allow her/him to affect the visibility of the object. One way of reducing the comic's visibility is through bleeding, of the type demonstrated by Scott McCloud in *Making Comics,* where the image is printed up to the corners of the page (i.e., there are no margins and no panel borders around the outer edges of the image).[57] As McCloud remarks:

> Bleeds [. . .] tend to *open up* a scene - - /- - not just because of the increased panel *sizes* - - /- - but also because they're no longer fully *contained* by the panel border and can, well . . . "bleed" into our world - - /- - or perhaps because we're conditioned by the *panel-as-window* experience - - /- - and if a window frame has passed beyond our peripheral vision - - /- - it

> usually means we're *through* it.[58] [Author's note: McCloud places these words within a succession of balloons. The use of a slash (/) here indicates where one balloon ends and the next begins. I use this mark in this way throughout this book.]

Bleeding serves to reduce the distinction between the diegetic environment and the reader's environment by removing the empty border between them, thereby minimising the reader's perception of the comic as object. The hierarchy of three:

Real World > Comic > Image

is reduced to a hierarchy of two:

Real World > Image

Of course this process is not absolute; the reader remains aware that (s)he is reading a comic, but the distinction between the comic and its images is made less clear. The opposite occurs when the page is emphasised, and there are a variety of ways in which this can be done but I will only consider two examples here for the purposes of brevity. In Kyle Baker's *Plastic Man: On the Lam!*, panel borders are wholly absent: the images sit upon white paper with very few solid lines, even where they are usually common (for example in word balloons). Here the whiteness surrounding the image is indicative of the distinction between page and image, and the page itself is emphasised by this whiteness, suggesting the hierarchy:

Real World > Comic > Page Surface>Image

This is further complicated when panel borders are rigidly enforced, as is the case in *Watchmen* and numerous other comics. Here the ever-present, geometrically consistent whiteness surrounding the panels serves to emphasise the frames as containers of the images, thereby adding another level to the hierarchy:

Real World > Comic > Page Surface > Panel > Image

In both these examples, the surface of the page is taken into account not simply in terms of its function within the comic's aesthetic paradigm, but as a physical entity that takes its meaning from a broad physical context. In the former example the primacy of materiality serves to indicate the malleable physicality of the lead character, something we will come back to in more detail when we consider touch in chapter 4. In the latter, the highly experimental, formalist nature of *Watchmen* is reinforced by the continual reassertion of the physical form as the manifestation of the narrative, although as we will see in chapter 6, this was not necessarily the author's intent.

While these examples are certainly interesting indications of the ways in which comics creators are able to emphasise the nature of comics as objects to the reader, more complexity begins to develop if we consider the role of motion as an integral component of the comic reading experience. Motion on the part of the comic (which I am distinguishing from motion on the part of the reader's eyes, the aforementioned FocusMotion) is extremely important to the comic reading experience, though it is frequently resisted by commentators who seek to distinguish comics from animation in a fairly stark fashion, asserting that a comic becomes a cartoon when it begins to move.[59] The field of motion comics has accordingly met opposition from fans and scholars alike, who argue that there is no place for motion within the field of comics proper, consigning these productions to existences as at worst bastardisations and at best hybrids of comics and animated cartoons.[60] While it is beyond the remit of this study to consider the ontological issues surrounding motion comics, it is nevertheless worth mentioning them when considering the roles that motion plays in comics because they provide both a point of comparison and an area that is likely to develop further in future as digital comics become more common. Yet the type of motion that is employed in productions such as *Watchmen: The Motion Comic* (dir. Jake S. Hughes) is not the kind I am speaking of here. Rather, I am speaking of the motion that is, and always has been, prevalent even in those works that *are* widely accepted as comics. Comic books and graphic novels alike require the reader to turn the page in order to advance through the narrative, and this kind of interaction does affect the ways in which that narrative is perceived. Furthermore, some artists require readers to interact in still more complex ways with the comic, and these are of interest to us here because they represent points at which the reader is drawn most comprehensively into the comic as performance (though not necessarily into the narrative). Finally, we must consider the realm of motion within the reader's peripheral vision, for this too can affect how the reader interacts with and comprehends the object with which (s)he is working.

In some media, the object of contemplation remains still while the spectator is free to move. In the field of painting, for example, conventional practice involves the piece being hung on a wall. Though there is perhaps a recommended viewing angle, this is only rarely a requirement of the act of viewing the image.[61] In cinema the spectator is more fixed, traditionally remaining in one seat throughout the presentation, but this too is more a social convention than one of necessity.[62] Where cinema tends to discourage the movement of the spectator, sculpture encourages it, presenting objects that are intended for viewing from multiple angles and unlike painting or cinema cannot be taken in fully without this requirement being met.[63] Comics, by contrast, allow the mobility of both the object and its spectator, and employing this can have a significant impact upon the perception of the object.[64] In printed comics both are employed regularly as readers are required to move their eyes and hands to progress through the comic's narrative, and to move the comic itself while turning the pages, changing its position, and so forth. On a very basic level, some particularly thick books require readers to move the head or the book or both in order to make out the content in the centre of the double page that can at times become obscured by the density of pages on either side of it.

There are ways in which the motion of the comic and/or the spectator can be integrated more fully, however, and it is here that we move once again into the realm of the performance as an explicit mode of understanding comics. One way in which the reader can be encouraged to move the comic is through the employment of 'puzzle pages' or the use of other devices that require the reader to reorient the comic in order to be able to comfortably read it.

In figure 2.2 we see a piece from David Mack's *Kabuki: Metamorphosis* (1998), in which the protagonist is attempting to navigate a labyrinthine facility, and the reader is required to do the same with the page, rotating it around in her/his field of vision in order to follow the words around the page.[65] This technique has also been used less ostentatiously in other works. After the first few pages of Chris Ware's *Jimmy Corrigan: The Smartest Kid on Earth,* which are presented in a portrait orientation, the reader is required to rotate the book by 90° to continue reading, which clearly marks out the existence of that book as a spatial entity that has a tangible substance upon which the reader is able to act. Still more inventive than these examples is Gustave Verbeck's short-lived *The Upside Downs of Little Lady Lovekins and Old Man Muffaroo* (1903–1905), which required the reader to read the comic from top left to bottom right once, then rotate it 180° and read it in the same way again to complete the narrative.[66]

In all of these examples the '[. . .] function[s] of space, light, and the viewer's field of vision' whose interactions were marked up by Robert Morris as being present in the best new work are clearly in evidence, and through these functions the comic is explicitly pushed from a two-dimensional text to be read into a four-dimensional work to be performed. The relative positions of reader and comic are actively engaged with by these comics' creators, who situate the works within the contexts of consumption. Were creators inclined towards a more controlling function, they might also seek to direct the reader's position relative to the page though anamorphosis. This has been implied in comics to some degree. In *Alice in Sunderland,* Bryan Talbot presents Colin Wilbourn's sculpture 'Passing Through', which does make use of anamorphosis in its representations of past, present and future.[67] These representations are depicted upon the page, but the anamorphosis effect does not come across particularly strongly in the book form. Nevertheless, it does suggest an area for development in comics; the effectiveness of anamorphosis would likely be increased if pieces were created specifically for comics.

Before moving on, it is worth noting that motion is not confined to the comic itself. Movement in the reading environment that is seen in the reader's peripheral vision, for example, contrasts sharply with the stillness

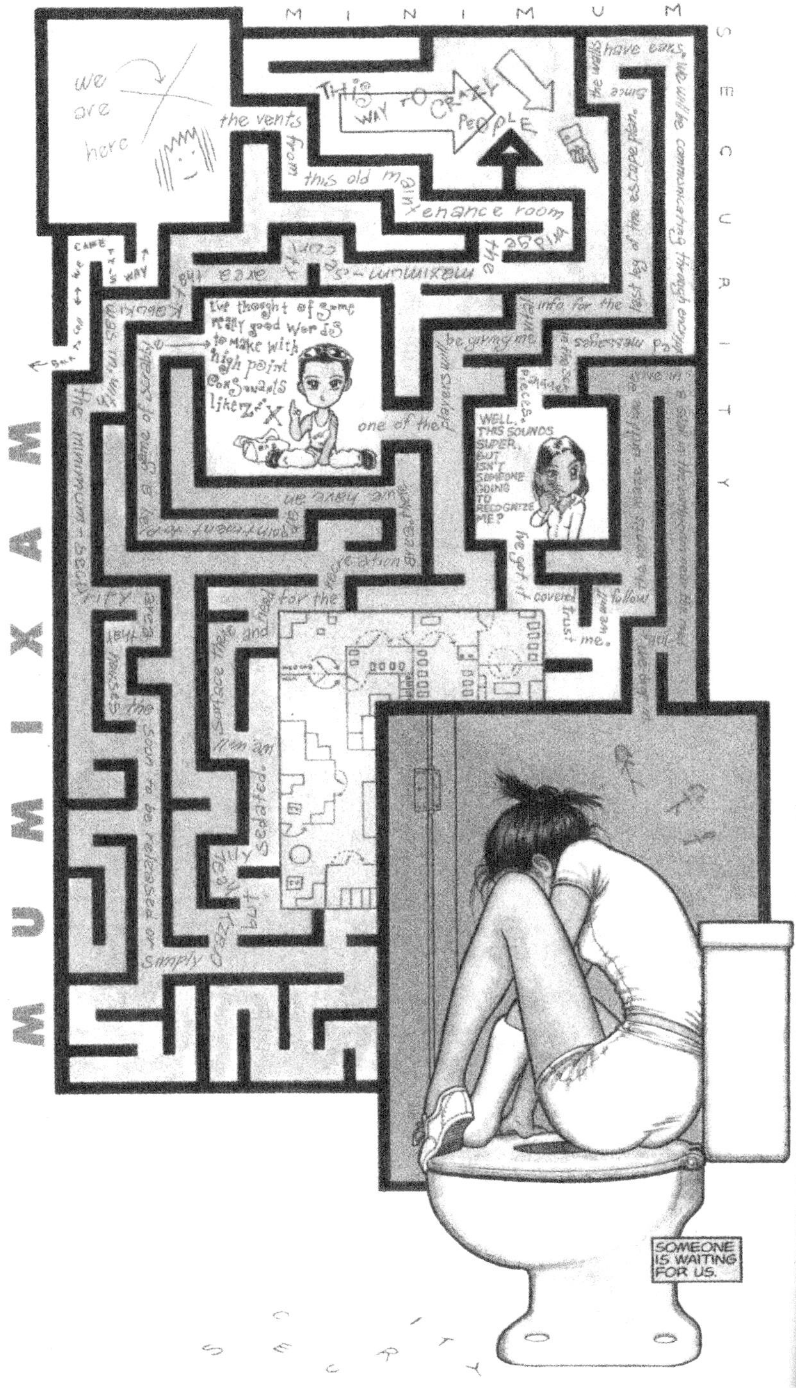

Figure 2.2 A puzzle page from David Mack's *Kabuki: Metamorphosis*. Image used with the kind permission of the artist.

of the images upon the page and can serve to distract the reader from the narrative with which (s)he is engaged. This distraction also has the effect of emphasising the physicality of the comic as an object because it is continuously situated within a broad visual context rather than being able to present an all-encompassing (or nearly all-encompassing) diegetic environment. The contrast between stillness and motion here serve to make the comic highly visible by emphasising its nature as an object. Of course, this mode of awareness is not something that is controlled by the comic's creator, but it is possible that a sufficiently inventive thinker could develop a means by which this type of control could be effected.

2.6 DIMENSIONALITY

One final element of sight that needs to be thought about before we can move onto the other senses is the fact that the eye is not a single object. That we have two eyes is an important consideration when we think about how comics are read because it is this that gives us the ability to perceive depth (i.e., the third dimension). Many of the considerations I have outlined above are implicitly predicated upon three-dimensional vision, but despite my assertion that we should view comics as a four-dimensional medium it is rare that an ability to perceive three dimensions is absolutely necessary for the understanding of comics. Nevertheless, there are some instances where binocular vision is a requirement; as in the case of 3D comics, which often use anaglyphs as a means of creating a three-dimensional image upon the page. Relatively little has been written on 3D comics, and they have generally been seen as a gimmick product with little function beyond increasing sales during their brief periods of popularity.[68] In recent years, however, some efforts have been made to employ anaglyphs with the express intention of generating particular narrative or philosophical effects. In Mathieu's *La 2,333e dimension* (part of the five-volume *Julius Corentin Acquefacques* series), the last few pages feature anaglyphs that add additional meaning to the protagonist's growing awareness of multidimensional reality.[69] Similar applications of the technology can be found in DC Comics' *Final Crisis: Superman Beyond 3D* series (Grant Morrison and Doug Mahnke), and *The League of Extraordinary Gentlemen: The Black Dossier* (Alan Moore and Kevin O'Neill, see section 6.1 for more on *The Black Dossier*).

As these examples all indicate, the most obvious benefit of the three-dimensional image is the possibility it provides for the images upon the page to expand along the z-axis and the implications this can have for the characters. Just as the character of A. Square learned to think 'Upward, not Northward' in Edwin A. Abbott's classic *Flatland: A Romance of Many Dimensions*, comic book characters can be presented as having an additional, even metatextual awareness when they come to operate outside the two-dimensional limits by which their ontologically challenged companions may be bound.[70] Certainly, there is room for further development in this area, and as digital technologies become more powerful it is probable that they will increase the ease with which images can be produced in or converted to 3D.

Yet it is worth sounding a note of caution here. 3D comics provide a particular touchstone for the issue of comics for blind and visually impaired readers because they are so dependent upon the reader having two fully functional eyes. Readers with sight loss in one eye or with certain forms of colour blindness will be unable to access a 3D comic in which the images are rendered using anaglyph techniques. As a slight aside, I would like to briefly consider this issue here. Comics, already conceived of as a primarily, if not exclusively, visual medium do not tend towards easy adaptations for the visually impaired. Where a textual work can be converted into spoken words or Braille, comics' use of images makes it extremely difficult to argue that a similar conversion would provide a satisfactory outcome in this medium. While it would theoretically be possible to create comics for the blind or visually impaired reader using raised images, this would also require a simplification of the image to ensure tactile clarity (though this would perhaps be easier in the field of comics than other types of illustration), which may eliminate certain meaningful elements, and would at any rate be very expensive and time-consuming. Although this latter condition should not deter creators and companies from producing such works, it is undoubtedly the case that in the commercial setting, it will. Thus, while it is tempting to advocate a development of comics along the technological lines that are proving popular in cinematic works such as *Avatar* (James Cameron, dir.), it is important to remember that comics' readership may well be reduced if such technologies were to become widespread. That said, other technologies have recently begun to develop that suggest ways in which comics' readership might well be expanded to include a broader range of readers, and we will come onto these in more detail when we consider the sense of hearing in chapter 3, and texture in chapter 4.[71]

2.7 CONCLUSION

Over the course of this chapter, I have sought to outline and complicate the notion of the ideal perspective, and to present a range of elements of comics that involve sight as a physical process rather than a conceptual understanding. While the ideal perspective is not an explicit analytical paradigm it is certainly implicit in much scholarship on the medium of comics, and although it is not a crippling problem it is nevertheless somewhat limiting. For this reason, it is worth considering the elements of comics that are overlooked (if the reader will pardon the expression) by the ideal perspective. This is what I sought to do by considering the nature of sight and the ways in which comics work to stimulate that sense. In doing so, I have presented a number of visual phenomena and processes (glossiness, accommodation) as well as visually affective devices and techniques (bleeding, puzzle pages, colouring, anaglyphs). Rather than simply seeking to attack the ideal perspective, what

I intended in presenting such a selection is to suggest productive possibilities by which sight might be incorporated into comics scholarship in a more holistic fashion through a better understanding of the sense and a greater emphasis upon the temporal nature of the experience of comics reading. In particular, I have sought to indicate through the processes discussed here that comics are not simply static objects that can be considered from an atemporal perspective. They change and are changed over time, modifying the space they occupy as they are being read as well as the physical condition of their reader (e.g., through FocusMotion). This changeability (on the part of both the comic and its reader) is critical to the act of reading comics, and it is here that we find the most productive possibilities for expanding upon the existing works in the canon of the mechanical project. I have therefore sought to expand upon the work of Eisner, McCloud, Hatfield, Groensteen, and so forth not simply by presenting new categories of meaning for already acknowledged visual elements but rather new visual elements (or more complicated forms of existing ones (e.g., colour)) to consider. The list of elements I have discussed here is not comprehensive, nor could it be even in a chapter as long as this book. This is the nature of sight; it is far too complex and wonderful to contain within a simple catalogue. Nor are all the terms I have discussed here exclusive to the sense of sight. Certainly, aspects such as size and shape can be reckoned by a multiplicity of senses, and we will return to these themes when we come to consider the other senses in later chapters. Nevertheless, I have sought to consider a series of elements that are at least primarily visually oriented (accommodation and colour in particular).

In the next chapter, we will move on to think about the second of the distance senses: hearing. As we will discover, while hearing has not been completely overlooked by comics scholarship in the way that the physical process of sight has been virtually eliminated in favour of a theoretical "transparent" mode of seeing, it too is filtered through an ocularcentric conception of the medium. The sounds of comics, it would seem, are visual phenomena; we 'listen with [our] eyes'.[72] Yet this immediate reaction, one propagated largely through the obvious use of visually represented sound effects in a wide range of comics, is not wholly valid because a number of creators have worked with actual, audible sounds in various ways to generate intriguing and stimulating works that have definite aural presences. In fact, even when sounds are not consciously manipulated by a creator they can play important epistemological and affective roles in our understanding of the medium.

NOTES

1. Sabin, Roger. 2000. "The Crisis in Modern American and British Comics, and the Possibilities of the Internet as a Solution." In *Comics and Culture: Analytical and Theoretical Approaches to Reading Comics*, edited by Anne Magnussen and Hans-Christian Christiansen, 43–57. Copenhagen, Denmark: Museum Tusculanum Press and University of Copenhagen. 52.

2. Nagel, Thomas. 1986. *The View from Nowhere*. New York, NY: Oxford University Press.
3. Cooley, Heidi Rae. 2004. "It's All about the Fit: The Hand, the Mobile Screenic Device and Tactile Vision." *Journal of Visual Culture* 3 (2): 133–155. 135.
4. MacLeod, Catriona. 2009. "Gazing at the Female in French-Language Comic Strips." *Women in Comics Conference*. Cambridge, UK. See also: Chute, Hillary L. 2010. *Graphic Women: Life Narrative and Contemporary Comics*. New York, NY: Columbia University Press. 91–92. And Baetens, Jan. 2011. "Abstraction in Comics." Edited by Jared Gardner and David Herman. *SubStance* 40 (1 (#124): 94–113. 109–110.
5. Barthes, Roland. 1977. *Image, Music, Text*. Edited by Steven Heath. London: Fontana Press. 157, 156.
6. Barthes, *Image*, 157.
7. Einstein, Albert. 2004. *Relativity: The Special and General Theory*. Translated by Robert W. Lawson. London: The Folio Society. 64–67.
8. Beaty, Bart. 2009. "Comics Off the Page: Towards a Theory of Performance in the Comics World." *International Bande Dessinée Society Sixth Bi-Annual Conference*. London; Di Liddo, Annalisa. 2009. *Alan Moore: Comics as Performance, Fiction as Scalpel*. Jackson, MS: University Press of Mississippi; Worth, Jennifer. 2007. "Unveiling Persepolis as Embodied Performance." *Theatre Research International* 32 (2): 143–160.
9. Sabin, Roger. 2009. "Ally Sloper: The First Comics Superstar?" In *A Comics Studies Reader*, edited by Jeet Heer and Kent Worcester, 177–189. Jackson, MS: University Press of Mississippi. 177.
10. Bruno, Giuliana. 2002 (2007). *Atlas of Emotion: Journeys in Art, Architecture and Film*. New York, NY: Verso. 45. Bruno's book *Atlas of Emotion: Journeys in Art, Architecture and Film* includes an excellent discussion of how cinemas affect the viewers' experiences of film. For more on the contexts of media reception, I would direct the reader to that text.
11. Jay, Martin. 1994. *Downcast Eyes: The Denigration of Vision in Twentieth Century French Thought*. Berkeley, CA: University of California Press. 7.
12. Ibid.; Schiffman, Harvey Richard. 1996. *Sensation and Perception: An Integrated Approach*. 4th ed. New York, NY: Wiley. 54.
13. Gross, Richard D. 1992 (1999). *Psychology: The Science of Mind and Behaviour*. London: Hodder and Stoughton Educational. 209.
14. Jay, *Downcast*, 7–8.
15. Rée, Jonathan. 1999. *I See a Voice: Language, Deafness and the Senses—A Philosophical History*. London: Harper Collins. 15.
16. It could be argued that the darkness itself presents an alternative to the film, and this is certainly true to an extent; however, it should be noted that darkness, as Jonathan Rée has suggested, is 'thick and full', and 'signifies the temporary invisibility of things you would otherwise be able to see: it is impenetrable, because it prevents you from seeing them' (Rée, *I See*, 43). Thus, darkness has a directive function and serves to focus the viewer upon the film because there is nothing else to see (darkness is also a visual 'nothingness' because it is caused by the absence of light).
17. The 'For Tomorrow' storyline, originally published in *Superman* #204–215 (2004–2005), was collected in the Absolute format in *Absolute Superman: For Tomorrow* in 2009. The six-issue *Green Lantern: Rebirth* series (2004–2005) was collected in *Absolute Green Lantern: Rebirth* in 2010. The first seven-issue series of *Danger Girl* (1998–1999) was collected in *Absolute Danger Girl* in 2004. All were published by DC Comics.
18. Millidge, Gary Spencer. 2009. *Comic Book Design*. Lewes, UK: ILEX. 132.

19. Pustz, Matthew J. 1999. *Comic Book Culture: Fanboys and True Believers*. Jackson, MS: University Press of Mississippi. 5. Sterling North quoted in: Hajdu, David. 2008. *The Ten Cent Plague: The Great Comic Book Scare and How It Changed America*. New York, NY: Farrar, Straus & Giroux. 40; Miller, Ann. 2007. *Reading Bande Dessinée*. Bristol, UK: Intellect Books. 34.
20. For more on the implications of artisanal versus mechanised production, see: Beaty, Bart. 2007. *Unpopular Culture: Transforming the European Comic Book in the 1990s*. Toronto, Canada: University of Toronto Press. Particularly 49 and 63–65.
21. See, for example: Sabin, Roger. 1993. *Adult Comics: An Introduction*. London: Routledge. 67–68; Wolk, Douglas. 2007. *Reading Comics: How Graphic Novels Work and What They Mean*. Cambridge, MA: Da Capo Press. 64–66.
22. Marx, Karl. *Capital: A Critique of Political Economy*. Translated by Ben Fowkes. Vol. 1 of 2 vols. London: Penguin Books, 1990. 163.
23. McCloud, Scott. 1993. *Understanding Comics: The Invisible Art*. New York, NY: HarperPerennial. 188.
24. Hajdu, *Ten*, 40–41.
25. Baetens, Jan. 2011. "From Black & White to Colour and Back: What Does It Mean (Not) to Use Colour." *College Literature* 38 (3): 111–128. 113.
26. Blanchard, Louis Gabriel. 1672 (2008). "Conference on the Merits of Colour." In *Art in Theory 1648–1815: An Anthology of Changing Ideas*, edited by Charles Harrison, Paul Wood and Jason Gaiger, 177–182. Oxford: Blackwell. 181.
27. Le Brun, Charles. 1672 (2008). "Thoughts on M. Blanchard's Discourse on the Merits of Colour." In *Art in Theory 1648–1815: An Anthology of Changing Ideas*, edited by Charles Harrison, Paul Wood and Jason Gaiger, 182–185. Oxford: Blackwell. 184.
28. Lefèvre, Pascal. 1999. "Recovering Sensuality in Comic Theory." Edited by John A. Lent. *International Journal of Comic Art* 1 (1): 140–149. 146.
29. Ibid.
30. Gross, *Psychology*, 209.
31. For examples of works where colour is incidental, consider *The Amazing Spider-Man*, the *Peanuts* Sunday strips and even *The Adventures of Tintin*, all of which have very bold and distinctive colour schemes but have nevertheless been published in black and white at various points, implying that the colour is not essential to their composition (numerous issues of *The Amazing Spider-Man* were reissued in black and white in Marvel's low cost *Essential Spider-Man* series (1996–present), the *Peanuts* Sundays appear in black and white in the ongoing Fantagraphics reprint series *The Complete Peanuts* (2004–present), and the first nine *Tintin* albums were originally published in black and white (1930–1941 (dates indicate collected editions; serialised publication of these albums took place between 1929–1941); the second to the ninth were subsequently reissued in colour (1943–1947 & 1955)). This is not to say, however, that colour is used ineffectively when it is present in the foregoing examples (see also: Baetens, 'From').
32. McCloud, *Understanding*, 185–192.
33. Barthes, *Image*, 163.
34. Gross, *Psychology*, 207.
35. Siegel, Jerry, and Joe Shuster. 2006. *The Superman Chronicles*. Vol. 1. New York, NY: DC Comics. 110.
36. Hatfield, Charles. 2005. *Alternative Comics: An Emerging Literature*. Jackson, MS: University Press of Mississippi. 32.
37. Ibid., 48.

38. Ibid.
39. Chute, Hillary L. 2006. "Decoding Comics." *Modern Fiction Studies* (Johns Hopkins University Press) 52 (4): 1014–1027. 1016. Versions of the ideas Hatfield presents here are outlined in: Witek, Joseph. 1989. *Comic Books as History: The Narrative Art of Jack Jackson, Art Spiegelman, and Harvey Pekar*. Jackson, MS: University Press of Mississippi, 34. And: McCloud, *Understanding*, 104.
40. Moore, Alan, Dave Gibbons and John Higgins. 1986–1987. *Watchmen*. Edited by Len Wein and Barbara Randall. 12 vols. New York: DC Comics. n.p.
41. For the layout plans for this page (and indeed the rest of the chapter) see: Gibbons, Dave, Chip Kidd, and Mike Essl. 2008. *Watching the Watchmen*. London: Titan Books. n.p.
42. Hatfield, *Alternative*, 65–66. This clarification also serves as something of a defence against Hillary Chute's argument that Hatfield's approach is overly prescriptive.
43. Talbot, Bryan. 2009. "Style and Storytelling Technique in 'The Tale of One Bad Rat'." *Possibilities and Perspectives: A Conference on Comics*. Leeds, UK.
44. Eisner, Will. 2006. *Comics and Sequential Art*. Paramus, NJ: Poorhouse Press. 41.
45. For a somewhat critical reading of the function of eye-guiding devices in comics, see: Groensteen, Thierry. 2007. *The System of Comics*. Translated by Bart Beaty and Nick Nguyen. Jackson, MS: University Press of Mississippi. 34–35. For a more sympathetic examination see: Witek, Joseph. 2009. "The Arrow and the Grid." In *A Comics Studies Reader*, edited by Jeet Heer and Kent Worcester, 149–156. Jackson, MS: University Press of Mississippi.
46. Witek, *Comic*, 34. For a scientific approach to the physical act of reading comics, see: Ecke, Jochen. 2010. "Spatializing the Movie Screen: How Mainstream Cinema Is Catching Up on the Formal Potentialities of the Comic Book Page." In *Comics as a Nexus of Cultures: Essays on the Interplay of Media, Disciplines and International Perspectives*, edited by Mark Berninger, Jochen Ecke, and Gideon Haberkorn, 7–20. Jefferson, NC: McFarland. 11–12.
47. For a particularly good example of this type of motion/focus understanding, see Mark Millar and Bryan Hitch's *Fantastic Four* #557, as it is analysed in Gary Spencer Millidge's *Comic Book Design* (86).
48. Witek, 'Arrow', 149.
49. Einstein, *Relativity*, 14.
50. In 2011, the conference 'Sculpture and Comic Art' took place in Leeds (UK) as part of that year's annual Comics Forum event.
51. Morris, Robert. 1966–1967 (2007). "Notes on Sculpture." In *Art in Theory 1900–2000: An Anthology of Changing Ideas*, edited by Charles Harrison and Paul Wood, 828–835. Oxford: Blackwell. 830.
52. At the bottom end of this spectrum we might place something like Shannon Wheeler's *Postage Stamp Funnies*, at the top *Kramer's Ergot #7*.
53. Morris, 'Notes', 831.
54. Ibid., 831–832. cf. Liotard, Jean-Etienne. 2000 (2008). "Treatise on the Principles and Rules of Painting (Extract)." In *Art in Theory 1648–1815: An Anthology of Changing Idea*, edited by Charles Harrison, Paul Wood and Jason Gaiger, 673–677. Oxford: Blackwell.
55. Barthes, Roland. 2000. *Mythologies*. Translated by Annette Lavers. London: Vintage.115.
56. Morris, 'Notes', 832.

57. McCloud, Scott. 2006. *Making Comics: Storytelling Secrets of Comics, Manga and Graphic Novels*. New York, NY: HarperCollins. 158, 162.
58. Ibid, 163–164.
59. The differences between comics and animated cartoons are outlined in: Taylor, Todd. 2001. "If He Catches You, You're Through: Coyotes and Visual Ethos." In *The Language of Comics: Word and Image*, edited by Robin Varnum and Christina T. Gibbons, 40–59. Jackson, MS: University Press of Mississippi. 42–43.
60. Gardner, Jared. 2012. *Projections: Comics and the History of Twenty-First Century Storytelling*. Stanford, CA: Stanford University Press. 213.
61. There are some paintings where the viewer's position is critical to the visibility of certain elements of the image, such as Holbein's 'The Ambassadors', which employs anamorphosis, whereby the representation of a skull on the floor is perceptible only from a particular angle.
62. Research at Senshu University (Japan) has shown that there may in fact be a benefit to sitting in a particular position within the cinema because it affects the side of the brain on which the film is processed. In right-handed people, the right side of the brain is thought to be responsible for visual processing and emotional information; thus, sitting on the right-hand side of the cinema improves right-handed people's ability to process the film. Nevertheless, the position in which one sits in a cinema is still largely driven by social/subconscious factors rather than necessity; all seats are assumed to be largely equal in terms of the visibility of the film. See: Anonymous. 2010. "News in Brief: Right-Handed People Choose the Best Cinema Seats for Themselves without Knowing It." *Focus*, March: 19. I am grateful to Andy Ridgway and Jheni Osman at *Focus* for their assistance in tracking this article down.
63. For a more detailed discussion of the differences between the perception of painting and sculpture specifically, see: Martin, F. David. 1978. "On Perceiving Paintings and Sculpture." *Leonardo* (MIT Press) 11 (4): 287–292.
64. Comics are not unique in this regard; some other art forms such as pottery also allow such mobility.
65. A similar technique was used by Jim Steranko in his work on Nick Fury, Agent of S.H.I.E.L.D. in Marvel Comics' *Strange Tales* #166 (1968). See: Steranko, Jim, Joe Sinnott, and Sam Rosen. 2004. "Strange Tales #166 [Excerpt]." *The Mighty World of Marvel* Volume 3 #23, December 1: 40–51. 45.
66. Horn, Maurice. 1996. "The Upside Downs of Little Lady Lovekins and Old Man Muffaroo." In *100 Years of American Newspaper Comics: An Illustrated Encyclopedia*, edited by Maurice Horn, 384–385. New York, NY: Gramercy Books.
67. Talbot, Bryan. 2007. *Alice in Sunderland, or, A Night at the Empire: An Entertainment*. London: Jonathan Cape. 103.
68. Gifford, Denis. 1984. *The International Book of Comics*. London: Deans International Publishing. 242–245.
69. Miller, *Reading*, 145.
70. Abbot, Edwin A. 2008 (1884). "Flatland: A Romance of Many Dimensions (Illustrated)." Vers. EPUB. *Project Gutenberg*. March 10. Accessed June 27, 2010. http://www.gutenberg.org/ebooks/201.epub.noimages. 77.
71. I am extremely grateful to Philip Jeffs of the Royal National Institute of Blind People (RNIB) for his generous assistance in assessing the possibilities of developing comics for the blind and visually impaired.
72. Pollmann, Joost. "Shaping Sounds in Comics." Edited by John A. Lent. *International Journal of Comic Art* 3 (1): 9–21. 15.

3 Hearing, or, Visible Sounds and Seeing with the Ears

3.0 VISIBLE SOUNDS

After sight, and arguably before touch, hearing is the sense that has most concerned scholars writing on comics. Though I have already addressed some of the reasons behind this in my fairly general discussion of the synaesthetic approach to the senses (see chapter 1), it will perhaps be beneficial here to draw out some of the specific characteristics of the sense of hearing as it is understood to work in relation to comics.

To open our discussion let us draw upon the work of Scott McCloud, who famously concludes a discussion of René Magritte's 'The Treachery of Images' (*La trahison des images*) in *Understanding Comics* with the question: 'Do you hear what I'm saying?', following up with: 'If you *do*, have your *ears* checked, because no one said a word.'[1] The implication here is obvious: comics are a silent medium and when we read a comic we never actually hear anything. Given the way that McCloud later goes on to conceptualise comics as a '*mono-sensory* medium', this understanding should come as little surprise to the reader.[2] Yet McCloud is far from alone in approaching sound in comics in this way, and in fact other writers have been still more explicit in their assertion that comics are a silent art form. Consider the words of Joost Pollmann in an article in the *International Journal of Comic Art*:

> [. . .] most comics are silent; perhaps the turning of their pages produces a whispering, but that's about it. In their own way, however, comics can be quite noisy.[3]

Pollmann is not using the term 'noisy' here to suggest that comics are literally audible. Rather, he is drawing the reader's attention to the implied cacophony that is represented upon the comic's pages through visual forms such as onomatopoeic words, word balloons, and similar devices. In an earlier article for the same journal, Pollmann outlined this position fairly concisely:

> What is the sound of a growing erection? BIIN. (Stretch the vowels.) This expression stems not from Japanese Zen-Buddhism, but from the

> Japanese *manga*, an artform [sic] that makes audible the most elusive things. Thus HIRA HIRA renders the sound of a falling leaf, PO the sound of blushing, and SHIN the sound of silence.
>
> Comics are a mix of visual and verbal elements and, therefore, the Japanese must have argued, each image should have its acoustic counterpart. So that what cannot be expressed in writing or drawing, can be suggested graphically.[4]

Despite his phrasing, which implies that 'the Japanese' are a discrete, homogenous and historically specific group that somehow came to a definite consensus on how sound should be represented in comics, the ideas Pollmann outlines here with regards to visually represented sound are characteristic of thinking on the medium. Essentially, to take a few final words from him, '[. . .] you can listen with your eyes'.[5]

There are numerous ways in which sounds are represented visually in comics. The most common mode of expression is probably through language. I have already mentioned Pollmann's discussion of terms like 'PO', 'HIRA HIRA' and 'SHIN' in Japanese manga.[6] To these examples we might add onomatopoeic terms such as 'TOOOT' and 'BOOM' and 'RRRING' which feature in the French *bande dessinée* tradition (specifically the Tintin series, these examples are taken from *Land of Black Gold*) along with 'ZIZZIST!', 'KRAKK!', and 'SHOOM!' from the American tradition (*Fantastic Four*) and 'PIP!', 'CRASH!' and 'PHEEP!' (*WHOOPEE! (and Wow!)*) from the British.[7] Indeed, as Suzanne Covey has noted, such devices are so heavily associated with comics that they 'have become a kind of cliché; journalists find it irresistible to include "Pow! Blam!" and the like in headlines when writing about comics'.[8] They are perhaps the most recognisable signs of "comicness" outside the form, and consequently they are regularly taken up in other media, most famously in the 1960s television series *Batman* and its spin-off *Batman: The Movie* (dir. Leslie H. Martinson), which incorporated sound effects such as 'Pow!' and 'Blam!' as intertitles and subtitles respectively. They also feature in the works of Roy Lichtenstein, for example in 'Whaam!' which of course takes its name from the onomatopoeic term that makes up a large part of the image. To these very explicit representations of sound we can add simpler forms, such as the text that features in word balloons, though we might exclude thought balloons and narration boxes depending on whether one considers the narration (and characters' thoughts) to take the form of a spoken voice-over (as in film) or not.[9] Will Eisner described the balloon as a 'desperation device' that 'attempts to make visible and capture an ethereal element: sound'.[10] Finally, musical notation and graphical forms can indicate the presence of sounds, more or less specifically depending on whether they are heavily structured or not. A consequence of this type of understanding is that word balloons and their contents have been identified as part of the comic's 'soundtrack' despite the complete absence of actual, audible sound that is associated with them.[11] Similarly, although the implication that sound is wholly absent from a comic's diegetic environment is extremely rare, and deaf and hearing-impaired characters are few and far between, the term 'wordless' has been taken to mean silent, and wordless comics have been compared to silent cinema.[12] This must surely be regarded as a double silence if we take into account Joost Pollmann's aforementioned dismissal of comics' actual sounds and description of the comic as a 'silent' object.

Sound in comics, then, would seem to be imagined rather than perceived, and for that reason it sits very firmly within the realm of what Don Ihde has called the 'auditory imagination'.[13] Although there are many similarities between imagined and perceived sound, Ihde notes that there are also 'distances and resistances' between them: imagined sound is more focused and directed, it does not drift 'lazily' around, while perceived sound can be highly intrusive.[14] Although perceived sound can of course be a powerful means for communication and learning, it can also fall into the category of noise, which as Paul Hegarty has observed 'is negative: it is unwanted, other, not something ordered'.[15] Despite Joost Pollmann's assertion that comics can be a 'noisy' art form, the imagined (and usually structured) nature of visually represented sounds means that there is no true analogue here between comics and the auditory environment. Intrusive visual "sound effects" may make it slightly more difficult to process visual information and to work out what is going on, but they do not defocus the mind as quickly and disruptively as perceived noises can.

Yet comics do have perceivable auditory characteristics. To the 'whispering' that Pollmann was so quick to dismiss, we might add the harsh cracking sound made by a new book's spine as it is opened to be read for the first time and the weary, creaking complaint of a well-worn hardback's cover. Though they could be classed as incidental, these sounds comprise elements of the comic's character, they tell the reader certain things about the progression of the text and the modification of the comic as an object, and they indicate 'distances and resistances'. Looking more broadly, we can observe that comics have made explicit use of auditory communication technologies since at least as early as 1945, when New York City Mayor Fiorello La Guardia read newspaper comics out over the radio to children who were unable to get their weekly fix of *Dick Tracy* (Chester Gould), *Little Orphan Annie* (Harold Gray) and the like due to a newspaper deliverymen's strike.[16] The presence of such technologies has only become greater as their costs have fallen. It would seem probable that as recording systems continue to develop and digital modes of distribution become more common, innovative artists will continue to work on expanding their uses of sound. Thus, while there is certainly plenty of work to be done with respect to the visual "sounds" of comics and the roles played by the imagination, I would argue that we might profitably spend time considering the actual sounds that are involved in the performance of comics and seeking to understand the soundscape(s) of the medium. This is the project I will undertake here in considering not visual means of showing sound such as the 'desperation devices' of which Will

Eisner spoke in *Comics and Sequential Art,* but rather the audible sounds that we really hear when we read comics.[17] Before doing so, however, let us first contextualise our discussion through an outline of the nature of sound and the functions of the ear.

3.1 A BRIEF INTRODUCTION TO HEARING AND THE EAR

Of all the senses, hearing is perhaps the least easily understood as a mechanism for differentiating between inside and outside the subject. The reason for this lies in the confusion that can arise when we try to work out what and where sound is, and the problems this causes for establishing a clear subject/object relationship. Where sight draws upon the interaction of photons with the eye, and touch, smell and taste relate to the specific objects we are interacting with when we experience them as sensory inputs, the object of hearing, sounds, are far more ethereal. 'Sound is defined as any pressure variation (in air, water or some other medium) that the human ear can detect', writes Barry McCormick, and in this definition we can identify some of the problems for studying sound.[18]

Essentially, the biggest problems stem from the difficulty of locating sound. We hear because the pressure variations of which McCormick writes (sound waves) enter the auditory canal and cause the eardrum (tympanum) to vibrate at the same frequency as them (see Figure 3.1 for an overview of the structure of the ear). The vibrations of the eardrum are transmitted to the ossicles, three small bones (the hammer (malleus), anvil (incus) and stirrup (stapes)) that make up the middle ear. They are then passed into the inner ear by the stirrup, which hits the oval window and causes changes in the pressure of the fluid that fills the cochlea. These pressure changes cause vibrations within the basilar membrane (which lines the cochlea), bending the tiny hairs that are attached to it against the tectoral membrane. This action creates nerve impulses that are transmitted to the brain via the auditory nerve (the vestibulocochlear nerve, comprising the vestibular and cochlear nerves).[19] As this description implies though, a question remains as to whether the sound can be called a sound if it is not registered by an ear. 'If a tree falls in a forest and there's no one around to hear it, does it make a sound?' to put it in simple terms. The answer to this question lies in whether one counts the pressure variations themselves as sounds (in which case the answer would be yes) or considers them to be sounds only at the point that they cause sympathetic vibrations in another object, whether this is the human ear or an electronic recording device (in which case the answer would be no because the sound is the vibration of the ear or the device).

Although the latter position is not quite the same as the auditory imagination, it is clear that both privilege an internal conception of sound. Each, in its own way, presents the sound as a product of the hearer (whether that sound is perceived or imagined). Accordingly, in seeking to reverse the

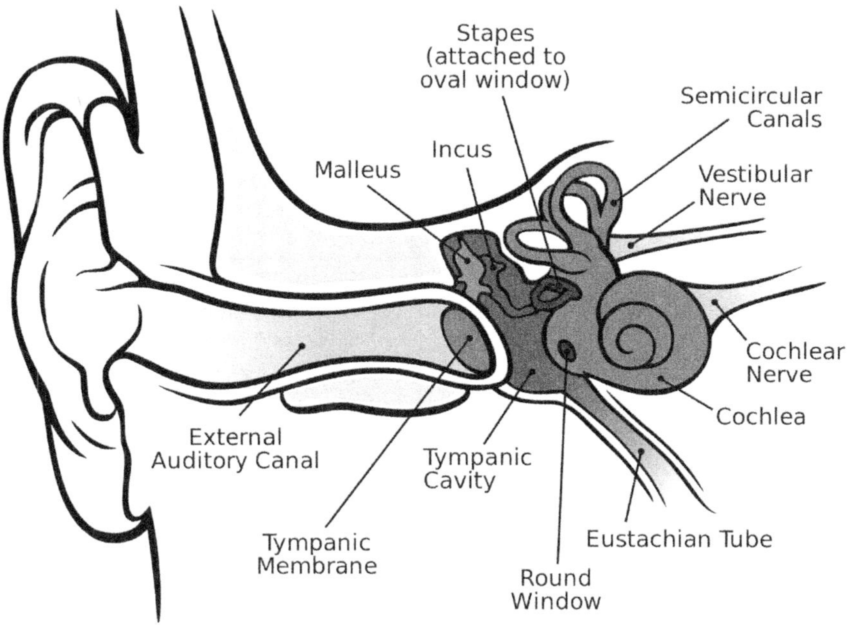

Figure 3.1 The structure of the human ear. Artists: Chittka, Lars and Axel Brockmann; image used under a CC BY 2.5 licence.

traditional position and present the sound as an emission from an external object (i.e., the comic), it behoves us to adopt the alternate mode of understanding. Thus, when I speak of sound over the course of this chapter I am speaking of it as arising and being emitted from an object. In truth, this fairly precise distinction should have little effect upon the reading of this chapter, and the reader could choose to refuse this position without disregarding the rest of the chapter. I make note of it here to avoid problems arising when I use phrases like 'the comic as sound source', which specify particular origin points for sounds that are external to the reader.

This terminological necessity having been dealt with, let us now move on to consider the natures of the sounds that comics emit, incorporate or work with. In so doing, we will need to pay particular attention to elements of materiality, but we will also emphasise the importance of time, which again reasserts the notion of performance as I outlined it in chapter 2. Of course we do not have space here to consider every sound that the reader is likely to hear while reading a comic, but we should be able to consider a number of interesting areas. We will begin by considering the comic itself as a source of sound, and think about three ways in which this might be interpreted (section 3.2 and subsections). Next we will move on to think about the possibility of sounds themselves being the substance of a comic (section 3.3) before giving consideration to the sounds that the readers hear around them over the course of the reading experience (section 3.4).

3.2 THE COMIC AS SOUND SOURCE

In describing the comic as a sound source, I am seeking to delimit a specific group of sounds that are produced by the comic, but which do not make up the entirety of the work. They can be considered loosely analogous to the film or television show's soundtrack, or the use of sound in sculpture (though this is distinguished from sound sculpture, which we will return to in section 3.3), in that the sound is an optional element of the form and does not challenge most definitions ('A film without sound remains a film; a film with no image, or at least without a visual frame for projection, is not a film').[20] Although those definitions of comics that present the medium as exclusively visual in nature (e.g., McCloud) explicitly reject the notion that sound can play a part in comics, knowingly incomplete definitions that identify visual components as a part but not the whole of the medium (e.g., Eisner, Groensteen) do not. Social definitions (e.g., Barker, Witek) present no significant reasons why we cannot include sounds within comics. For these reasons, this type of sound should be fairly uncontroversial and I will therefore proceed to discuss it without considering whether it challenges notions of "comicness" (again, this will be a more pressing issue in section 3.3).

We can further subdivide these types of sounds into three categories: sounds *of* comics, sounds *in* comics, and sounds *with* comics. The first category includes the sounds produced by the body of the comic as an object (e.g., page turns). The second involves those sounds that are integrated into the narrative of a comic and are produced by a component of the object that was installed for that specific purpose (e.g., electronic sounds created by button presses). The third includes those sounds that are packaged with the comic but produced separately to it, perhaps on another device (e.g., sounds produced from CDs and records). While the boundaries between these three categories are not absolutely impenetrable, they are largely valid and do provide us with a means of conceptualising the comic that allows for a structured discussion.

3.2.1 Sounds of Comics

The sounds that comics make can tell us a lot about the objects with which we are interacting. Nevertheless, it is worth sounding a note of caution. Although it has traditionally been the case that 'the epistemological status of hearing has come a poor second to that of vision', we must be wary of expecting too much of the sounds produced by comics.[21] Seeking to remedy visual bias by constructing a structured epistemological understanding of comics' audible qualities will not necessarily yield many new insights. This is particularly true because of the fairly standardised production techniques employed in the creation of most works. Sounds may allow us to know certain things about a comic, for example its age (the thin, coarse paper of the type used in Marvel and DC comics of the 1960s produces a different sound to the glossier materials used for modern comics pages) but the knowledge that we gain from this type of interaction is both imprecise (we could not tell one 1960s comic from another by this method) and more easily obtained by some other means (e.g., sight, touch or smell). Thus it would be extremely difficult, if not impossible, to create sound-based taxonomies of comics.

But sounds do have some important functions with regard to comics reading, perhaps the most significant being the emphasis of temporality. John Shepherd has argued that:

> Sound is more symptomatic of the flow of time than any other phenomena impinging on our senses. Although all other phenomena occur within the stream of time, the fact that they may be generally isolated and examined at leisure demonstrates that, *as far as their influence on the arrangement of people's sensoria is concerned*, they are not so inexorably tied to that stream as sound is.[22]

Despite Shepherd's oversimplification of the roles of time in relation to the other senses (we have already seen how important it is in influencing the visual aspects of the comic in our discussions of colour in section 2.3 and motion in section 2.5), his marking up of the importance of time to sound is valid. Sound is bound to time, and despite what many a tall tale might indicate, it cannot be frozen and converted into a purely spatial entity.[23] Thus, the sounds that comics produce tell us about the comic in time. They inform us of the motions of the comic, the changing positions and configurations of its composite elements. The nature of sounds as motions (in air or another medium) produced by motions (in objects) means that they serve as stark reminders to the reader that comics are not, indeed they cannot be, stationary while they are being read: they move through both space and time.

For these reasons, sounds represent a critical element of the *performance* of comics as I outlined it in chapter 2 (even their absence is indicative of certain things). They serve to implicate both the reader's body and the physical composition of the comic within the act of reading. The reading environment will also play a significant role in modulating the sounds of comics, and therefore affect the performance, though I will not have space here to give detailed consideration to the multitude of environments in which readings take place (see section 3.4 for more on this). Sounds emphasise that reading comics is a physical and productive process because the sounds a comic emits originate with the reader as well as with the work. They indicate change (in fact, they *are* change). The importance of the sounds of comics now outlined, let us move on to consider a selection of such sounds and think about their more specific meanings for the experience of reading comics.

Perhaps the first sound the reader comes across when reading a comic originates primarily with its packaging. While it would clearly be impossible to incorporate all forms of packing materials into our discussion, we can consider a few here. One of the most common forms is the soft plastic wrapper. In some instances this is fixed tightly to the shape of the comic (shrink wrapping, most common with hardback volumes), while in others it is looser and is generally not sealed (as in the comic bag). In the case of the former, accessing the comic requires a deformation of the wrapper through stretching, tearing and/or cutting. The harsh, strained sounds of a plastic wrapper as it is stretched until it breaks attest to the potentially violent nature of these acts. Conversely, cutting the wrapper with a knife or scissors results in a more continuous tone whose pitch changes as the cut is made, suggesting the progression from the start of an action to the end. Each of these sounds indicates a nascent interaction between work and reader, and the dismantling of the work's protection, whether this is undertaken carefully or otherwise. The character of such sounds is almost always one of resistance (given that the plastic's material composition resists being stretched), though this resistance is less substantial where the surgical precision of a knife is used. The sounds of resistance, however, are both fleeting and unique. Once one has removed the wrapper the comic will not make this sound again because the wrapper cannot be reapplied and will usually be discarded.

This is not always the case with the loose plastic wrap. Although some such wrappers are sealed, the form more commonly associated with comics is the comic bag, associated with the practice of bagging and boarding (preservation of the comic in a specifically sized bag with a stiff piece of cardboard in it to keep the comic straight). The most common sound emitted by such bags comes when the adhesive tape used to hold it shut is pulled away from the bag. Like the sounds discussed earlier, these sounds indicate a shift from purchaser or addressee (a person to whom a text's *title* is addressed) to reader (the person for whom the *text* is intended).[24] In so doing, they also denote a move from comic as commodity to comic as text. The sound of the wrapping being removed is a sign that the comic is shifting from an object to be purchased to one to be read. Where more substantial preservation devices are employed, such as the hard plastic capsules used in the process of slabbing, the sounds of disassembly are sharper and louder still (see section 4.0 for more on slabbing).[25] Given the criticism that the commoditisation of comics has come under from some, we can only assume that these auditory indicators of the shift away from the comic as commodity are greeted with satisfaction by comics scholars.[26] Additional sounds made by the packaging of comics must also include the sliding sound that can be heard when a comic in a slipcase or box is removed from this solid packaging. Such modes of packaging are not particularly common except in fairly expensive works like the Absolute Editions I mentioned in chapter 2, or in works that are comprised of multiple pieces that may or may not have been published separately earlier. Examples of the latter would include

The Actus Box: Five Graphic Novellas (Actus Tragicus) and the minicomics of Tempo Lush, which have been collected in a box/slipcase shaped like a bear. Nevertheless, as Gérard Genette has observed, the modes of packaging and presenting books have been evolving since the early years of the printed book, and the slipcase has at times taken on some of the functions formerly assigned to the cover.[27] As the complexity of such items continues to grow, they will undoubtedly alter the sounds we experience on our way to the text.

Upon reaching the core components of the comic, the reader is confronted with those noises I mentioned earlier: the sounds of the cover and the pages being particularly obvious. Because these elements are physically attached to each other they are mutually affective in terms of sound production. For this reason I will not seek to differentiate them too starkly here. As I discussed above, the sounds a comic makes are generated by its motion, and the most common type of motion involved in reading comics is the page turn. Because the cover of a paperback is soft and flexible, it can be bent slightly by the reader to prompt the forward movement of the page, the speed of which is regulated by the thumb, which releases one page and then adjusts its position slightly (almost imperceptibly) to hold back the next page while it is read. Here the most audible sound is produced by the interaction of the thumb with the side of the page (right-hand page in Western comics, left-hand page in manga). This sound has a number of interesting qualities. In character it is somewhere between a click and a flip, the sound being produced by the motion of the edge and a tiny amount of the surface of the page interacting with a small section of the skin on the thumb; the page is almost being plucked. The type of surface the page has will affect the sound significantly. Glossier pages tend to slide more than flip, which gives them a smoother sound as they pass over the surface of the thumb. Matte pages are slightly rougher; they grate on the finger's surface instead of sliding smoothly over it, and produce a harsher (and sometimes louder) sound than glossy ones as a result. The stiffness of the page also has an effect. Softer pages tend to flop, while stiff ones click.

The pitch of the sound is controlled by the number of pages below the one being turned. Though it is barely discernible when individual pages are turned, and almost nonexistent in short works, it can be observed that when the pages of a thick book are allowed to turn quickly, the pitch of the sound this produces increases as the listener moves from the front of the book to the back (i.e., as the number of pages below the one being read decreases). The pitch of the sound that the page makes as it is being turned (assuming the book is held in the hands) therefore increases as the reading goes on. This characteristic is particularly interesting because moving from the front of a book to the back tends to be associated with finishing the book, but in terms of sounds a high or increasing pitch is often connected to incompleteness (think, for example, of how we raise the pitch of our voice when we ask a question), whereas a low or falling pitch tends to suggest completion.[28] The sound of the performance, then, inverts the expected soundscape and contrasts directly with the cultural/anthropological norm. In this sense, the sound of a turning page emphasises the "objectness" of the comic as a thing that does not conform to human conventions, even if it is produced by them. A slight variation in the character of this sound can be heard when the position of the thumb upon the page is altered, though this is so minute as to be almost undetectable and may only have any noticeable impact in extremely large books such as *Kramer's Ergot #7* (ed. Sammy Harkham) and *Little Nemo: So Many Splendid Sundays* (Windsor McCay), both of which are sixteen inches wide by twenty-one inches high.[29] Most books on this scale, however, tend to be published in hardback only (these examples included), which limits the possibilities for this type of sound to be investigated, given that the less flexible cover makes it more difficult to "pluck" the page. A more definite modification can be achieved by altering the positions of the other fingers and the hand upon the cover of the book because they fix or release different sections of the overall shape of the work, thereby affecting the density of the pitch-controlling area, and consequently the pitch itself.

Plucking the page is by no means denied to readers of the hardback, as they can simply take the book's pages (not including the cover) and hold them, flicking through them as they progress through the comic. There are also other options available to them, which produce a different sound altogether (but are not necessarily denied to paperback readers). Because the hardback sits more easily upon a flat surface without closing (this is also a characteristic of comic books because they are extremely thin and usually made completely of paper), the hardback reader is able to turn the page by either taking each one individually and moving it over to the other side of the book, or by inserting her/his finger at the top (or bottom) corner of the page and sliding it down the front of the next (verso) page, lifting it away from one side and placing it onto the other. This method creates a very different sound to plucking; it is more akin to the type of sound produced when a bow is drawn across a string. Because the page is held slightly apart from the rest of the pages, there is less opportunity for a density of pages to create a lower pitched sound, and the page's material and texture play a more important role here. Of even greater importance, however, is the nature of the finger's interaction with the page. If a smooth motion is used in the progression of the finger along the page, the sound will have a similarly smooth quality. Where a greater pressure is applied, or the fingertip has some form of moisture on it, it will drag over the page creating a squeakier sound (though not necessarily at a higher pitch) and a staccato rhythm.

Finally, one of the least consistent, and least controllable, sounds comics produce is created when pages interact with each other as the reader allows one to fall onto the previous one. This is again a sliding sound; however, here the effect is created by the sliding of one material over another (rather than the finger over the page or vice versa). The specific type of material (usually but not necessarily paper) is critical. The materials of composition are similarly important to the sounds made by the cover and its appendages (e.g., dust jackets, bands, etc.). Hardness and density have obvious effects here, but the surface can also play a role. One only need compare the sounds made by the smooth plastic cover of *Jack Cole and Plastic Man: Forms Stretched to Their Limits!* (Art Spiegelman and Chip Kidd) with the rough, hard cardboard cover and loose, smooth paper dust jacket of *Asterios Polyp* (David Mazzucchelli) to realise the extent of the influence wielded by different materials.

Scott McCloud has asserted that 'One nice *side effect* of interactivity is that sound and motion can actually *sneak in* through the back door as a *byproduct* of reader interaction'; specifically, the sound and motion produced by a reader's hand upon the page of a comic.[30] What is important about this comment is not only that it identifies a type of sound we would not ordinarily discuss, but its implicit acknowledgment that reading comics is an inherently physical action that involves the human body coming into contact with an object and producing new phenomena, such as sounds. These sounds comprise an element of the performance/reading of comics, and if we are seeking a more holistic understanding of the reader's experience of comics it is important to neglect as few elements of that experience as possible. Furthermore, it is important to remember the possibility for additional meaning to be conferred upon the comic through these ostensibly throwaway sounds: significance can '*sneak in* through the back door', and in order to ensure the validity of a reading it is worth being vigilant here. This means incorporating sounds and developing our understanding of how they affect the dynamics of the reader/comic relationship, and the deployment of meaning within a work. It may also be the case that the nonlinear mode of reading that is common in comics (as readers move backwards and forwards through the comic), means that comics are already a louder form of book than, for example, prose fiction, which promotes a fairly conventional mode of monodirectional, linear reading. Finally, as the physicality of comics grows in importance to both creators and critics, the sounds that they make will change along with their visual, textural, olfactory and gustatory components. Given the strength of the link between sound and time, and the ways in which sound serves to structure spatial and temporal relationships between reader and work, the sounds comics make will play an important role in tracking the changing forms of comics.

3.2.2 Sounds in Comics

A second category of sounds produced by comics can be identified in those sounds that are part of the diegesis, and are consciously integrated into the work to supplement or even facilitate the narrative (though the latter application is rare). Such sounds tend to be produced electronically, either through a dedicated physical unit attached to the device or, in the case of digital comics, through a generic system like speakers. This latter category may appear to slip into the realm of sounds *with* comics, but I have included it here because the sounds themselves are integral components of the comic and the information necessary for their production cannot be physically separated from its body. In truth, such sounds are relatively rare and do not feature in many comics, though this situation may begin to change with the increasing prominence of digital comics that allow for the easy transmission of audio content.

Perhaps the greatest prevalence of sounds of this type has come in works involving licensed characters such as Spider-Man. Indeed, it is a discussion of this very type of sound that opens Joost Pollmann's article on the visual sounds in comics. He writes:

> In 1995, Marvel published a "Golden Sound Story," starring Spider-Man. It's a book with a "Touch 'n' Listen" system that makes it possible to actually hear what you read. The so-called *tingling* of the Spider-Sense, that triggers Peter Parker into putting on his costume; the buzzing of the Neogenic Recombinator, a powerful and sophisticated weapon; the terrifying growl of the Lizard . . . all these sounds can be made audible by the mere push of a button. Thank God, most comics are silent [. . .].[31]

Pollmann's tone here is interesting. He evidently considers the book's sounds to be noises, which as I have already mentioned are 'negative' and 'unwanted'.[32] Yet in this capacity they also serve the function of generating distances and resistances because they refuse the reader the privilege of complete control. Of course in this instance readers are required to press a button to generate the sound and for this reason they do have a measure of control over the work's production and employment of sounds. Nevertheless, the nature of sound as a temporally deployed phenomenon, something that can only exist in time, means that it confers upon the comic something that no other sensory input easily can: duration.

Although we may experience visual inputs, tastes, smells and tactile qualities for a particular duration of time, the sounds a comic makes are *essentially* temporal; they necessarily have existence for a limited duration. 'The basic truth about sounds [. . .]' writes Jonathan Rée, 'is that they never last. You cannot collect and keep a beloved sound, as you can a letter or a flower or a lock of hair'.[33] Sounds are always in motion; even recorded sounds cannot wait in a particular place or go backwards (playing a sound backwards is not the same as the sound itself going backwards because it is a separate manifestation and therefore a different sound). In this sense they are contrary to the conventional understanding of comics creation and reading. In *The System of Comics,* Thierry Groensteen writes of 'the operation of breaking down (*decoupage*)', as the means by which the narrative is divided into segments that are deployed temporally within the restrained arthrology.[34] Though this action serves to 'confer [upon the panel] its temporal coordinates', these coordinates can quickly be subverted, because the reader is not bound to obey the artist's wishes; the speed and even direction of comics reading is entirely down to the readers, who can move around the work as they so choose.[35] As Frank Miller has observed: '[. . .] movies control pace; a cartoonist has to be really smart to slow you down, a filmmaker just has to leave the camera where it is for a long time'.[36] Contrarily, sounds in comics limit the readers' ability to read the comic in their own time because they must hear (if not listen to) a sound for a particular amount of time. By integrating sounds, the comic's creators take back a measure of control over the work and instruct readers to perform that work in a particular way. Sound therefore offers creators a very powerful tool for renegotiating the contract between producers and receivers of which I spoke in chapter 1.

This tool has begun to have a presence in some comics, and the greater availability of comics on a number of different sound-capable platforms will likely increase its spread. While the deployment of specific sound-production systems of the type used in Touch 'n' Listen books is very limiting (given that few are able to construct such devices on a scale appropriate to distribution), digital media forms offer more possibilities. To give one example: in their adaptation of Bryan Lee O'Malley's *Scott Pilgrim* for mobile platforms (e.g., mobile phones), Robot Media make use of an audible guitar solo on the opening panel of the first volume.[37] This fast-paced sequence is described by its creator, 'Noise Collector', as '[r]ogue electric strat clone through Zoom guitar effects', and runs for eleven seconds.[38] Unlike the buttons on the Touch 'n' Listen Spider-Man book, this sound is fully integrated into the comic; it plays when the reader advances from one panel to the next. Readers are not directly responsible for producing it (they do not directly cause the sound to play) and it cannot be extracted from the panel and played independently (the Touch 'n' Listen book would allow the owner to play the sounds at any time, without her/him having to have a particular page open). In presenting this fairly loud, complex piece of music in the first moments of the reader's engagement with the text, and in maintaining its presence (it runs for the full eleven seconds whether the reader moves to the next panel or not), Robot Media stresses to readers that this comic is not solely visual in nature, and that there are certain elements that must be deployed at certain speeds. This is further emphasised by the presence of haptic feedback later in the comic (see section 4.3 for more on this). In this way the comic is not only reformatted for the new mode of presentation, it is *adapted* (with all the connotations of that term).

This adaptation is, however, some way from fully realising the potential for multisensory comics in digital formats. The auditory and haptic elements are integrated in only a very small way: the single track I have already mentioned is the only sound in the *Scott Pilgrim* adaptation. But there are digital comics that more comprehensively integrate sounds. One approach to integrating sounds into comics that has met with some success is the motion comic, which involves the creation (or adaptation) of comics using limited animation and usually a full soundtrack of some description (whether this includes music, acted dialogue, narration and sound effects depends upon the title). Motion comics are generally released in a video format, in some cases on DVD or a similar platform, and offer no more control than a standard film in terms of the navigation of the text; the use of the term "reader" to describe the consumer of motion comics is perhaps somewhat inaccurate—"viewer" would be more appropriate. Although this format did gain some popularity in the mid to late 2000s, with both Marvel and DC comics (among others) releasing highly publicised motion comics, there are relatively few titles available in this format and it has so far failed to establish a strong position for itself in the field, possibly because it is unclear whether it is a comic with a lot of animation or an animation with very little. More nuanced integrations of sound in digital comics include AveComics' adaptation of Reinhard Kleist's *Johnny Cash: I See a Darkness* for Apple's iPhone and iPad systems (iPhone version 2009, iPad version 2010), which includes not only the full image-text sequence from Kleist's original graphic novel, but also integrates songs by Johnny Cash into the body of the work itself.[39] If readers have specific songs by Cash in their iTunes library they can play them at relevant moments in the narrative as they are reading, and if they do not there is the option to purchase them through the app. Going beyond the relatively simplistic integration employed in *Scott Pilgrim,* here we see a much more sophisticated use of sound within the comic that supplements and expands upon the visually presented material in a relevant and potentially very powerful way (note also that this example blurs the boundaries between sounds *in* comics and sounds *with* comics, demonstrating one of the most challenging aspects of applying multisensory theory to digital comics). More complex still than *Johnny Cash: I See a Darkness* is Cognito Comics' *CIA: Operation Ajax,* which integrates an original soundtrack and sound effects throughout the image-text sequence. Here, the sound system is set up in such a way that the soundtrack responds to the reader's position in the narrative, replaying sound effects or adjusting the soundtrack to fit the relevant panel if the reader moves backwards in the image-text. Unlike *Scott Pilgrim* or the motion comic, then, the reader is here given control over the way in which the soundtrack functions, although this type of system does require a relatively modular approach to sound design and may not work so well with a lyric-heavy setup of the type used in *Johnny Cash: I See a Darkness.* The approach used in *CIA: Operation Ajax* is not unique to that title, and similar soundtrack systems can be found in works such as Galvin Scott Davis and Alexis Hall's digital graphic novel *Stricken* and the digital adaptation of Sean O'Reilly and Pedro Del Gado's *The Gwaii.*

Nevertheless, it is still too early to argue that these titles represent the direction that digital comics are likely to move in future. Although these examples do suggest a number of different routes that comics creators could seek to develop, from increasing the verisimilitude of the environments they present to directing the actions of the reader, titles of this type are still few and far between.[40] They therefore represent only the first tentative steps in what sounds in digital comics could become, and it will be interesting to see if these approaches gain a more substantial foothold in time, or if sounds remain a relatively rare phenomenon in digital comics.

3.2.3 Sounds with Comics

Sounds *with* comics present another interesting set of relationships between audio content and image-texts. In using the phrase 'sounds with comics', I am speaking of those comics that come with audio content attached to them, but which rely on an external device such as a CD player to play it back. In some ways, this category could be combined with sounds *in* comics but the different ways in which sounds tend to be used in the two forms mean that their separation is perhaps helpful here. I have therefore elected to keep them distinct. Such sounds tend to be present only in printed comics, since it is more logical to integrate sounds directly into digital productions, though this is not to say that it is impossible for nonintegrated/attached sounds to feature in digital productions, and *Johnny Cash: I See A Darkness* arguably represents an example of this type of sound in digital comics, since the audio tracks it uses can either be played independently of the narrative or integrated into it if the reader chooses. Examples of sounds with comics can be further subdivided (albeit loosely) into two categories. In the first we can place those comics whose audible content reproduces its visual content more or less directly (e.g., the Marvel/Golden Records *Marvel Age Comic Spectaculars* sets of the 1960s). In the second are those comics whose audible content does not directly reproduce the majority of the visual (e.g., Dominique Grange and Tardi's *1968–2008 . . . N'Effacez Pas Nos Traces!*).

Where sounds with comics directly reproduce the language and sound effects presented visually upon the pages of the attached comic, their primary function can be understood as one of direction. In the first instance, this direction is temporal. Like the examples discussed above, the presence of sounds within a comic will serve to specify the performance time of the comic. Here, however, the far more comprehensive audio content and the fact that it is separate from the image-text (i.e., readers cannot navigate the two simultaneously as they can with *CIA: Operation Ajax*) means that the whole of the performance is normalised to the audio standard (cf. motion comics). The visual content of the comic is subordinated, in temporal terms, to the audible, which directs the speed at which the performance should take place.

The second mode of direction surrounds the voices in which the readings take place and the voices as the reader encounters them. In presenting the voices of particular characters, fictional or otherwise, products like the Marvel/Golden Records *Marvel Age Comic Spectaculars* series specify the voice in which a character speaks. They also add information regarding the vocalisation of things like narration boxes. This series, released in 1966, comprised four LPs, each of which was packaged with a reprint of a particular Marvel Comic.[41] Advertisements promised readers the opportunity to 'listen to the voices of [their] heroes in action!', and the audio content provided this and more in reproducing every single word and sound effect in the comic.[42] This was beneficial in terms of sales because it allowed the records to be marketed as educational tools, and indeed a third directive function is in evidence here: the comics directed the children who learned from them as to the correct pronunciation of the words they were reading. Remaining with the voice for the moment though, it is worth noting just how influential these audio elements may have been. Experimental research by Jessica D. Alexander and Lynne C. Nygaard has indicated that when readers are exposed to a speaker's voice before they hear something they believe to have been authored by her/him, they reproduce that speaker's voice within their auditory imagination as they read. 'We propose', the researchers write, 'that when specific representations are accessed, they contribute to a form of auditory imaginary for speech that includes properties of the vocal characteristics of the assumed author'.[43] This suggests that the voices employed in the production of the record may well have served to influence the reader's conception of the characters' voices in subsequent editions of the comic, even if they were without a record.

A fourth and final directive function of sound as employed here comes in the specification of the speaker, which can be understood as an addition of information that was not previously present (though without stepping outside the realm of the language in the comic). In his review of the Golden Records version of *Amazing Spider-Man* #1, Al Sjoerdsma writes:

> Ever wonder who is speaking in the panel that only shows Reed's lab and one word balloon reading, "We just keep enough money to pay our expenses. Every other cent goes into developing the most effective super-crime-fighting apparatus we can create!" and the other balloon reading, "Besides, aren't you wanted by the police? This isn't Outlaws Anonymous!" In other words, which of the Four rags on Spidey about being wanted? Well, in this version, Mr. Fantastic reads the first balloon (makes sense) and the second one comes from the Invisible Girl. Somehow I always visualized that ragging coming from the Human Torch. The disembodied "Wait! Come back!" in the next panel is also voiced by Mr. F.[44]

In his review, Sjoerdsma astutely identifies another function of sound in comics: the addition of information that is not conveyed visually. While this is of course evident in the other directive functions to some degree, sound here plays a role in developing the reader's understanding of the narrative (though it should be noted that it is hardly nonsense without the voices). The possibilities for such a function are substantial, given that they allow for the insertion of new information without requiring the disruption of the *mise-en-page*. It should be noted, however, that it is possible to visually indicate the identity of an off-panel speaker. In David Mazzucchelli's *Asterios Polyp,* for example, every character in the book has an individual balloon and text style that are employed consistently throughout, which allows Mazzucchelli to indicate to the reader who is speaking, even when they are off-panel. Thus, the identifying role of the voice is not exclusive to comics' audible components. Nevertheless, the informative function of sound here is clear, and were comics creators to take up the challenge of developing this type of sound more concertedly there would undoubtedly arise some intriguing and powerful works, particularly once the voice was used to convey more nuanced intonation, a critical element of speech that is frequently overlooked.[45]

The second category of sounds with comics bears some consideration too. In this field we can include works such as Dominique Grange and Tardi's *1968–2008 . . . N'Effacez Pas Nos Traces!* which is an album in two senses of the word, first as a *bande dessinée,* second as a compact disc.[46] The CD presents a selection of antiestablishment songs composed by Grange in May 1968. Although some of the words of the songs are reproduced in visual form on the book's pages, the music and the voice (both inherently aural elements) are not. Consequently, there is a fairly significant difference between the two elements. Yet they are physically packaged together and it is not difficult to see that each is somewhat incomplete without the other, particularly given that the CD's track listing appears on a page of the book, not on the CD holder. The publisher's website asserts: 'A double reading of this book is essential for the reader who has the task of listening to Dominique Grange's songs with her/his eyes focused on Tardi's pictures'.[47] Indeed, upon perusing the book the reader may well be struck by how reliant it is upon the CD. Each of the CD's fifteen tracks (which range in length from two minutes thirty seconds to six minutes five seconds) is accompanied by a short *bande dessinée* sequence (the strips range from two to five pages in length). The length of these strips is interesting because rather than reading to "keep up" with the progression of the music, the reader is encouraged to linger over the images, absorbing the messages of the work both visually and aurally (this effect is further contributed to by the scarcity of written words). In this sense, the work associates not only (perhaps not even) Grange's *lyrics* with the images of revolution and repression, but the sound of her *voice,* that ineffable quality of aurality that transcends speech; '[s]ound infuses the image', to borrow a turn of phrase from Michel Chion.[48] The emotive qualities of sounds are here drawn out, and serve to give the work a greater affective power over readers; they make readers *feel* the images they are confronted with in the emotional sense of that term. The sounds afford the images a visceral power that they might not otherwise possess.

There are other examples of sounds with comics, and we certainly do not have space to cover them all in depth here. What I hope to have demonstrated are some of the effects that sound can have in combination with visual images, and the potential for further areas of development.

3.2.3.1 Producible Sounds

Before considering whether sound can work in isolation to express the medium, it is worth a brief aside to consider another type of sound with comics. I am hesitant to position the category of producible sounds here because a valid argument can be made for its inclusion in the majority of the categories I have outlined; however, the requirement for an external mode of sound production has directed my choice in this instance.

In using the term 'producible sounds' I am referring to a category of perceivable sound that is generated by the reader in response to visual stimuli. The most obvious category of such sounds is music, which when rendered accurately upon the page can allow the reader to produce sounds in a specific fashion. In the first volume of *Scott Pilgrim,* for instance, a narrative sequence involving a rehearsal for the titular character's band 'Sex Bob-omb' provides the setting for the deployment of guitar music. A narration box proclaims: 'Hey Kids! Now you can play along with Sex Bob-omb at home! It's easy, because they're kind of crappy! Look, this whole song only uses 3 chords!'[49] The box then provides tab notation for three chords, and the song's lyrics are presented at the bottom of the succeeding panels along with the markers for the chords in the musical sequence. The narration box describes the rhythm as '4/4 rock, fast, hard, sloppy'.[50] Other examples, such as *V for Vendetta* and the Tintin story *The Castafiore Emerald* present musical notation upon the page that could, in theory, be played, though they are less emphatic in suggesting that the reader do so (see section 6.1 for more on *V for Vendetta*).[51] This is not to say, however, that the producible sound must be musical in nature. We can also include the dialogue of comics when it is read out, or even more generic sounds. In his one-page story 'Don't Get Around Much Any More', Art Spiegelman provides an example of the latter, instructing the reader that the comic is '[t]o be read to the accompaniment of a dripping faucet, slowly', an ideal aural accompaniment to the strange domestic narrative, which revolves around an isolated outsider.[52] Like the musical sound, such instructions implicate the reader not just in *receiving* the text, but in *performing* it (Spiegelman is well aware of the power of sounds with comics as well, as *MetaMaus,* a companion to his noted graphic novel *Maus,* demonstrates through its inclusion of extensive audio content from the interviews that provided the background for *Maus*).

Of all the sounds presented here, producible sounds are perhaps the most indicative of the potential for the performance of the medium. They serve to extend the physical boundaries of the work not just in terms of the space that it occupies (as is the case with CDs and records) but also in the employment of readers, whose productive relationship with the text is made explicit by their presentation of the sound. The reader is tasked, in this relationship, with the *conversion* of sounds from visual representations to audible manifestations. They are therefore required to negate the work's representative function through action; abstraction is refused because the abstract, arbitrary form (language) is transformed into that which it represents. Produced sounds constitute a rejection of the auditory imagination (though they may later contribute to it). A further shift away from the auditory imagination can be found in sounds *as* comics.

3.3 SOUNDS AS COMICS

Having now addressed the fairly noncontentious areas of sounds as *components* of comics and sounds that come *with* comics, we can move on to consider a more striking development of the medium: the idea of sounds *as* comics. To put the point of discussion in simple terms: Can a sound (or set of sounds) be a comic?

A fairly traditional understanding of comics as a means of telling stories through a sequence of pictures (and possibly words) is unlikely to offer much support to the notion of a comic composed purely of sound. Part of the reason for this is that comics tend to be understood as presenting time spatially; to borrow Scott McCloud's most concise phrasing, 'space equals time'.[53] Even those definitions that are slightly looser fall into line with this basic idea through their emphasis upon the spatial juxtaposition of images to communicate a narrative (e.g., Groensteen's concept of iconic solidarity). As I outlined in my discussion of the visual process of accommodation in section 2.4, this gives comics the ability to work in two ways at once, manipulating the tension between what Charles Hatfield identifies as the sequence and the surface in both a mental sense (through cognition) and a physical one (through FocusMotion). This duality would seem to be negated in the auditory field given that '[s]ound is more symptomatic of the flow of time than any other phenomena impinging on our senses'.[54] This is what Ferdinand de Saussure was getting at when he wrote:

> Unlike visual signals [. . .] which can exploit more than one dimension simultaneously, auditory signals have available to them only the linearity of time. The elements of such signals are presented one after another: they form a chain.[55]

Though the idea of sound as monodimensional is inaccurate (sounds are spatial in character as well as temporal) Saussure's general argument here is valid.[56] Because sounds are reliant upon, indeed they are comprised of, motion, they cannot exist in an atemporal way as visual phenomena (apparently) can. It would seem, therefore, that sound is bound to the sequence and cannot be understood in terms of the surface. While it may serve to drive the reader forward (as in the examples discussed above), this drive is not capable in and of itself of being a comic.

Yet there are some good reasons to think that comics could be entirely auditory in their composition. Particularly obvious is the development of the sound sculpture as an auditory manipulation of space, as embodied in facilities such as AUDIUM in San Francisco, 'variously described as a theatre of sound-sculptured space or a sound space continuum', which has been open since 1975.[57] Composer Stan Shaff, the co-creator of AUDIUM, '[asks] listeners to see with their ears', a neat inversion of Joost Pollmann's argument that 'you can listen with your eyes'.[58] In so doing, Shaff emphasises the spatial character of sound, though of course those remarks about the temporariness of sound mentioned earlier still stand. In working with sounds as spatial entities, Shaff points towards a means by which a surface could be developed for audible comics, though I have yet to encounter any works that could truly be said to display the formal properties of comics through sound.

In a simpler and less formal sense though, it is entirely possible that auditory comics might be validated by social definitions of the types advanced by Martin Barker and Joseph Witek. The *Julius Knipl: Real Estate Photographer* RealAudio Cartoons/Radio Cartoons based on the series of the same name by Ben Katchor and produced by David Isay are one example of works that challenge the idea that comics and cartoons are necessarily visual.[59] The series comprises fourteen audio files ranging in length from one minute twenty-one seconds to three minutes thirty-six seconds, distributed over the Internet in RealPlayer format.[60] They have no visual content whatsoever, which would bring them into conflict with most formal definitions of comics, but they do have some characteristics that might allow us to incorporate them.

Firstly, the character of Julius Knipl has appeared in numerous newspaper comic strips and collections. While this is not enough, in and of itself, to lead us to call the audio files cartoons or comics (just as we would not call a pair of trainers with the Batman logo on a comic), it does serve to situate them within a context of comic strip production and reception. That they are linked to from Katchor's own website (though they are hosted externally) further embeds them in that context.

A second, more substantive reason why we might accept the *Julius Knipl* audio pieces as comics can be found within the printed strip. As Frank L. Cioffi has noted:

> In Katchor's Julius Knipl comic strips, the words and images interdepend [. . .] the words appear to be an extension and explanation of the images, but in fact offer little help at all in explaining the overall paraworld that Katchor has created. The images without the words would be disembodied here, would form a confusing non-sequential series with little connectedness at all.[61]

Critiquing Cioffi's ideas, Nathalie op de Beeck suggests that Katchor's comics lack a drive for resolution; they are not a satisfyingly coherent synthesis between words and images, rather they 'require readers to maintain a productive, though melancholic, limbo'.[62] Whichever side of the argument one falls on regarding the function of the relationships between text and images in *Julius Knipl: Real Estate Photographer*, even a cursory reading reveals that the textual elements, particularly those in the caption boxes, do have a narrative flow that could convincingly be separated from the visual context through a conversion into speech. Though this conversion divests the words of their visual qualities and removes the possibility for slippages between words and images, it imparts to them a powerful alternative for communication: voice. As we have already seen, the natures of sounds and the voice are such that they can both provide information and stimulate emotion in different ways to visual elements, and voice is used very effectively for both purposes in the audio pieces. We might also note that the voice brings with it a 'grain'. This grain is a part of the sound that goes beyond the aural expression of language (i.e., speech). While it is difficult to express this *in* language, the grain of the voice is that which is generated by the meeting of the (aural) tone and the language; it is what results from their interface, but is at the same time embedded within and constituted of that interface. In a sense, it is the texture of the voice. Roland Barthes describes this in the following way:

> The 'grain' [of the voice] is [. . .] the materiality of the body speaking its mother tongue; perhaps the letter, almost certainly *significance*.
> [. . .]
> The 'grain' of the voice is not—or is not merely—its timbre; the *significance* it opens cannot better be defined, indeed, than by the very friction between the music and something else, which something else is the particular language (and nowise the message).[63]

Thus, although the audio pieces lose the potential for a text/image friction, or *tension* to use the term employed by Katchor, when the words acquire a voice they gain an alternative, aural dimension that is similarly capable of dissonance.[64] The texture of the voice can make familiar words difficult for the hearer, and thereby open up gaps between the listener's expectations and her/his experiences of the words as they are spoken. It is worth noting, however, that the seemingly disparate natures of words and images in this particular series suggest that the Julius Knipl strips are unusually well suited for this kind of literal separation and for this reason they may benefit more than most from the presence of the grain of the voice. The already strange rhythms and language structures of the *Julius Knipl* series are perfectly suited to the aural form, and benefit from the audible effects that form can employ. Cioffi does identify other examples in which words and images are somewhat divergent, though, which suggests that the Julius Knipl series is not unique in its transferability.

We might also suggest that the Julius Knipl audio cartoons represent an extension of Katchor's ideas in the series to their fullest extent. The printed Julius Knipl strips often refer to spaces that were once full or objects that were once present, and people's reactions to them as they become empty or are lost (for good examples of this, see 'The Vacant Storefront' and 'Misspent

Youth Centre').[65] It could be argued that in the audio cartoons we have a physical embodiment of this principle: a drawn strip without a drawn strip, so as to speak.[66] The audio series becomes a reference to something that was once present (the visual strip) but no longer is, and in so doing it perhaps serves as a comment on the decline of the newspaper comic strip (which is of course only part of the larger decline of newspapers in general).[67]

Perhaps the most substantial argument for the audio files as cartoons comes in their being named as such by the producers, calling to mind Martin Barker's assertion that '*a comic is what has been produced under the definition of a "comic"*'.[68] The works are listed on the website from which they can be downloaded as both 'realAudio Cartoons' and 'Radio Cartoons'.[69] Calling the works cartoons in this way indicates that they can be considered alongside the other manifestations of the Julius Knipl character; they are no more or less cartoons than the newspaper strips, though they are determinably *different* to them, a fact attested to by the presence of the words 'realAudio' and 'Radio' as specifying terms. Reader-oriented social definitions such as Joseph Witek's may also allow for this type of understanding, depending on whether one feels it is possible to read with the ears (given Pollmann's assertion that we can listen with our eyes this is perhaps not such a leap). The implication that these works can be considered as comics does not sit easily with all comics readers, however, many of whom remain wedded to the concept of visuality as a defining characteristic of the medium, and Bart Beaty has provided some anecdotal evidence to suggest that most of his students are unwilling to make the leap in this case.[70]

Whether we accept the Julius Knipl pieces as comics or not, they nevertheless present an intriguing possibility for the medium and demonstrate the breadth of objects that producers and readers are willing to accept as constituents of the field. The presence and significance of sound as an artistic medium continues to grow and increase in its cultural prominence, even if this prominence is attended by controversy. In 2011 a work by Susan Philipsz became the first sound installation to win the Turner Prize, an event that Channel 4 News Culture Editor Matthew Cain described as a 'a shot in the arm for sound art'.[71] If the aural arts do indeed continue to develop along more experimental lines, it is entirely possible that we will see a shift in this direction from comic artists as well. We have already witnessed the beginning of this type of activity in Katchor's works; it remains to be seen whether this is the start of a new approach to comic art, or both the beginning and the end of audio cartoons.

3.4 SOUNDS AROUND COMICS

A final category of sounds involved in the experience of comics is that of sounds *around* comics. In this category we can include those sounds to which readers are exposed when they read a comic that are not a part (or the whole) of the comic, and which do not necessarily relate directly to it. This type of sound has been noted (albeit very briefly) by Randy Duncan and Matthew J. Smith in their application of a communications model to comics. In their discussion of 'noise', which they describe as 'any interference which distorts the message', Duncan and Smith identify the category of 'Environmental noise'.[72] This identification is not hugely helpful to us, however, because they use it in a way that would lump together a number of the categories I have already discussed under the description 'physical noise in the receiver's surroundings'.[73] Nevertheless, they do go on to remark that: 'A person reading a comic book while babysitting is likely to experience some environmental intrusions'.[74] Although the communications model they use has been strongly criticised, Duncan and Smith's point about the audible differences in reading environments is well taken.[75] In a broader sense, the sounds of the time period in which comics are read can also contribute to their character in the reader's mind.[76]

The biggest problem with this type of sound is its almost limitless variety. The number of places in which comics are or can be read is huge, and certainly goes beyond the boundaries of what any academic study could hope to cover. Though there are certainly some common locations that might be worth investigating (bookshops, libraries, comic shops) and there may be some value in using comparative site-specific research to determine how different perceivable soundscapes affect reading experiences, we could never catalogue and/or describe the vast complexities of sounds around comics.[77] This is not to say that sounds around comics are entirely valueless, however, and there are two major points worth noting here.

Firstly, sounds around comics can have a significant impact upon the categories of sounds that I have already discussed. In a very quiet environment, the sounds *of* comics will be more keenly perceived. The production of sounds *in* or *with* comics or the performance of producible sounds may be discouraged (as in the stereotypical library setting) or at least be understood as a disruption that pushes the sound into the category of noise as it is outlined by Paul Hegarty. The reverse will be true in a setting that is already very loud and noisy, since the structured sounds *in* or *with* comics may constitute an order that is contrary to the audible cacophony, while the sounds *of* comics could well be drowned out altogether. Though difficult to be consistent about, the ways in which the sounds of the setting affect what we hear from comics are worth mentioning, and they should be taken into account in any application of the foregoing categories.

A second aspect of sounds around comics that bears consideration is that readers are not wholly absent from their creation. We should not fall into the trap of thinking that the sounds around comics are somehow "outside" the experience of reading or the performance of the comic. In fact, the sounds to which readers are listening when they read a comic can be consciously selected to aid in that reading experience. To give one example, in a letter printed in *RASL* #8, reader Jason Warzecha asked writer/artist Jeff Smith if he ever thought of a 'soundtrack' to his comics, stating that he had had difficulty deciding on what to listen to while reading the second collection of the *RASL* series, to which Smith replied[78]:

> I don't really picture a movie soundtrack for it, exactly, but I can tell you what I was listening to while writing it: Chihei Hatakeyama's Minima Moralia, Carbon Based Lifeforms' Hydroponic Garden, Bob Dylan's Modern Times, and as I write this . . . Pink Floyd's Wish You Were Here—really, really loud at midnight. [sic][79]

Here then, the choice of music does not serve as a soundtrack as such but it may help the reader to reconstitute the context of the comic's production, and thereby bring him closer to that work, seemingly connecting him to the artistic processes involved in its creation. Sounds and music can also serve to reflect the themes and contents of the comic itself. When one reader of the UK reprint comic *The Mighty World of Marvel* (volume 4) wrote to ask what type of music he should listen to while reading, editor Scott Gray replied[80]: 'I used to listen to movie soundtracks. John Barry, Jerry Goldsmith, Howard Shore and John Williams were my favourite composers!'[81] The editor's identification of these composers as the ones he enjoyed listening to is particularly interesting because it suggests strong links between film and comics, and specifically between common genres within each medium. Each of these composers has worked on films that could be said to fall into the action genre, as could the comics reprinted in *The Mighty World of Marvel*. In this instance then, the comic's content does somewhat suggest a type of music that would be appropriate to it, though the knowledge and genre associations of this music may well be drawn from other fields, such as film. Soundtracks to filmic adaptations of comics, or even comic-based works such as the *V for Vendetta* EP released (separately to the comic) by Alan Moore and David J may also be influential here (see section 6.1 for more on *V for Vendetta*).[82]

Suggestions within the comic of musical types or of pieces that are more or less specific may also direct the reader to select a particular type of music or sound effect. In Marvel's *Invincible Iron Man* #2, for example, the protagonist's narration boxes make such a suggestion: 'Rostropovich doing *Bach* inside the helmet. Discreet Dolby 7.1 holophonic sound. / If they yell, I can't hear it'.[83] Similar references can be found in Kieron Gillen and Jamie McKelvie's *Phonogram* series, which makes numerous allusions to Britpop music, and in Gilbert Hernandez's *Love and Rockets X*.[84] More specific direction of the comic's soundtrack can be found in Brian Wood and Ryan Kelly's *Local*, each issue of which included a track listing for the issue and in some cases additional pieces, such as music to cover the transition between issues ('my segue to Minneapolis') or a 'Roll credits song'.[85] The songs listed were existing pieces by known artists, so readers could employ them in their reading if they so chose, demonstrating a very simple means for integrating sounds into narratives without significant cost to either creators or readers. In such examples though, we cross over slightly into the territory of the producible sound, the major difference being that these directions for the readers' ears are generally more implied than instructional. Whether we count them as producible or not, it is clear that sounds around comics are a key means of environmental control for readers, and should not simply be dropped into the category of 'noise', as Duncan and Smith are inclined to do.

3.5 CONCLUSION

In approaching the role of hearing in comics as we have here, it is clear that for the large part sounds serve as supplements to the visual elements of the medium. Ben Katchor and David Isay's works aside, sound artists have not yet sought to comprehensively displace the visual in favour of a new, audible sequential art. Yet it is also clear that employing sounds enables the transmission of information and meaning in fundamentally different ways to the purely visual mode, and that that information and meaning can be substantively different in nature from what can be expressed visually. Audible sound transcends the possibilities of visually represented "sounds" and allows for the specification of information such as the voice, as well as a certain degree of control over elements like the duration of the reading. More than a simple gimmick, the most accomplished uses of the sounds of, in, with, as and around comics enable their creators to communicate information in a truly multimodal fashion that expresses meaning in a fundamentally different way to what the visual or aural representation alone would provide. Rather than visuality or aurality taking priority, in works such as *1968–2008 . . . N'Effacez Pas Nos Traces!* the combination of sounds with still images enables new nexuses of meaning to develop. Just as the relationships between text and image in comics have long been seen as productive areas for study, the various ways in which sound and images/texts can be integrated or juxtaposed in the medium offers a fruitful area for future development. This is something we will take further when we consider the roles of music in *V for Vendetta* in section 6.1.

As we move now to discuss touch, 'our most elusive yet most vital sense', it will be important to remember this idea of comics as a multimodal medium, one that is capable of expressing different types of meaning in a variety of ways.[86] Like sounds, the tactile elements of comics can in some senses be understood as supplements to a visual image-text, but they also strengthen the idea that comics are *fundamentally* multisensory because tactility so clearly emphasises the "objectness" of the comic; it makes clear to readers that the text they are reading is physically embodied, not just an abstract idea. While the sounds made by a comic may not always be consciously picked up on by readers as indicators that they are interacting with a physical object, touch is not so subtle in its functionality.

NOTES

1. McCloud, Scott. 1993. *Understanding Comics: The Invisible Art*. New York, NY: HarperPerennial. 25.
2. Ibid., 89.
3. Pollmann, Joost. 2001. "Shaping Sounds in Comics." Edited by John A. Lent. *International Journal of Comic Art* 3 (1): 9–21. 9.
4. Pollmann, Joost. 1999. "An Art of the Real: About the Adulthood of Contemporary Comics." Edited by John A. Lent. *International Journal of Comic Art* 1 (2): 107–126. 107.
5. Pollmann, 'Shaping', 15.
6. For more on sound effects in manga see: Petersen, Robert S. 2009. "The Acoustics of Manga." In *A Comics Studies Reader*, edited by Jeet Heer and Kent Worcester, 163–171. Jackson, MS: University of Mississippi Press.
7. Hergé. 2003. "The Adventures of Tintin: Land of Black Gold." In *The Adventures of Tintin Volume 5*, by Hergé, 3–64. London: Egmont Books. 3, 7; Lee, Stan, and Jack Kirby. 2010. "Fantastic Four #64: The Sentry Sinister." *Fantastic Four Adventures* Volume 2 no. 10, November 12: 52–72. 55, 58; Anonymous. 1984. *WHOOPEE! (and Wow!)*. London: IPC Magazine, October 27. n.p.
8. Covey, Suzanne. 2006. "Beyond the Balloon: Sound Effects and Background Text in Lynn Johnson's For Better or For Worse." *ImageText: Interdisciplinary Comics Studies* 2 (2). Accessed January 18, 2012. http://www.english.ufl.edu/imagetext/archives/v2_2/covey/.
9. It is worth noting that not all visual sound effects apply to actual sounds, and may be intended to indicate or make explicit other aspects of an aural environment, as in Pollmann's examples of SHIN, which indicates silence, and BIIN, which suggests a certain aurality to a growing erection but this is more likely to be in the sense of a nondiegetic sound effect than something that is genuinely audible to the characters in the narrative.
10. Eisner, Will. 2006. *Comics and Sequential Art*. Paramus, NJ: Poorhouse Press. 26.
11. Khordoc, Catherine. 2001. "The Comic Book's Soundtrack: Visual Sound Effects in Asterix." In *The Language of Comics: Word and Image*, edited by Robin Varnum and Christina T. Gibbons, 156–173. Jackson, MS: University Press of Mississippi.
12. Kunzle, David. 2001. "The Voices of Silence: Willette, Steinlen and the Introduction of the Silent Strip in the Chat Noir, with a German Coda." In *The Language of Comics: Word and Image*, edited by Robin Varnum and Christina T. Gibbons, 3–18. Jackson, MS: University Press of Mississippi. Beronä, David A. 2008. *Wordless Books: The Original Graphic Novels*. New York, NY: Abrams. 12. Of course there are some well-known deaf and hearing impaired characters in comics, for example Marvel Comics' Echo, and Professor Calculus from *The Adventures of Tintin*, but representations of deafness and hearing impairment are very limited.
13. Ihde, Don. 2003 (2005). "Auditory Imagination." In *The Auditory Culture Reader*, edited by Michael Bull and Les Back, 61–66. Oxford: Berg. 61.
14. Ibid., 62.
15. Hegarty, Paul. 2007. *Noise/Music: A History*. New York, NY: Continuum International. 5.
16. Manilla, Ben. 2008. *The Sounds of American Culture: NYC Mayor LaGuardia's Legendary Radio Readings*. MP3 (downloaded from http://www.npr.org/player/v2/mediaPlayer.html?action=1&t=1&islist=false&id=97621982&m=97621965, December 15, 2010).

17. Eisner, *Comics*, 26.
18. McCormick, Barry. 1988 (1992). "Basic Acoustics." In *Constructing Deafness*, edited by Susan Gregory and Gillian M. Hartley, 84–86. London: Pinter Publishers in association with the Open University. 84.
19. Gross, Richard D. 1992 (1999). *Psychology: The Science of Mind and Behaviour.* London: Hodder and Stoughton Educational. 206–207.
20. Chion, Michel. 2008. "Sound Film—Worthy of the Name." In *Visual Sense: A Cultural Reader*, edited by Elizabeth Edwards and Kaushik Bhaumik, 249–254. Oxford: Berg. 250.
21. Bull, Michael, and Les Back, eds. 2003 (2005). *The Auditory Culture Reader.* Oxford: Berg. 1.
22. Shepherd, John. 1991. *Music as Social Text.* Cambridge: Polity Press. 20. Italics in original.
23. For a summary of numerous tall tales dealing with the idea of frozen speech, see: Hansen, William F. 2002. *Ariadne's Thread: A Guide to International Tales Found in Classical Literature.* Ithaca, NY: Cornell University Press. 146–147.
24. Genette, Gérard. 1987 (1998). *Paratexts: Thresholds of Interpretation.* Translated by Jane E. Lewin. Cambridge: Cambridge University Press. 75.
25. Wolk, Douglas. 2007. *Reading Comics: How Graphic Novels Work and What They Mean.* Cambridge, MA: Da Capo Press. 66.
26. Ibid., 65–66; Sabin, Roger. 1993. *Adult Comics: An Introduction.* London: Routledge. 62–69.
27. Genette, *Paratexts*, 31–32.
28. On this aspect of sound see: Nuckolls, Janis B. 1999. "The Case for Sound Symbolism." *Annual Review of Anthropology* 28: 225–252.
29. See: Kramer's Ergot. 2008. *Kramer's Ergot 7: About.* Accessed December 15, 2010. http://www.buenaventurapress.com/KE7/about.php. And: Sunday Press Books. n.d. *What the World Is Saying about LITTLE NEMO IN SLUMBERLAND—SPLENDID SUNDAYS.* Accessed March 22, 2011. http://www.sundaypressbooks.com/testimonials.htm.
30. McCloud, Scott. 2000. *Reinventing Comics.* New York: Paradox Press. 229. Emphasis in original.
31. Pollmann, 'Shaping', 9.
32. Hegarty, *Noise*, 5.
33. Rée, Jonathan. 1999. *I See a Voice: Language, Deafness and the Senses—A Philosophical History.* London: Harper Collins. 23.
34. Groensteen, Thierry. 2007. *The System of Comics.* Translated by Bart Beaty and Nick Nguyen. Jackson, MS: University Press of Mississippi. 22.
35. Groensteen, *System*, 35.
36. *Men Without Fear: Creating Daredevil.* 2003. DVD. Produced by Eric Young.
37. O'Malley, Bryan Lee. 2010. "Scott Pilgrim's Precious Little App." Compiled by Robot Media SL. London: HarperCollins. 1.
38. Noise Collector. 2005. *Sample: Guitarsolo1.wav.* July 8. Accessed November 26, 2010. http://www.freesound.org/samplesViewSingle.php?id=3649.
39. Kleist, Reinhard. 2009. "Johnny Cash: I See a Darkness." Ave!Comics Production. Accessed July 2, 2013. https://itunes.apple.com/us/app/johnny-cash-i-see-darkness/id341297746?mt=8. p. 217. Apple Application.
40. The educational value of audio elements attached to comics was recognised by the EduComics project (part of the European Union Life Long Learning Programme) in 2009. They note particularly the role audio could play in the tuition of languages. See: EduComics. n.d. *Edu Comics Project.* Accessed December 13, 2010. http://www.educomics.org/.

41. The reprinted comics were: *Amazing Spider-Man* #1 (1963), *Avengers* #4 (1964), *Fantastic Four* #1 (1961), and *Journey Into Mystery* #83 (1962).
42. Golden Records. n.d. *Golden Book & Record Sets Advert.* Accessed December 13, 2010. http://www.neatstuffsite.com/npics/300–1110–204b.jpg.
43. Alexander, Jessica D., and Lynne C. Nygaard. 2008. "Reading Voices and Hearing Text: Talker Specific Auditory Imagination in Reading." *Journal of Experimental Psychology: Human Perception and Performance* 34 (2): 446–459. 457.
44. Sjoerdsma, Al. n.d. *Audio: Golden Records: Amazing Spider-Man #1 [Review].* Accessed December 13, 2010. http://www.spiderfan.org/audio/reviews/spiderman_record_comics/golden_records_asm1.html.
45. Bolinger, Dwight, ed. 1972. *Intonation: Selected Readings.* Harmondsworth: Penguin.
46. The same creators, along with Jean-Pierre Verney, also used the BD/CD format for *Des Lendemains qui saignent.*
47. Casterman. n.d. *1968–2008 . . . N'effacez pas nos traces!* Accessed May 10, 2010. http://bd.casterman.com/albums_detail.cfm?id=11764. Translation by Hayleigh Nash (2010) from original text: 'Une double lecture de cet ouvrage s'impose donc au lecteur qui aura la tâche d'écouter les chansons du CD de Dominique Grange le regard rivé sur les dessins de Tardi !'
48. Chion, 'Sound', 251.
49. O'Malley, 'Scott', 16.
50. Ibid.
51. Moore, Alan, and David Lloyd. 1990. *V for Vendetta.* New York, NY: DC Comics. 89–93; Hergé. 1995. "The Adventures of Tintin: The Castafiore Emerald." In *The Adventures of Tintin Volume 7*, by Hergé, 1–64. London: Methuen Children's Books. 53–55.
52. Spiegelman, Art. 2008. *Breakdowns: A Portrait of the Artist as a Young %@&*!* London: Penguin. n.p.
53. Harvey, Robert C. 1995. "Round and Round with Scott McCloud." *The Comics Journal* (179): 52–81. 64.
54. Shepherd, *Music*, 20.
55. Saussure, Ferdinand de. 1983 (2005). *Course in General Linguistics.* Translated by Roy Harris. London: Gerald Duckworth. 70.
56. I am grateful here to Simon Grennan for his comments on the spatial qualities of sound and the ways in which this subverts Saussure's ideas.
57. Shaff, Stanley. 2002. "AUDIUM: Sound-Sculptured Space." *Leonardo* (The MIT Press) 35 (3): 248.
58. Audium. n.d. *What Is Audium?* Accessed December 14, 2010. http://www.audium.org/omhpp.cgi?src=what_is_audium.hpp. n.p.
59. I am here using the term 'cartoon' as if it were equivalent to 'comic' because both are generally taken to be necessarily visual entities (even animated cartoons must have the 'visual frame' marked up by Michel Chion (see: Chion, 'Sound', 251)). I am aware of the discrepancies between the two terms in the broader sense.
60. See: Isay, David. n.d. *Julius Knipl: Real Estate Photographer Audio Cartoons.* Accessed September 20, 2010. http://hearingvoices.com/webwork/isay/knipl.html.
61. Cioffi, Frank L. 2001. "Disturbing Comics: The Disjunction of Word and Image in the Comics of Andrzej Mleczko, Ben Katchor, Robert Crumb, and Art Spiegelman." In *The Language of Comics: Word and Image*, edited by Robin Varnum and Christina T. Gibbons, 97–122. Jackson, MS: University Press of Mississippi. 105.

62. Beeck, Nathalie op de. 2006. "Found Objects (Jem Cohen, Ben Katchor, Walter Benjamin)." *MFS Modern Fiction Studies* (Johns Hopkins University Press) 52 (4): 807–830. 821.
63. Barthes, Roland. 1977. *Image, Music, Text*. Edited by Steven Heath. London: Fontana Press. 182, 185. Italics in original.
64. Cioffi, 'Disturbing', 105.
65. Katchor, Ben. 2000. *Julius Knipl: Real Estate Photographer: The Beauty Supply District*. New York, NY: Pantheon Books. 23, 55–56.
66. I am grateful to Hugo Frey for pointing out this interpretation of the audio cartoons to me.
67. For more on the changing nature of newspaper comics see: Watterson, Bill. 1995. *The Calvin and Hobbes Tenth Anniversary Book*. London: Warner Books. 6–9.
68. Barker, Martin. 1989. *Comics: Ideology, Power and the Critics*. Manchester, UK: Manchester University Press. 8. Italics in original.
69. Isay, *Julius*, n.p.
70. Beaty, Bart. 2009. "Comics Off the Page: Towards a Theory of Performance in the Comics World." *International Bande Dessinée Society Sixth Bi-Annual Conference*. London.
71. BBC. 2010. *Turner Prize: Susan Philipsz Wins with Lowlands Away*. December 7. Accessed December 14, 2010. http://bbc.co.uk/news/entertainment-arts-11928557.
72. Duncan, Randy, and Matthew J. Smith. 2009. *The Power of Comics: History, Form and Culture*. New York, NY: Continuum. 12.
73. Ibid.
74. Ibid.
75. Beaty, Bart. 2010. "Review: The Power of Comics: History, Form and Culture, Randy Duncan and Matthew J. Smith (2009)." Edited by Julia Round and Chris Murray. *Studies in Comics* (Intellect Ltd.) 1 (1): 179–181.
76. Hajdu, David. 2008. *The Ten Cent Plague: The Great Comic Book Scare and How It Changed America*. New York, NY: Farrar, Straus & Giroux. 7.
77. For an indication of the type of study that might be able to usefully incorporate a discussion of auditory elements, see: Gibson, Mel. 1993. "Too Graphic? Graphic Novels in a Dual Use Library." In *Graphic Account: The Selection and Promotion of Graphic Novels in Libraries for Young People*, edited by Keith Barker, 24–27. London: Youth Libraries Group.
78. Warzecha, Jason. 2010. "Untitled Letter." *RASL* #8, July. n.p.
79. Smith, Jeff. 2010. *RASL* #8. Columbus, OH: Cartoon Books. n.p.
80. Fisher, Adam. 2010. "Untitled Letter." *The Mighty World of Marvel* Volume 4 #12, September 1: 75.
81. Gray, Scott, ed. 2010. *The Mighty World of Marvel* Volume 4 #12. Tunbridge Wells: Panini. 75.
82. Gray, Maggie. 2010. "'A Fistful of Dead Roses . . .' Comics as Cultural Resistance: Alan Moore and David Lloyd's *V for Vendetta*." Edited by Joan Ormrod and David Huxley. *Journal of Comics and Graphic Novels* (Routledge) 1 (1): 31–49. 44, 48.
83. Fraction, Matt, and Salvador Larroca. 2010. "Invincible Iron Man #2." *Marvel Legends #51*, November 17: 3–25. 2. Emphasis in original.
84. Hernandez, Gilbert. 2008. *Beyond Palomar: A Love and Rockets Book*. London: Titan Books. 191–251.
85. Wood, Brian, and Ryan Kelly. 2008. *Local*. Portland, OR: Oni Press. 321, 325.
86. Classen, Constance, ed. 2005. *The Book of Touch*. Oxford: Berg. Back cover.

4 Touch, or, The Taboo/Fetish Character of Comics and Tactile Performance

4.0 THE TABOO/FETISH CHARACTER OF TOUCH IN COMICS

It would certainly be possible to discuss the role of touch in comics in the same way as I discussed the auditory imagination in relation to hearing. Philosophy scholar Christopher Perricone has followed Bernhard Berenson in asserting the importance of the 'tactile imagination' in painting.[1] This approach is clearly not restricted to that medium, having become fairly prominent in film criticism in recent years as well, with thinkers such as Thomas Elsaesser and Malte Hagener, and Tarja Laine, arguing for the importance of touch and the skin in cinema.[2] Approaching film in this way privileges notions of affect and metaphor; the skin is appealed to only through the eye and tactility becomes visual. 'The "touching eye"', writes Laine, 'is an openness waiting to touch and be touched, to be sensitive to touch with an affective and affecting component, for without affect there can be no touch in a reciprocal sense, as an open totality and a mutual enrichment'.[3] While this formulation may be considerably more complex and precise than Scott McCloud's argument that 'Comics [. . .] relies on only *one* of the senses to convey a *world* of experience', it is not fundamentally different.[4] Laine, following Derrida, goes on to argue that 'affect charges vision so that it becomes an "affected act of touching"'; there is still an emphasis here upon the sense of sight as the *conveyor* of stimulation that would otherwise be experienced directly by another sense.[5] Touch itself cannot be stimulated directly by film, it would seem, only through the eye as intermediary. Comics scholarship has also begun to gesture towards this type of discussion, indeed Scott McCloud himself mentions touch and feeling on more than one occasion in *Understanding Comics*, and more recent work by Charles Hatfield has also moved in this direction, considering the ways in which materiality is evoked in the medium through expressive line work.[6] Therefore, there is no reason to believe that we could not here follow the same structure of discussion as chapter 3, first outlining the existing approaches to touch as a visual phenomenon in comics, and then going on to consider the realities of tactile experiences.

Yet there are two reasons why, although it would be *possible* to do this, it is not necessarily desirable or representative. The first is that, unlike sound, tactile aspects of comics are rarely discussed in isolation. While visual manifestations of aural phenomena through things like sound effects and word balloons are so well known as to have become iconic representatives of the medium itself, tactile qualities have not achieved the same status. Of course we can recognise indicators of things like pain and some thinkers, such as Charles Forceville, have begun to work towards cataloguing and understanding such indicators, but these are not so well regarded as objects for study in and of themselves as sound effects are.[7] Indeed, the study by Forceville that is cited above mentions representations of pain in comics only very briefly, before going on to discuss broader issues of representation through pictorial runes. Furthermore, it is debatable whether the ability to feel things such as pain and temperature truly fall into the realm of touch at all, although following the Aristotelian five-sense model that we are here it is fairly safe to say that pain would be classed more surely as an aspect of touch than of taste, smell, sight or hearing.[8] Studying existing approaches to visual representations of touch in comics would be difficult because tactile elements are not generally parsed out from other modes of synaesthetic communication. The second reason why it is not hugely desirable to approach touch through a critique of visually oriented approaches is that the reality of touch *is* itself discussed in some limited ways, and this provides us with more fertile ground for development than would a restatement of the arguments I made in chapter 3.

Discussions of comics' tactile elements tend to ascribe one of two characters to touch, which are ultimately two sides of the same coin; presenting it as either a taboo or a fetish. On the one hand, touching comics is identified as something to be avoided to the greatest extent possible. This position is represented most strongly in the collector's market that has developed, particularly in relation to American comics, since the 1980s. Consider the following comments, taken from the third edition of *The Official Overstreet Comic Book Grading Guide* (2006):

> [. . .] there are other, more devastating opponents railing against collectors than the many machines and individuals who make up the chain of manufacturing and distributing comics—and they are the collectors' younger selves and peers! As Walt Kelly said in 1971 (through his comic creation, Pogo), "We have met the enemy and he is us." Kelly was referring to humanity's degradation of the environment through apathetic littering, and the observation can be just as easily applied to the actions of young comic book readers who—unaware of the emotional and financial value they would one day attach to their precious comic—would treat these future collectibles with all the disdain that quickly-read, rapidly decomposing paper pamphlets deserve. Running roughshod over

> their comic books, tearing covers, patching holes with tape, applying name tags, cutting coupons, rolling them into tight tubes and stuffing them without a second thought into pants pockets, stuffing them into bureau drawers—all this and more might have been perpetrated on a comic by the very same people who would one day spend months or even years desperately seeking a high grade copy of the same issue. In the quest for perfection, the most frequent and pernicious enemy is the collector's own past.[9]

The anti-touch position is also emphasised by companies that facilitate collection and preservation, and is visible in the widespread availability of bags designed specifically for comics, which limit the possibilities for the fingers of the reader to damage the comic inside (though of course bags also help the comic to resist other forms of dirt and damage). The process of slabbing, which I mentioned briefly in section 3.2.1, is also relevant here since it goes beyond even the limited form of protection from touch offered by the comic bag, and for this reason it is worth expanding a little on that process.

Slabbing is carried out by the Certified Guaranty Company (CGC) in America. It involves the inspection of comics in minute detail for the purposes of describing their condition as accurately as possible, before sealing them in a hard plastic case for protection and preservation. I will not go into the entirety of the process here but it is worth quoting a small section from the company's website to give the reader an idea of the type of physical examination being carried out[10]:

> After being examined by a Restoration Detection Expert, a [comic] book then passes to a pre-grader [. . .] The pre-grader begins the grading process by counting the book's pages and entering into the computer any peculiarities or flaws that may affect a book's grade. Some examples of this would be "a tear on third page," "a corner crease—does not break color," "a 1/4" inch spine split," and so forth.[11]

As with those comments from the *Overstreet* guide cited above, what is notable here is the absolute resistance to tactile interaction with the comic. Those 'peculiarities' and 'flaws' that CGC's graders are looking for, and which can so greatly affect the value of the comic once it reaches the open market, are predominantly caused by the movement of the comic.[12] This movement is of course partly an element of, for example, shipping, but it is also (perhaps primarily) an aspect of *reading*, and of interacting with the comic using the hands and the fingers.[13] Reading a comic changes it; indeed reading a comic is reliant upon changes, and it results in traces of the reader's presence upon the comic's pages. Taking this to its logical extreme we might even say that these traces become part of the comic. It should therefore come as little surprise that elements such as the grease on the reader's fingers that leave marks on the pages, the way that opening the comic creases the spine, and the way in which pages are occasionally torn through a too-quick turn, are strongly implied to be negatives by the CGC approach given its emphasis upon the fixing and preservation of the comic in the "best" condition possible. To the collector, touch is taboo.[14]

Standing in stark contradistinction to this position are those readers who are so enamoured of the tactile experience of comics that they seek to emphasise it as a positive aspect in and of itself. As the commoditisation of comics tends to be resisted by academics and critics who privilege reading over consumption or see comics as commodities that warrant critical enquiry rather than unmitigated support, it is unsurprising that these are the groups, along with readers themselves, in which we can observe the most support for tactile interactions with comics.[15] Let us recall once more Roger Sabin's mention of the ways in which '[Comics] can be bent, rolled-up, roughly opened or whatever. They can be held in different ways: cradled in your hand or gripped at the edges. We know how far into a comic we've read because we can feel how many pages are left', and Mel Gibson's mention of how readers' discussions of the comics they read as children '[. . .] included titles and narratives alongside physical aspects of the texts, including paper quality, feel, scent and size'.[16] Yet what is notable about these discussions is that they do not go very far beyond the idea that touch is interesting. There is little attempt made to generate a nuanced interrogation of different experiences of touch or to explore the complexities of the reader's tactile interaction with comics, though some of the functions of touch (changing the comic's configuration, facilitating recall (if not nostalgia)) are hinted at.[17] Touch, it would seem, is important but essentially simple and oriented around what are largely emotional concerns. In this sense, touch becomes a *fetish* as that term is defined by Gamman and Makinen: 'Fetishism, we would argue, is by definition a displacement of meaning through synecdoche, the displacement of the object of the desire onto something else through processes of disavowal'.[18] In comics scholarship the part (the affective power of touch) is very much taken to stand for the complex whole, and touch is thereby simplified and fetishized.

This simplification tends towards favouring certain types of comic. Roger Sabin's remarks above are oriented exclusively around printed comics, and he clearly feels that digital comics are inferior in terms of the tactile experience they are able to provide, asserting: 'Compared to this very sensual experience, clicking a mouse just isn't the same'.[19] While it is worth noting that these remarks were published in 2000, some years prior to the present writing and well before digital comics had achieved their current level of development, Sabin's comments do have echoes in modern debates surrounding the print/digital divide and the shift from printed comics to digital ones, and indeed books in general.[20] The tactile (and olfactory) elements of comics are most commonly mentioned when they are undergoing a process of change or believed to be in jeopardy, usually through processes of technological development. Readers tend to lament the supposed negation of the contact senses that comes with the development of new kinds of 'support' for the sequence of images that would seem to comprise the comic.[21] This is likely due in part to the memorable/nostalgic elements of the medium marked up by Mel Gibson and others, and in part to the fact that '[t]he communication process between humans and objects [. . .] is so familiar in ordinary life that we seldom notice it unless things go wrong', or, I would suggest, unless they change.[22] Whatever the reason, it is clear from even a cursory glance at reader forums such as Internet message boards that changing the material form of a comic is frequently resisted by those who would prefer to retain the 'sensual experience' of comics reading, with the increasing digitisation of the medium a particular concern.

It is here that concerns begin to arise surrounding the fetish character of touch in relation to comics. In simplifying the notion of touch to relate primarily, if not exclusively, to printed comics, scholars and readers sustain a broader divide in modern media, one which is perhaps most concisely enunciated by Laura U. Marks as '[. . .] a bifurcation between, on the one hand, the increasingly mediatized and virtualized experience, and on the other, an increasing desire for immediacy, the actual, or the material [. . .]'.[23] Yet as she goes on to emphasise, virtual media is not without its own materiality, and materialist approaches to that media can yield important insights. '[. . .] what unifies my materialist approach to virtual media', Marks writes, 'is a belief that reality is interconnected in multiple ways, and that it is valuable to restore the complexity of these interconnections to the false transparency attributed to digital media'.[24] While I will not be following Marks' approach *per se,* it is important to make note of it because it emphasises that materiality matters, even in a virtual environment, and digital or ostensibly virtual media is just as dependent upon material components as nondigital media is for its existence, though the forms these components take may be quite different. For this reason it is unwise to lament the shift to digital comics on the basis that it represents a negation of elements such as tactility. Over the course of this chapter I will begin to address (and hopefully challenge) this 'bifurcation' through a discussion of the sense of touch that takes in both printed and digital comics. Both forms require readers to interact with them in tactile ways, and both stimulate tactile experiences. While there are some important distinctions to be made about the types of tactility they use, they are not fundamentally different in the sense that they both affect and/or employ the reader's sense of touch. This is not to say that I will always make reference to both forms, merely that my discussion should provide avenues of approach that are not exclusive to one form or another.

The remainder of this chapter, then, will present a selection of ways in which we can begin to develop a new understanding of touch in comics. This understanding will acknowledge the importance of tactile interaction with comics, and thereby overcome the taboo position on touch. At the same time it will seek to be more precise and analytical than previous approaches that *have* indicated the value of touch, eliminating the simplicity of the fetishistic approach and allowing us to understand the uses and value of comics' tangibility more satisfactorily.

4.1 A BRIEF INTRODUCTION TO TOUCH AND THE SKIN

While sight and hearing allow us to *perceive* the world around us, it is arguably touch that *connects* us to that world most definitely, dispelling illusions and concretising our notions of the spaces we inhabit. As Jonathan Rée has remarked: '[. . .] eyesight on its own does not always enable you to distinguish appearances from realities, and when in doubt it is wise to call on the sense of touch to settle the matter'.[25] This is not to say that our sense of touch cannot be tricked, as sufferers of phantom limbs will attest, but rather that touch would seem to give us access to a realm of objects that are more certain than the distance senses can. For this reason it can to some degree negate symbolism and afford the feeler a level of direct access to things, something that is at times particularly important in comics, as we will see later in the chapter. Yet although it has been argued that '[a]mong all the senses, touch stands paramount', it should not be assumed that it is wholly separable from those other senses.[26] Touch underpins all of our senses because the skin, the largest of the sense organs, covers the whole of our body (a layer of modified skin even covers the transparent cornea in the eye).[27] While we *learn* to employ the other senses in understanding the world around us and even ourselves, touch is the first and most fundamental mode we have of comprehending our environment and the objects with which we are confronted.[28] Betrand Russell has even gone as far as to assert that 'our whole conception of what exists outside us, is based on the sense of touch'.[29] It is therefore unsurprising that it has been described as 'the bass line to the melody of sight and hearing in the arts,' as the thing that 'keeps the work of art coherent and grounded'.[30] Before we go on to discuss the nature of this coherence in more detail, though, let us first develop our understanding of how touch works.

We feel things because sensory receptors in our skin and deeper tissues detect them either as they come into contact with the skin itself, or as they stimulate the hairs that grow out of it, and transmit the sensations generated by these contacts to the brain and spinal cord.[31] Estimates place the number of sense receptors in the skin at around 50 per 100 square millimetres, giving a total of 640,000 across the body as a whole, though this number decreases with age.[32] As I have already mentioned, there are some who advocate the separation of sensations like heat and cold from touch per se, but I will include these categories here for the sake of simplicity.

It is interesting to note that touch is in some ways both the most and the least intimate of our senses; the most intimate because it requires the direct physical interaction of two bodies that are literally in contact with one another. Though this has obvious implications in terms of sexuality, to the point that it is deemed curious that touch is not a central concern in discussions of that theme, the intimate nature of touch is also evident in the descriptions of acts such as reading of the kind presented by Roger Sabin and others, who present tactile interactions with books as desirable and pleasurable.[33] 'A book in the hand is worth two on the screen', writes Constance Classen, upholding the idea that to touch something is to establish a uniquely intimate relationship with it.[34] Yet touch could also be reckoned the least intimate and least close of our senses, given that it is the only one that relies upon resistance and impact rather than penetration for its functionality. While the objects of sight (photons), hearing (sound waves), smell and taste (chemicals in both cases) must enter into the body before they can generate the sensations that are transmitted to the brain, tactile sensation is generated by contact between the object and the sensory receptor. Because the receptor is embedded in the skin, the object need not penetrate the skin to effect a response. Thus, while the other senses blur the boundaries between the sensing individual and the sensation (hearing is perhaps the most effective in doing this, as I discussed in section 3.1), that is, between subject and object, touch resolutely reinforces them. The 'realities' on which Jonathan Rée commented are surely due in part to the way in which touch defines the limits of the physical bodies that are being brought into contact. In the case of comics, touch prevents us from entering into the diegesis too completely because it emphasises the material context in which that diegesis sits. While the visual, auditory, olfactory and gustatory content may serve to detach us from our physical environment and the comic as object (albeit in quite different ways), touch continually reasserts that materiality; it does not allow us to slip too far away from the reality of the situation. As we will see, this reality is at times extremely important in the field of comics, and creators have begun to develop a variety of innovative ways to play with the tactile properties of comics.

There are two major areas to think about in relation to the role touch plays in reading comics. The first comprises what we might call the passive tactile elements of comics: those properties of comics that stimulate particular sensations in readers when they come into contact with them. These properties are physical in nature, and include texture, material composition, hardness, flexibility, weight and temperature. We will consider these areas in section 4.2 and its subsections. The second major area involves those elements of tactility that are involved in the *performance* of the comic, which are either culturally determined and relatively conventional (e.g., the turning of pages), or stimulated specifically by the individual comic itself through direct or implied instructions (e.g., for the assembly of flat-pack furniture). We have already thought about some of these areas in our discussion of producible sounds in section 3.2.3.1, but the number and variety of ways in which touch is involved in the performance of comics are significant enough to warrant further attention here. We will cover them in section 4.3 and its subsections.

4.2 PROPERTIES OF THE OBJECT

4.2.1 Texture

Even a gentle touch can tell us much about the nature of a comic and begin to establish a relationship between reader and object that can supplement and in some cases go beyond what visual expression can convey. Perhaps the most obvious elements of the comic's composition in this regard are its textures, whether these are the cover and pages of a printed comic, or a mouse or touch screen used to access digital comics. My use of the plural, *textures*, here is important because relatively few comics have only one texture (exceptions to this general idea being comics in newspapers, and more unusual examples such as *Cardboard Comics* (Proof Spirit), whose composition comprises only a single sheet of cardboard). The medium is therefore to be understood as comprising a multiplicity of textures overlaid upon and interlaced with each other, in more or less complex configurations depending on the comic. Each of these textures, however, is itself a combination of elements, as Cathryn Vasseleu observes:

> Texture is a disposition or characteristic of anything which is woven into a fabric, and comprises a combination of parts or qualities which is neither simply unveiled or made up. Texture is at once the cloth, threads, knots, weave, detailed surface, material, matrix and frame.[35]

While I would expand on this perspective somewhat by going beyond woven fabrics in my discussion of texture, indeed, I would suggest that all materials have textures, this description is essentially sound. It is also quite useful because it highlights the complex mesh of elements that contribute to the textures we perceive in objects.

In some regards, texture serves a similar function to gloss (see section 2.2), in that it implies a level of cultural prestige in a manner that exceeds the artwork upon the page. The glossier the page is, the smoother it will feel, and given that the application of gloss is often part of the material "upgrade" that I discussed in chapter 2, it is clear that to many, smoother textures imply a more prestigious item. We should not underestimate the extent to which paper quality does matter to readers. In 2007 Mark Williams, a reader of Panini Comics' *Astonishing Spider-Man* (volume 2) indicated this quite clearly in a letter to the publication, stating that his interest in Marvel comics had dropped off in the 1980s as 'the print quality went downhill'.[36] He cited a decline in the quality of colouring and the use of 'poor quality newsprint' as contributing to his disillusionment with the company's products.[37] While visual qualities such as colour are clearly important to this writer, it is clear that the quality of the paper is not only responsible for its ability to convey images. The tactile qualities of newsprint, being thin and rough, likely contributed to a general feeling that the material being presented in those comics of the early 1980s was not being treated respectfully. No matter how well written or drawn it may have been, it was not satisfactorily manifested in a physical sense, and this was off-putting for the reader quoted here. Paper texture and qualities such as thickness can also suggest other ideas as well. Two months prior to the letter quoted above, another reader of the same publication took a reduction in the paper thickness used in the comic to mean that the publishers were 'going green'.[38] While it is clearly unwise to follow this assumption per se, it is interesting to note the ways in which a comic's consumers read not only its visual content but its physical form, and this can in some instances lead them to believe that publishers have particular ethical, financial or other concerns, whether this belief is validated by other factors or not. In this instance the comic's editor made no response to the remark on 'going green' so the motivation for changing the paper stock was not clarified.

To return to gloss more specifically: it could be argued that glossy pages feel less like paper because they are coated in a sheen that does not possess the properties of the paper itself. This implies protection, suggesting (as do the comic bag and the plastic capsule mentioned in section 4.0) that the comic itself should not be touched and thereby (arguably) reasserting the commoditised nature of that comic.[39] Conversely, rougher pages tend to imply either a lower-quality item or one that has more authorial input (again, see section 2.2). This latter attribution may of course serve to make an item *more* prestigious than a smooth object, depending on the interpreter. The letter from Mark Williams cited above is from a reader of an American-originated superhero comic; one wonders whether the same interpretation would be applied to something like the aforementioned *Cardboard Comics,* which is relatively rough but evidences a great deal of authorial input (each of the twenty-five copies is signed and numbered by hand, and the narrative of the comic concerns its own production). It is interesting to note, however, that if we look beyond printed comics this textural paradigm disappears. In digital comics, whether they are operated via mouse and keyboard or touch screen, smoothness has no inherent (or rather no inherited) value. Because we employ devices such as computers and mobile phones for a wide range of tasks, the actions we perform in reading comics on them do not generate substantively unique textural experiences; we interact with roughly the same textures every time we operate the same device (though, as I will discuss in section 4.3, there are other ways in which they can present unique tactile experiences in a more general sense). This is in contrast to printed comics, where each instance may be texturally unique even if the actions employed in reading them are identical and the shapes and sizes of the books are not hugely different. For this reason, digital comics are perhaps more egalitarian than printed ones in a physical sense as well as in terms of their distribution.[40] There is no way to tell, either through texture or visible gloss, how prestigious a digital comic might be deemed by its creators and/or publishers. Thus, while digital comics may well divest the form of some of those elements to which critics are currently nostalgically attached, they also enable a greater level of accessibility to both producers and consumers, and thereby (potentially) open comics up to new audiences.

4.2.2 Compositing Materials

What is critically important in determining the texture of a comic is the material of which it is composed. In the case of printed comics this is conventionally taken to be paper at this point in time but of course this is only a convention borne of the historical development of printed formats and there is no reason to believe that comics cannot be made from fabric, stone, or pottery.[41] As digital formats develop it is necessary to expand the catalogue of materials to account for the technologies employed in that realm as well; glass, metal and plastics will thereby gain ground as primary materials involved in the composition of comics, since these are common materials used in the production of devices such as computer monitors, mobile phones and tablet computers. Although, as I have already mentioned, the material element of comics is generally deemed to be a 'support' to the images, what examples such as the Bayeux Tapestry, Trajan's column and classical Maya pottery emphasise is that images are not somehow abstract and distinct from their material conveyance.[42] It has been argued that:

> What is lost in translation, one might say, is the artist's "touch." What is perfectly translatable, if such exists, is the perfectly abstract; it is what would speak to a bodiless mind, to what is remote and beyond human reach.[43]

Yet the images of comics do possess the textures of the materials of which they are composed, and the conscious manipulation of those materials by artists can affect how we understand the images, in terms of both visual information and tangible character. While this may not be a means of conveying the artist's touch per se, it is a means by which the artist can signify things *using* touch. The materials of which a comic is composed can serve to fundamentally alter the representational status of the works in question and even challenge the notion that comics *are* representational. To explicate this notion further and gain a better understanding of the importance of texture at the same time, let us now turn to consider two examples, one in some detail, and the other more briefly.

In Art Spiegelman and Chip Kidd's biography of Jack Cole, *Jack Cole and Plastic Man: Forms Stretched to Their Limits!*, which includes a number of Cole's pages from *Plastic Man*, designer Kidd masterfully manipulates materiality. 'The design approach to me was obvious: what if Plastic Man had turned himself into a book?' he has remarked.[44] Accordingly, the book features a plastic cover, a huge variety of paper stocks with numerous textures, and rounded corners. The effect of this is to make the reading experience very changeable and inconsistent; readers are constantly reminded that they are reading a book because their sense of touch is actively drawn into the reading process, and through this the 'realities' upon which Jonathan Rée remarked are continuously brought back to their attention. We cannot simply look at the comics on the book's pages and see them as visual narratives because we are also repeatedly told by our sense of touch that this is a book, even that this is a page that is very different from those that came before it or will come after it. This changeability is ideally suited to the character of Plastic Man, whose superpower is an inhuman malleability (he is able to stretch and transform himself into outlandish shapes and sizes), a power that is replicated within the book itself and accessed by readers through their sense of touch just as much as, if not more than, through their sense of sight. This emphatic physicality is further strengthened by the selection of materials employed in the book's design. While the interior pages are made of paper (albeit with varying levels of thickness, smoothness and glossiness), the book's covers are plastic; precisely the same material that the protagonist is supposed to resemble. It does not simply *represent* plastic, it *is* plastic, and touch here serves to negate the abstraction required of the looking individual by evoking a direct link between the reader and the work that cannot be replicated by any other sense. Plasticity as a concept, and plastic as a material, permeate the entire work and serve to strengthen the expressions of narrative therein without simply restating them. We are presented with a tactile experience that exceeds the visual one without overwhelming it, and in this sense the ostensibly conventional book format transcends the role of a 'support' to the visual images; the visual components support the tangible just as much as the material elements support the visual.

A similar technique was employed, albeit in a more restricted fashion, in the 2004 collection of the first six issues of the 2004–2006 *Plastic Man* series in *Plastic Man: On the Lam!*, which also had plastic covers but used a consistent paper stock in its interior.[45] Throughout the book, the character's physicality is displayed as mutable to say the least, and his sidekick Woozy Winks draws attention to some of his more unusual characteristics, stating at one point: 'Wow. You got no pores in your face'.[46] What is interesting about this is that very few comic book characters have visible pores, but it is only when this is drawn attention to through a comment about a character that would not have any by the nature of his powers, that this is noticed. The smooth, nonporous plastic cover also contributes to the effect of this statement, allowing the reader to understand the character's texture as well as his visual appearance. Again the properties of the character are present within the material form of the book, ironically allowing the reader to come closer to the diegetic environment by emphasising the real world. The effect of this becomes more pronounced if we compare the first collection to the second, which has a more conventional construction and is relatively unremarkable in a physical sense.[47]

4.2.3 Hardness, Flexibility and Weight

Going beyond what we might call the surface aspects of touching, the texture of the comic and what it is made of, we can observe that when we grip a comic more firmly, whether to pick it up or to read it, we encounter another set of tangible qualities. Comics can be hard or soft, stiff or flexible, heavy or light. In many instances these properties and their implications track closely to book publishing in general; hardback editions are usually more prestigious than paperback ones, for example. Again, there are similar issues at play here to those discussed in sections 2.2 and 4.2.1, but in some instances the emphases are slightly different. Where gloss serves to catch the eye and may also imply protection, the dense covers of a hardback comic more certainly stress that protective element than the comic's prestige (although of course part of the prestige is derived from the level of protection a comic is afforded). A format whose pages are ensconced safely away between solid walls more surely indicates that the images within are worthy of protection than a paperback format does. Those contained within the literal shell of a slipcase, into which the comic is supposed to retreat when it is not being read, magnify this effect still further. Weight is similarly capable of suggesting solidity, density (both of the physical material of which the comic is comprised and the meaning it conveys through language forms) and prestige. These properties also play important roles in storing and organising materials, and to some extent dictate both how comics are kept and where. In preservation terms, it is clear from the modes of storage employed by collectors that stiffness is an important aspect of maintaining the integrity of an item, thus we witness the deployment of preservation materials such as backing boards (to be put into comic bags with comics to keep them straight) and at the more extreme end of the scale the aforementioned plastic capsules provided by the CGC. These processes do of course serve to preserve the commercial value and physical composition of comics, but they also make them amenable to archiving and are therefore important elements of the uptake of comics into fields like academia and perhaps also fine art.[48] It is not surprising that many of comics' earliest scholars came out of the fan communities that surround the medium; a number of the early comics scholars were also extremely fastidious fans and performed critical work for the field by cataloguing and archiving material effectively, projects continued in new ways today by user-generated projects such as the Grand Comics Database.[49]

Even in a less specialised sense, though, increasing the stiffness of a comic also increases the possibilities for storage and display. The size, shape and composition of soft, flexible comics such as American comic books means that they are essentially unable to maintain their physical form when they are stacked in close contiguity; they require a stiffer support to hold them up. While collectors are able to store their comics in boxes that minimise the amount of space they take up, this is not always an option in a commercial environment, and comics tend to be stacked on racks that display their covers to potential purchasers. This leads to a relatively small number of comics being put on display at any one time (particularly in locations where comics are situated within a general arrangement, less so in specialist comic shops). Where comics are thicker and stiffer, as is the case when they are collected into graphic novels, it becomes possible to stack them side-by-side with their spines facing outwards rather than their covers. This vastly increases the number of titles it is possible to store in a given space, and it is probably this physical change more than any elements of content that led to the uptake of graphic novels into general bookshops around the 1980s.[50] This would seem to be well known to publishers today; the popular manga digest format that has taken America and Europe by storm did not originate in manga's native Japan; it was specifically created to fit Western bookshop layouts.[51] Within the home too it is clear that the possibility of storing comics in the same places as conventional books provides a greater variety of options than a format that requires more specialised storage; digital comics remove even the requirement for more space within the home than the computer or other display device requires. They therefore allow for a greater integration of comics content into the domestic environment. As we will see in section 4.3, these qualities have implications for the use and performance of comics as well.

But properties such as hardness can serve other functions in comics, and if we turn to another work by Art Spiegelman, *In the Shadow of No Towers*, we can see some of these in use. *In the Shadow of No Towers* is Spiegelman's response to the attacks on the World Trade Centre in New York on the 11th of September 2001. It comprises a series of ten double-page comic spreads commenting upon the events and Spiegelman's reactions to them, which were originally published serially in the German newspaper *Die Zeit*, amongst other publications, and an appendix providing a brief history of American newspaper comics along with a plethora of example pages and strips.[52] One of the things that is particularly interesting about the work is its publication format: it is a large board book printed on fairly hard cardboard pages rather than soft paper. Surprisingly, this has to some extent been ignored by critics such as Hillary L. Chute, who focuses upon its serialised newspaper publication over the later collection:

> Spiegelman's trauma takes the form of innovative representation and expression in serialized comics, and yet this approach is contingent upon an anti-transcendent recognition of ephemerality—something Spiegelman takes pains to underline in presenting the correspondence of comics and buildings that both are all too destructible.[53]

What this argument overlooks is the way that the later presentation of the work in a hard physical format makes a powerful statement: in *In the Shadow of No Towers* hardness serves to suggest permanence and significance partly in a physical sense, but also in a mental one. Spiegelman presents the events of 9/11 as physical memories that are literally too hard to efface, just as the black on black silhouette of the World Trade Center that serves as the book's cover suggests the ever-present absence of the twin towers themselves. In making the book physically hard he gives the memories a permanence, which reflects the permanent changes wrought upon American society, and the American psyche, by the relatively brief but significant events of that day. He challenges the reader not only to 'read back and forth between images and words . . . [revealing] the visuality and thus the materiality of words and the discursivity and narrativity of images', but to acknowledge the tangible physical and mental traumas that the events inflicted.[54] Laura U. Marks has pointed out that '[t]o appreciate the materiality of our media pulls us away from a symbolic understanding and toward a shared physical existence', and this is particularly evident in *In the Shadow of No Towers*.[55] By making the work unusually inflexible, and indeed unusually large, Spiegelman forces the reader to remain aware of its (often uncomfortable) presence in her/his hands or upon the table in front of her/him at all times.[56] There is no escaping this black box of encrusted memories and histories; it is something that must be dealt with and thought about, despite the fact that this will not always be a comfortable process. He makes history literally too hard to crumple up and dispose of as we might otherwise do with the seemingly ephemeral newspaper comic strip, which is usually '[. . .] consumed, then discarded [with the newspaper]'.[57]

It can be seen, therefore, that the properties of comics that we detect through touch have a number of applications in terms of publishing, collecting and organising comics, as well as in presenting narratives in the medium. While these in some cases supplement visual elements such as gloss, they are also able to provide uniquely tactile experiences that more definitively emphasise ideas such as protection than other features might. As we will see in section 4.3, these elements also play major roles in the ways in which comics are performed, and to a large extent determine both what and how stories are told. Before we go on to discuss touch and performance though, it is important to mention one factor that underlies all our tactile interactions with comics and affects all the categories I have discussed so far: temperature.

4.2.4 Temperature

Though it may seem exceedingly basic to assert that comics exist at certain temperatures, this point is not one that should be forgotten because the temperature a comic is at determines the arrangement and nature of almost all the elements of that comic to some degree. In the case of printed comics, warmer temperatures will generally result in a softer object, perhaps one that is more easily manipulated. Colder temperatures will make materials stiffer and less easy to move (these modifications will also impact upon the sounds that comics make (see section 3.2.1)). At extreme levels, either type of temperature can lead to a deterioration of the comic's physical integrity; heat melting the glue that holds the pages in place, cold resulting in an increased level of brittleness. The humidity of the environment can also play a role here, and it and temperature are critical considerations when it comes to archiving and cataloguing comics. In this context the maintenance of specific safe temperatures is extremely important. Temperature is significant for digital comics as well, since computers and other electronic devices are often dependent upon a particular temperature range for their operation. While cooling systems become more efficient all the time it is worth pointing out that an overheated or overcooled computer will tend to operate more slowly, and this can impact the reading experience.

These are, generally speaking, relatively minor concerns, and I make note of them here only for the sake of completeness. In reality, discussing the temperature of a comic is so seldom likely to be of value (or even possible, in a widely generalizable sense) that it stands alongside sounds around comics (see section 3.4) as a subtle but nonetheless present aspect of the comics reading experience that may occasionally prove useful for analysis but is unlikely to be discussed regularly. This is not to say, however, that it is entirely pointless to consider temperature, because when a comic is composed of a particular material for the purposes of producing meaning, as is the case in the two Plastic Man books discussed above, we can discern some functions for temperature variation when they are tied into the comic's narrative. In *Plastic Man: On the Lam!*, the protagonist is heated and cooled at various points during the narrative.[58] Warmed by the reader's fingers, and cooler in places that it is not in contact with them, the book's plastic cover displays the properties of increased/restricted malleability that the lead character experiences, and thereby further enhances the extension of the visual narrative into the tactile field.

More explicit use is made of temperature in Jordan Crane's 2011 book *Keep Our Secrets*. In this small board book, sections of each page's images are covered with a heat-sensitive ink. Opaque black at room temperature, when the ink is heated it becomes transparent, revealing a number of concealed items within each scene. In this way images are fragmented into at least two states: (1) room temperature, and (2) warm; and this offers an interesting mode of juxtaposition whereby images are not juxtaposed within *space* along the x/y axes (because they both occupy the same space), but in *time*, since the temperature of the page at a particular time will determine which image is visible. Importantly, since both images are present in the same space *at the same time* (but they are not equally visible) this is not quite the same as film, where individual images are juxtaposed temporally within the same space, but never occupy that space simultaneously.[59] An alternative way of reading this mode of juxtaposition would be to suggest that the images are juxtaposed along the z axis, that is, they are juxtaposed in depth, rather than upon a flat plane. In this example this would mean that the first image (room temperature) lies partly on top of the second (warm). Heating allows the reader to *penetrate* through the first image to the second, and this term is, I think, an important one to remember as the technology employed in the presentation of comics becomes more complex. At a conference in 2011, Joe Sutliff Sanders outlined a range of transition effects employed in moving between panels in the digital comic *Valentine* (Alex de Campi and Christine Larsen), and some of these do suggest the notion of juxtaposition through depth whereby the reader passes through one image to get to the next. As *Keep Our Secrets* demonstrates, this type of movement between panels is not restricted to digital media, but it is certainly common in it, and the concept of penetration will therefore be an important one to keep in mind as the modelling of the comic as a multidimensional object becomes more important.[60]

Furthermore, where the reader is conventionally taken to be able to see the whole of an image at once with the revealing of information linked to the action of turning the page, in *Keep Our Secrets* objects are concealed even within ostensibly single images.[61] Readers are refused complete control over the page itself as aspects of it are hidden from them and they must work to uncover them. The cover of the book bears a sticker reading, 'For best results read this book with a hairdryer', which not only implicates readers in *performing* the work, physically modifying it over time in order to access information, but in performing it in a particular way and even providing equipment in order to do so. As we will see when we move on to consider touch and performance more concertedly below, *Keep Our Secrets* is not alone in employing this mode of interaction. At present though, temperature variations are usually taken to be incidental elements of a comic, save when they are particularly noteworthy or unique.

Yet when taken together, what the various components of comics that I have discussed so far emphasise is the tremendous potential of touch as a conveyor of meaning in the medium of comics. This potential is of course partly realised within the characteristics as I have outlined them here, simply as things that possess connoted meanings derived from the social and cultural contexts in which they are consumed; smoothness implies cultural prestige, for example. But it is important to note that, like the other qualities identified in the book, these properties are not static; they change over time as the comic is read. Touch is therefore not just an element of the comic itself, but an element of the *performance* of the comic, and it is to this performative aspect that we now turn.

4.3 TOUCH AND PERFORMANCE

The act of performing comics always involves touch to some degree, whether this means the contact readers make with their fingers upon a printed page, or the manipulation of an image on a computer screen with a mouse. As I have already noted, it is unwise to present these two processes as wholly distinct solely because one engages with printed media and the other with electronic. Both are generic physical processes that tend to apply just as much to other media forms as to comics specifically; the actions involved in turning the pages of a prose book are no more different to those involved in reading a graphic novel than is the clicking of a mouse to advance through a digital comic distinct from other applications of the mouse technology. Yet we should also be wary of discarding a particular process simply because it is generic. The mere fact that processes of performance, or processes of progression, are similar or identical between media forms does not inhibit the possibility for them to be meaningful (though it does potentially widen the applications of any analysis of them). If 'the meaningfulness of objects unfolds through interaction', then it behoves us to consider as many elements of this interaction as possible, even those that are not ostensibly unique to the form.[62] There are a number of elements of comics' physical makeup that determine how they can be performed, and affect the reader's tactile interaction with them. The size and shape of the comic are particularly obvious aspects, since these determine to a large extent the relative positions of the comic and its reader over the course of the reading, and also the ways in which they are able to move relative to each other. I have already discussed the importance of these aspects for the visual experience of reading comics (see section 2.4) and I will not repeat myself here, but it is worth marking up some additional points in relation to touch.

In general, it can be said that the progression of a comics' narrative usually requires the repetition of a particular action: turning the page, clicking through to the next screen, or touching the screen to advance. As Tim Dant has remarked, '[. . .] most gestures lead to repetitions or further gestures to achieve an accumulating effect in transforming the object'.[63] In the case of the printed comic these repetitive gestures and the transformation they bring about is easily observed in the turning of the pages and the modification of the shape of the object as the comic is read. In general, the function of this action is to progress through the narrative or move between sections within a book. It is interesting to note, however, that the processes of repetition and transformation do not necessarily sit well together because one subverts the other. While the repetitive action of turning the page suggests the possibility of an endless sequence, an infinite series of similar page turns, the material form of the printed comic denies this notion of eternal action precisely because it is transformed. Just as the reality of tactile sensation denies us the possibility of escaping completely into a diegetic world, so too does the limited modification of the comic as a physical object negate the seeming infinity of the *process* of modification. The changing shape of the comic indicates the progression of the narrative, and in some cases time itself, from start to end. This aspect of the page turn's character was noted in a particularly astute review of the collections of Frank O. King's *Gasoline Alley* in a series of hardback volumes entitled *Walt and Skeezix:*

> The ineffable grace and infinite gentleness of King's art takes on an increasing poignancy as you make your way through [*Walt and Skeezix 1923 & 1924*]. It's life presented as a gift, slipping away bit by bit each time you turn the page.[64]

Given that *Gasoline Alley* is not only published as a daily comic strip but also depicts only one day per strip this comment is strikingly sharp, and it is unsurprising that the book's publishers decided to feature it on the book's attached band. In this case, the simple action of turning the page indicates progression through not only the readers' and the creators' lives, but the characters' lives as well, because the characters in the strip grow and age in what is more or less real time. The baby Skeezix is discovered on Walt Wallet's doorstep on February 14, 1921, and by February 14, 1924, he is able to walk and talk at around the level a real three-year-old might. Thus the repetitive action of turning the page and the familiar sensation that action generates in the reader's fingers establishes a regular sensation of the passing of time; every page turn is equivalent to the passage of four days (the book is printed with two strips on each side). While every page *looks* different, the tactile similarity of the page turns lend the strip what we might call a tangible regularity: they underpin the fact that while each day may appear unique, in truth it is as temporary as the one that preceded it. When coupled with the transformation of the book over the course of the reading, this tangible element emphasises the inexorable forward motion of the strip. The diminishing number of pages left to read as they move from the front of the book to the back indicates the passage of time to readers, as does the shifting of its weight from one of their hands to the other. While readers can of course turn back and read strips from previous days, they always remain aware that they are literally going backwards in time: in this case, delving into the archives effectively means witnessing the past.

In the case of digital comics, things are quite different. Although the act of turning the page can be replicated with varying degrees of accuracy through the clicking of a mouse or the movement of the finger across the screen, we do not witness the 'accumulating effect in transforming the object' that we see in the printed comic because the digital comic is contained within a single space: the screen. While the comic is transformed visually, there is no sense of accumulation because the object upon which the comic is being viewed is not noticeably changed through interaction. The digital comic truly does exist on what Scott McCloud has called 'the infinite canvas', and the actions involved in reading can therefore continue, in theory at least, forever.[65] The tactile experience too lacks a sense of accumulation and progression. The weight of a digital comic remains constant throughout the reading, it does not shift from one hand to the other, and the reader cannot feel how many pages remain so there is not necessarily the sense of tactile engagement with the work as a progressively changing object that one experiences with the printed comic.

This is not to say, however, that the digital comic is unable to access the reader's sense of touch while it is being performed. In fact, modern technologies in some instances offer modes of communication that are arguably more powerful than the relatively conventionalised tactile experiences that we can find in the standard book form. Digital comics often allow the reader to transform the image in various ways, using different types of gesture to navigate images with page viewers, zoom in on panels, limit the view to a single panel and so on. The use of a mouse and/or keyboard to navigate through a digital comic on a computer can lead to a sense of physical detachment given that the control of the image-text is physically separated from the image-text itself, but this sense of detachment is perhaps revealed as illusory if we remember Heidi Rae Cooley's remark that 'screenic seeing encourages an experience of encounter'.[66] When we look at a digital comic, we are not looking at an image on a screen, we are looking at an image that is composed of the screen; we look *at* the screen not through it, and the image does not exist independently of the screen (except perhaps in a different (i.e., nonimage) form as data to which we have no access without the screen). In the case of a comic on a touch screen, the material nature of the image as an arrangement of light on glass is emphasised because the visual encounter is supplemented by a tactile one. Tapping, pinching and swiping are common movements when interacting with a touch screen. This multiplicity denies the monotony of the conventional page turn (though a standard route through a digital comic is usually available), and enables the reader to more fully interact with the image-text, even if it arguably minimises the importance of the whole network by emphasising small sections such as panels over larger elements such as page layout. Nanna Verhoeff has gone as far as to argue that the touch screen implicates the user in *producing* the image. Writing on the touch screen used in Nintendo's DS handheld games console, she asserts:

> Viewing is no longer a matter of looking alone, nor of perceptually receiving images; it entails movements with the hand that holds the [Nintendo DS'] stylus. This simultaneity of touching, making, and viewing connects the viewing experience of the cinematic, to the television viewing as live, to the installation-art experience of performativity, and to the physical experience of drawing.[67]

Although Verhoeff's comments here relate to the playing of computer games, which has until recently been a somewhat different type of physical activity to reading, her remarks are nonetheless applicable to experiences of digital reading, particularly given the convergence of media interactions that has taken place in recent years. We now regularly read, watch and play on the same object or type of object (computer, mobile phone, tablet computer), and use similar types of gestures in doing so. The screen therefore represents an important area of study in terms of digital comics, because it is the site at which the user encounters them, and the site at which comics encounter other media forms. Although the mapping of these types of convergent interactions is beyond the remit of this text, it does represent an area that multisensory research could look to pursue in future.

The screen is not the only site of interaction between readers and digital comics, however, and there are other systems that are explicitly (and arguably exclusively) employed to stimulate the reader's sense of touch. Tactile technology has not yet reached the level of the 'Feelies' featured in Aldous Huxley's *Brave New World,* which feature '[t]he most amazing tactual effects' and realistically reproduce the sensations of objects such as a bear-skin rug, but there are a number of options open to creators in using digital technologies to express meaning.[68] Mark W.D. Paterson identifies three types of haptic technology:

> (a) Basic force feedback devices, such as videogame controllers and tactile mice, that operate in two dimensions; (b) More sophisticated haptic "displays" that simulate shape and texture in three dimensions; (c) Increasingly popular exoskeletal or external devices for exerting tactile pressure on the skin, operating within a larger, free-flowing space for the user.[69]

While it is not impossible that comics could employ systems that fall into the second and third of these categories, the adoption of such systems within the medium is, at this point, some way in the future. Yet comic creators have begun to work with the first of the categories Paterson identifies. In its digital presentations of *Robot 13* (Thomas Hall and Daniel Bradford) and the *Scott Pilgrim* series (Bryan Lee O'Malley) for the Android mobile phone platform, the publisher/complier Robot Comics/Media makes use of force feedback/vibration technology at specific points within the narrative to varying effect. In *Robot 13,* the protagonist, a sentient robot, engages in combat with a kraken. During the battle and in a later flashback sequence involving a dropped crate, major impacts are registered on the phone through vibrations; the device literally shakes to indicate the force of the collisions.[70] In this way, Robot Comics makes use of a fairly common piece of technology, the phone's vibrator system, to translate visual information into a tactile experience. Like the plastic used in *Jack Cole and Plastic Man* and *Plastic Man: On the Lam!*, the vibrations here serve to go further than the visual symbolism employed in the comic. In *Robot 13* vibrations are not just *represented* upon the page, they are actually present within the physicality of the reading experience. These vibrations go beyond the physical properties of the object that were discussed in section 4.2 and its subsections, though, because they are not qualities of the comic's material composition per se;

they are movements of that composition that occur at particular times and in particular ways, and it is perhaps here that the performative aspect of touch in comics comes through most strongly. More than that though, the vibrations serve to powerfully indicate the nature of things like violence as disruptive phenomena. The phone is physically still for the majority of the narrative, only vibrating at four specific points. Consequently the vibration physically shocks the reader that is unprepared for it by the previous stillness of the phone. While it is relatively unlikely that a comic could make a reader jump through its visual elements alone, haptic (and auditory) systems do offer means by which stronger emotional responses can be generated because they are able to embed in the comic things that the reader literally cannot see coming (though making the reader jump is only one possible application of these types of technology).

In *Scott Pilgrim* we encounter the same generic technology being used, albeit to different effects. In one instance the (physical) phone vibrates repeatedly when a (depicted) phone is ringing in the narrative.[71] The pacing here is particularly interesting. Visually, we "hear" the phone (i.e., a version of the 'RIIIING' sound effect appears) four times upon the page. In the first panel, we see the exterior of Scott Pilgrim's residence with the sound effect emanating from the door. The next panel is similar but the viewing position is closer to the door, a close-up on the handle. The third panel cuts to an interior view: we see Pilgrim lying in bed with the phone ringing next to him, and it is here that the (physical) phone vibrates for the first time. In the fourth panel Pilgrim is reaching out to pick up the still-ringing phone, and the (physical) phone vibrates a second time. Thus it is only as we move into the private environment of the home's interior that we begin to access the tangible reality of the events taking place therein. In the first two panels, we are held slightly apart from the situation; the phone is still so the reader is only engaging with the scenario visually and through the interaction of her/his fingers with the phone in a normal way. There is no attempt on the part of the creators to actively engage the reader's sense of touch here (though the passivity of the reading experience at this point is itself meaningful when juxtaposed with the later, more active mode of engagement). When the phone does vibrate, it is at a point when the reader is inside the home, and consequently it serves to imply a level of intimacy and connection between the reader and the protagonist that would be difficult to represent in a purely visual fashion. Both the reader and the character experience disruptions and vibrations that serve to connect them to each other quite strongly: the reader experiences more or less directly and immediately what the character does. In this way, readers can become *immersed* in the reading experience far more completely than they might through a less nuanced use of haptic technology, and the digital version of *Scott Pilgrim* arguably goes beyond the printed version for this reason.[72]

It is important to avoid suggesting, however, that digital comics are automatically superior to printed ones simply because they have these types of technology available to them. As we saw in the case of the *Walt and Skeezix* series, it is entirely possible for printed comics to make use of the physical form and the reader's tactile interaction with it to potent effect. What *is* worth marking up, though, is the growing importance in the cases of both design and programming of making conscious efforts to utilise the various media as effectively as possible. This means thinking carefully about not just *what* is being presented but *how* it is presented, and ensuring that when a comic is presented in book form, it is in this form for a reason. Similarly, when a comic is presented digitally the various aspects of platforms and their capabilities must be taken into account. This is becoming increasingly important in all fields of media as the ease with which content can be uploaded and distributed over the internet becomes substantially greater. Where it was once enough to produce comics as purely visual media presented in a standardised physical format, and indeed some viewed it as a commercial hindrance to deviate from material norms, this is not necessarily a sustainable approach in a period when images can easily be scanned in and distributed online.[73] It is therefore becoming just as important for artists to produce works that are desirable as objects worthy of purchase and preservation as it is for them to create an entertaining series of words and pictures.[74] While this does of course have practical value in that it serves to limit the possibilities for pirates to steal and distribute intellectual property (one cannot (yet) scan in and upload the texture of a cloth-bound volume to a file-sharing website, although technology that could facilitate such behaviours is in development at the time of this writing), it also pushes artists to acknowledge that they are creating works that are more than simply visual in nature and encourages a greater level of input into the design and physical nature of the objects they are producing in order to develop their relationship with the reader as a human being rather than an abstract ideal.[75] In short, it forces them to acknowledge that their works will be *performed* by the reader, and to consider the ways in which they want that performance to take place.

4.3.1 Directed Touch

Yet we should not assume that the tactile elements of comics performances lie solely in the relationship between a reader and a specific physical object. Certainly, the digital comics I have already mentioned serve to challenge this conception because they employ fairly generic systems (albeit in quite specific ways) in communicating the comic's narrative, and so go beyond the idea that we are dealing only with a particular set of tangible things. In fact, the *visual* elements of comics can also be important in generating tactile experiences through more direct means than synaesthesia. As was the case with sound (see section 3.2.3.1), the reader can play an active role in not only *receiving* tactile sensations but in *producing* them. There are also other similarities between what we might call directed touch and producible sounds, in that both can be more or less specifically instructed by the visual stimulus. In the case of hearing, we have already discussed how the sounds produced by the reader may be quite generic (as in the example of a dripping tap taken from Art Spiegelman's *Breakdowns*) or quite specific (as is the case with printed music to be played). While the border between the two types is clearly not wholly discrete, these categories do provide us with a means for developing a broad understanding of the ways in which comics work to provoke their readers to take particular actions, and it applies to touch at least as much as to hearing. Therefore I will discuss the two areas separately here, although it is important to remember that the boundary line is more of an implication than a definite cut-off.

4.3.1.1 Generic Directed Touch

The category of generic directed touch is one that we might assign to those works where the production of particular tactile sensations are indicated, more or less explicitly, but without the sequence and nature of these sensations being defined as particularly as in examples of specific directed touch. In many cases, such modes of touching are entirely conventional. The act of reading a book, for example, conventionally involves the reader opening the cover and then leafing through the pages one by one, which will produce a particular set of tactile sensations in a given order, but this action is rarely specified within (or upon) the book itself (one exception to this being Scott McCloud's *Reinventing Comics,* although McCloud focuses more on the sounds generated by the page turn than he does its tactile effects).[76] Thus, although the action is directed, it is only directed by social norms and not by an explicit instruction. Yet there are some types of comic, and some creators, who do actively encourage certain actions without indicating *how* those actions should be carried out. While this is not a hugely common phenomenon, one *might* consider instructions to do things like playing music (as discussed in chapter 3) to fall into this category, although such instructions are very broad and could not convincingly be argued to be purely tactile in nature. One genre in which *tactile* experiences are more commonly directed is pornography and/or erotica, which is often produced with the explicit intention of stimulating the reader to masturbate or engage in other forms of sexual activity. Speaking at the Comica festival in 2008, the erotic/pornographic comic artist and writer Robin Ray, who works under the pseudonym Erich von Götha (among others), asserted that character, humour and masturbation on the part of the reader were the three most important elements for him in producing comics, and that he was extremely pleased when readers told him that they enjoyed masturbating to his works.[77] It should therefore come as little surprise that he refers to his comic book series *Torrid* as 'the World's Most Wanked-Over Magazine' and encourages readers to 'remove the trousers [and] position your beloved within (her) reach' in his editorials.[78] Here then, a very clear relationship is established between the comic and a tactile experience, but the specific nature of that experience is left up to the reader, who is also free to reject the possibility of enacting it if (s)he so chooses. Going beyond this limited example, thinkers such as Catherine MacKinnon have asserted that the intention to produce masturbation is inherent in all pornography, and it is therefore worth thinking about in relation to the vast body of pornographic and erotic works that constitutes an important part of comics history.[79] If we accept MacKinnon's premise that pornography stimulates its consumer to masturbate as correct, then we must also accept that pornographic comics entail an intended tactile experience that plays a role in the ways in which those comics are read, and may determine how they are perceived in a broader sense.[80] Ashley Montagu has observed: 'Two of the great negative achievements of Christianity have been to make a sin of tactual pleasures, and by its repression to make of sex an obsession', and this type of thinking has led to the roles played by masturbation in human sexuality being overlooked, even in areas where it would seem to be of critical importance, such as sexual health.[81] Furthermore, discussions of the sense of touch are curiously absent from discussions of sexuality and sexual activity.[82] Yet I suspect few could convincingly argue that sex and the culture of sex do not involve touch, whether this is touch of the other or touch of the self, and understanding the ways in which comics serve to modulate these touches can provide us with significant insights.

That said, masturbation is in some comics encouraged for reasons other than sexual gratification, and it is therefore important to avoid presenting it simply as an aspect of sexuality per se. In one issue of his renowned comic book series *The Invisibles*, Grant Morrison asked readers to engage in a 'wankathon', which he describes as 'a magically charged global masturbation session initiated in order to increase the sales of *The Invisibles*'.[83] While this may seem somewhat offbeat, it is worth noting that Morrison is a practicing magician and magical rituals and other such themes feature prominently in a number of his other works as well.[84] In this instance the ritualistic, rather than sexual, nature of the action recontextualises masturbation and gives it an economic purpose rather than directing it solely towards the stimulation of tactile pleasure. For Morrison, this purposiveness divested the act of masturbation of certain associations that it might have possessed had it been viewed as a solely pleasurable action: 'It gives everybody that sanction to wank. It's that one non-guilty wank—[sic]'.[85] Here then, Morrison seeks to transcend the social mores described by Ashley Montagu by repositioning what might traditionally be understood to be a sexual action as a magical (and perhaps commercial) one. We see a very strong instruction from the creator to the reader, which seeks to generate an action in many different places at the same time and thereby pushes *The Invisibles* and the tactile experience of it beyond the limitations of the physical object and its properties and into the realm of *performance* proper. Those who participated in the 'wankathon' were not solely accessing a tactile experience embedded in the text of the work, they were participating in a social performance of the text and thereby accessing a different kind of reality than we might find in other comics. As Douglas Wolk has written: 'The point of [Grant Morrison's] comics isn't to subvert or invert the traditions and clichés of the mainstream; it's to revel in them and amplify their power through art, with the ultimate goal of making his reader's world evolve'.[86] In this example from *The Invisibles*, Morrison does this by providing the possibility for readers to be bound together by shared tactile experiences across great distances, and thereby reaffirms the idea that touch is both the most and the least intimate of the senses, requiring both contact and division (see section 4.1).

4.3.1.2 Specific Directed Touch

In the category of *specific* directed touch, we might include things like instruction books that use sequences of images to instruct the reader on how to put together furniture or carry out other manual operations. Such comics have existed for many years, with some of the most notable examples being works produced by Will Eisner Studios for the United States of America's Department of Defense in the 1950s and 1960s. Features such as 'How to Strip Your Baby' showed military officers how to take their rifles apart and put them back together, using a combination of sequential art and accompanying text.[87] The use of comics for such purposes is perhaps unsurprising given that research conducted by the US Defense Department in around 1981 found that from a variety of options ('plain text, illustrated text, text with photos and comic strips'), 'comic strips proved the most effective in getting the information across'.[88] This is likely due in part to the way in which comics can clearly indicate where the reader should touch an object and how to move it, in a way that is not impaired by things like lighting levels (as photographs would be) and in part to the illustration of the sequence, which directs the reader's tactile experience in a particular way. This latter quality is more obvious where the instructions correspond to things that must be felt rather than seen, as with certain elements of car maintenance.

Yet sight does play an important role here, as Tim Dant, writing on one user's experience of building flat-pack furniture using diagrammatic instructions observes:

> [. . .] when Rachel read the diagram, the images helped her to read the array of objects on the floor which began to make sense as signs [. . .] and their relationship to the completed object meaningful. The diagrams hinted at gestures that would transform the bits materially.[89]

This is a very important point. In presenting instructions, comics can use visual cues to enable a directed tactile relationship to develop, but working in concert with sight that relationship becomes significantly easier to regulate. Although it has been argued that '[t]ouch on its own should enable us to understand our world in much the same way as with a full set of five senses', the act of '[feeling] our way towards the idea of a spatial world' would take a very long time were we dependent solely upon that sense because touch is limited in its remit, allowing us to access only the part of an object that our skin (or the hairs upon it) are in contact with.[90] Vision, by contrast, allows us access to a far greater quantity of the object at once (though we rarely have a view of the whole of anything), and this allows our partial tactile experiences to cohere into a unified whole. In the case of instructions then, the *sequence* is partially tactile and partially visual, while the *surface* is visual, and in this sense we begin to move towards a fairly clearly multimodal understanding of the comic that acknowledges the various input channels involved in reading and does not necessarily tend towards privileging vision over the other senses.

4.4 CONCLUSION

If hearing was a supplement to the visual elements of comics, touch is surely the foundation that underlies them. While we may not always listen to a comic, it is very rare that we do not touch the comic (or the technology that conveys it) in some fashion while reading. Touch and sight, then, have an interdependent relationship. Yet to some extent that relationship applies to the other senses as well. The sounds of comics are caused by a tactile interaction between reader and object, and the various other types of sound described in chapter 3 are also likely to be reliant upon the reader touching objects of various kinds (from musical instruments to music players) for their existence. Similarly, the smells produced by comics, and the tastes they are capable of employing, necessitate tactile interaction, as we will see in chapter 5. Yet what I hope to have emphasised over the course of this chapter is that while touch does serve to underpin the other senses, it is more than a simple, discrete and normative element of the comic reading experience. Rather, it is capable of expressing complex types of meaning that work with and perhaps even exceed comics' visual components, without simply replicating them. The vibrations in *Robot 13* and *Scott Pilgrim* do refer to aspects of those texts, but they do not only represent the visual content upon the page, they *translate* that content into the "language" of touch. Similarly, the heat-sensitive ink in *Keep Our Secrets* makes use of a uniquely tactile quality of the book (we cannot see, hear, smell or taste temperature) to deploy a fundamentally different mode of image arrangement to the norm. *In the Shadow of No Towers*, *Jack Cole and Plastic Man: Forms Stretched to Their Limits!* and *Plastic Man: On the Lam!* and the other examples I have discussed over the course of this chapter are all likewise emphatic in their employment of tangibility to go *beyond the visual*. Thus, while tactility is a fundamental element of reading comics, this is not a reason to take it for granted. While it may be tempting to assume that because we hold a graphic novel the same way we hold a prose novel they are essentially the same thing, this is not a satisfactory understanding because comics and graphic novels use space and materials in different ways and for different purposes to other media. They are *performed* differently.

As we move to discuss smell and taste, it is important to remember this dualistic mode of understanding the relationships between comics and the senses. The multisensory elements of comics are at once fundamental and active in the production of meaning in the medium. The olfactory and gustatory aspects of comics may seem to be even more basic and unremarkable than their tactile qualities, simply properties of an object that are usually subtle and unnoticed except for a few rare occasions. Yet like the sounds comics make and their tangible qualities, these elements are persistent and can be meaningful; subtlety does not necessarily imply insignificance. Furthermore, there *are* a number of creators who have actively worked with these senses to bring additional meaning to the comic in a wide variety of ways. Like touch and hearing, these senses can be drawn into the performance of the comic using techniques ranging from simple visual cues to attached content, and thereby serve to emphasise the multisensory nature of the medium. To explicate these ideas further, let us now turn to consider the final two senses in earnest.

NOTES

1. Perricone, Christopher. 2007. "The Place of Touch in the Arts." *Journal of Aesthetic Education* (University of Illinois Press) 41 (1): 90–104.
2. Elsaesser, Thomas, and Malte Hagener. 2010. *Film Theory: An Introduction through the Senses.* New York, NY: Routledge. 108–128.
3. Laine, Tarja. 2007. "'It's the Sense of Touch': Skin in the Making of Cinematic Consciousness." *Discourse* (Wayne State University Press) 29 (1): 35–48. 44.
4. McCloud, Scott. 1993. *Understanding Comics: The Invisible Art.* New York, NY: HarperPerennial. 89.
5. Laine, 'Skin', 44.
6. McCloud, *Understanding*, 89, 118–137. Hatfield, Charles. 2005. *Alternative Comics: An Emerging Literature.* Jackson, MS: University Press of Mississippi. 58–65.
7. Forceville, Charles. 2004. "Visual Representations of the Idealized Cognitive Model of Anger in the Asterix Album La Zizanie." *Journal of Pragmatics* 69–88.
8. Howes, David, ed. 2009. *The Sixth Sense Reader.* Oxford: Berg. 24.
9. Overstreet, Robert M., and Arnold T. Blumberg. 2006. *The Official Overstreet Comic Book Grading Guide.* 3rd ed. New York, NY: Gemstone. 42.
10. For a detailed discussion of the collector market that has developed around comics and the ways in which it reflects art markets more generally see chapter seven of: Beaty, Bart. 2012. *Comics versus Art.* Toronto, Canada: University of Toronto Press.
11. CGC. n.d. *Grading.* Accessed July 5, 2012. http://www.cgccomics.com/grading/grading.asp.
12. Gerber, Ernst W. 1991. *The Photo-Journal Guide to Marvel Comics.* 2 vols. Minden, NV: Gerber. B5.

13. Overstreet and Blumberg, *Grading*, 41–42.
14. One obvious exception to this rule is the touch of the author: a creator's autograph on a comic may serve to make it more valuable to the collector. This is not universally true, however, and signatures are in some instances considered to be 'defects' (Overstreet and Blumberg, *Grading*, 87). They also pose problems of authenticity that can lower the value of an autographed comic (CGC. n.d. *CGC Signature Series*. Accessed July 5, 2012. http://www.cgccomics.com/grading/SignatureSeries.asp).
15. Sabin, Roger. 1993. *Adult Comics: An Introduction*. London: Routledge. 67–68; Wolk, Douglas. 2007. *Reading Comics: How Graphic Novels Work and What They Mean*. Cambridge, MA: Da Capo Press. 64–66;. Gordon, Ian. 1998. *Comic Strips and Consumer Culture: 1890–1945*. Washington, DC: Smithsonian Institution Press.
16. Sabin, Roger. 2000. "The Crisis in Modern American and British Comics, and the Possibilities of the Internet as a Solution." In *Comics and Culture: Analytical and Theoretical Approaches to Reading Comics*, edited by Anne Magnussen and Hans-Christian Christiansen, 43–57. Copenhagen, Denmark: Museum Tusculanum Press and University of Copenhagen. 52, cf. Overstreet and Blumberg, *Grading*, 42. Cf. also: Gibson, Mel. 2008. "What You Read and Where You Read It, How You Get It, How You Keep It: Children, Comics and Historical Cultural Practice." *Popular Narrative Media* 1 (2): 151–167. 151–152.
17. Gibson, 'What', 152.
18. Cited in: Dant, Tim. 1996. "Fetishism and the Social Value of Objects." *Sociological Review* 44 (3): 495–516. Accessed May 15, 2013 at http://eprints.lancs.ac.uk/33407/1/Fetishism_eprint.pdf; all page numbers refer to this version. 5.
19. Sabin, 'Crisis', 52.
20. Gelles, David. 2011. "Action Heroes' Digital Challenge." *Financial Times*, November 8: 14. Classen, Constance, ed. 2005. *The Book of Touch*. Oxford: Berg. 7.
21. Groensteen, Thierry. 2000. "Töpffer, the Originator of the Modern Comic Strip." In *Forging a New Medium: The Comic Strip in the 19th Century*, 107–114. Brussels, Belgium: VUB University Press. 108.
22. Dant, Tim. 2007. "The 'Pragmatics' of Material Interaction." *Journal of Consumer Culture* 8 (1): 11–33. 15. See also: Groensteen, Thierry. 2009. "Why Are Comics Still in Search of Cultural Legitimization?" In *A Comics Studies Reader*, edited by Jeet Heer and Kent Worcester, 3–11. Jackson, MS: University Press of Mississippi. 11.
23. Marks, Laura U. 2002. *Touch: Sensuous Theory and Multisensory Media*. Minneapolis, MN: University of Minnesota Press. 177.
24. Ibid., 178–179.
25. Rée, Jonathan. 1999. *I See a Voice: Language, Deafness and the Senses—A Philosophical History*. London: Harper Collins. 20.
26. Montagu, Ashley. 1986. *Touching: Human Significance of the Skin*. 3rd ed. New York, NY: Harper. 17.
27. Ibid., 3–4.
28. Lacan, Jacques. 1966 (2002). *Ecrits: A Selection*. Translated by Bruce Fink. New York, NY: Norton. 3–9.
29. Russell, Bertrand. 1997. *The ABC of Relativity*. London: Routledge. 10.
30. Perricone, Christopher. 2006. "The Aspiration to the Condition of Touch." *Philosophy and Literature* 30 (1): 229–237. 230.
31. Montagu, *Touching*, 6–7.

32. Ibid., 7.
33. Classen, *Book*, 3.
34. Ibid., 7.
35. Vasseleu, Cathryn. 1998. *Textures of Light: Vision and Touch in Irigaray, Levinas and Merleau-Ponty*. New York, NY: Routledge. 12.
36. Williams, Mark. 2007. "Untitled Letter." *Astonishing Spider-Man* Volume 2 #9, August 22: 75.
37. Ibid.
38. Campbell, Dean. 2007. "Untitled Letter." *Astonishing Spider-Man* Volume 2 #6, July 11: 75.
39. In support of my previous argument in section 2.2, it should be noted that the use of a very thick gloss can itself add meaning to a work by drawing attention to its materiality (particularly where it is sufficiently thick as to be unusual). An example of this practice can be found in Harold Koda and Andrew Bolton's *Superheroes: Fashion and Fantasy*, the catalogue for the exhibition of the same name that ran at New York's Metropolitan Museum of Art from 7 May to 1 September, 2008. While not a comic itself (hence I mention it here rather than in the main body of the paragraph text) the catalogue does draw on comics in its '[examination of] the influence on fashion of superheroes [. . .] as represented in comic books, film, and television' (7). Its cardboard covers are overlaid with a thin layer of metal, and its pages are so thickly laminated that they seem to be made of plastic. The overall effect of this is to draw the reader's attention to the fabrics and other materials of which superhero costumes (and the fashion items inspired by them) are made, albeit in a relatively generic sense. Koda, Harold, and Andrew Bolton. 2008. *Superheroes: Fashion and Fantasy*. New York, NY: The Metropolitan Museum of Art and Yale University Press.
40. Online comics can be said to be relatively egalitarian in their distribution because it costs nothing for an individual with an Internet-capable computer (and perhaps a scanner) to make her/his comics available online. While we have in recent years seen the rise of centralised digital comics distributors such as Comixology, which may limit the possibilities for equal visibility, the medium is not as financially prohibitive as print and therefore does provide reasonable possibilities for independent creators to distribute their works effectively and in competition with more financially powerful groups/publishers.
41. McCloud, *Understanding*, 12–13; Nielsen, Jesper, and Søren Wichmann. 2000. "America's First Comics? Techniques, Contents, and Functions of Sequential Text-Image Pairing in the Classical Maya Period." In *Comics and Culture: Analytical and Theoretical Approaches to Reading Comics*, 59–77. Copenhagen, Denmark: Museum Tusculanum Press and University of Copenhagen.
42. Groensteen, 'Töpffer', 108.
43. Perricone, 'Place', 99
44. Kidd, Chip. 2005. *Book One—Work: 1986–2006*. New York, NY: Rizzoli International. n.p. See also: Millidge, Gary Spencer. 2009. *Comic Book Design*. Lewes, UK: ILEX. 128–129.
45. Baker, Kyle. 2004. *Plastic Man: On the Lam!* New York, NY: DC Comics.
46. Ibid., n.p.
47. Baker, Kyle. 2006. *Plastic Man: Rubber Bandits*. New York, NY: DC Comics.
48. For more on value and the transient object, see: Thompson, Michael. 1977 (2006). "An Anatomy of Rubbish." In *Arts in Society*, edited by Paul Barker, 40–46. Nottingham, UK: Five Leaves.

49. Sabin, Roger. 2009. "Mavericks and Zinesters: Comics Scholarship in the UK before 'Comics Scholarship.'" *Possibilities and Perspectives: A Conference on Comics*. Leeds, UK; Bottorf, Michael Rhode Ray, Jr. 2001. "The Grand Comics Database (GCD): An Evolving Research Tool." Edited by John A. Lent. *International Journal of Comic Art* 3 (1): 263–274.
50. Sabin, *Adult*, 245–248.
51. Brienza, Casey. 2010. "Naturalizing Foreign Comics: How Book Publishing Companies Made Manga American." *Graphic Novels and Comics: An International Conference*. Manchester, UK.
52. Chute, Hillary L. 2007. "Temporality and Seriality in Spiegelman's *In The Shadow of No Towers*." *American Periodicals: A Journal of History, Criticism, and Bibliography* (Ohio State University Press) 17 (2): 228–244. 230.
53. Ibid., 242.
54. Hirsch, quoted in: Whitlock, Gillian. 2006. "Autographics: The Seeing 'I' of the Comics." *MFS Modern Fiction Studies* 52 (4): 965–979. 966. For more on the visual representations of trauma in *In the Shadow of No Towers*, see: Versluys, Kristiaan. 2006. "Art Spiegelman's *In the Shadow of No Towers*: 9/11 and the Representation of Trauma." *MFS Modern Fiction Studies* 52 (4): 980–1003.
55. Marks, *Touch*, xii.
56. See section 2.4 for more on the importance of size in comics, which also has relevance here.
57. Carrier, David. 2000. *The Aesthetics of Comics*. University Park, PA: Pennsylvania State University Press. 63.
58. Baker, *On the Lam!*
59. McCloud, *Understanding*, 7.
60. Thierry Groensteen's distinction between the 'site' and the 'place' as described in *The System of Comics* (34–35, 147–149) is a useful starting point for any attempt at modelling comics as three-dimensional objects. For Groensteen, the site is the position of the panel upon the page, while the place is the position of the panel within the comic. The former term is evidently two-dimensional; it can be described in terms of an x, y coordinate that serves to locate the panel upon a given page. The place adds the dimension of depth to the coordinates in order that a panel might be understood relative to panels on different pages. Groensteen, Thierry. 2007. *The System of Comics*. Translated by Bart Beaty and Nick Nguyen. Jackson, MS: University Press of Mississippi.
61. See: Genette, Gérard. 1987 (1998). *Paratexts: Thresholds of Interpretation*. Translated by Jane E. Lewin. Cambridge, UK: Cambridge University Press. 33; Groensteen, *System*, 35. See also section 6.1 in this book.
62. Dant, 'Pragmatics', 13.
63. Ibid., 27.
64. King, Frank O. 2006. *Walt and Skeezix: 1923 & 1924*. Montreal, Canada: Drawn & Quarterly Books. Band.
65. McCloud, Scott. 2000. *Reinventing Comics*. New York, NY: Paradox Press. 200.
66. Cooley, Heidi Rae. 2004. "It's All about the Fit: The Hand, the Mobile Screenic Device and Tactile Vision." *Journal of Visual Culture* 3 (2): 133–155. 143.
67. Verhoeff, Nanna. 2009. "Theoretical Consoles: Concepts for Gadget Analysis." *Journal of Visual Culture* 8 (3): 279–298. 288.
68. Huxley, Aldous. 1932 (2004). *Brave New World*. London: Vintage. 29.
69. Paterson, Mark W.D. 2005. "Digital Touch." In *The Book of Touch*, edited by Constance Classen, 431–436. Oxford: Berg.432.

70. Hall, Thomas, and Daniel Bradford. n.d. "Robot 13 #1." Compiled by Robot Comics. *Blacklist.com*. 10, 15, 19, 22.
71. O'Malley, Bryan Lee. 2010. "Scott Pilgrim's Precious Little App." Compiled by Robot Media SL. London: HarperCollins. 21.
72. Lister, Martin, Jon Dovey, Seth Giddings, Iain Grant, and Kieran Kelly. 2003. *New Media: A Critical Introduction*. Abingdon, UK: Routledge. 21.
73. Windsor-Smith, Barry. 2003. *Young GODS & Friends*. Seattle, WA: Fantagraphics Books. n.p.
74. I am grateful here to Bryan Talbot, who marked up the importance of materiality as an antipiracy device in conversation at London's Comica Festival in 2009.
75. Vance, Ashlee. 2011. *Haptics Adds New Dimensions to Touchscreens*. June 16. Accessed June 27, 2011. http://www.businessweek.com/magazine/content/11_26/b4234043549730.htm; Kelly, Stephen. 2013. *How Helsinki-Based Startup Senseg Creates Touchscreens You Can Feel*. April 11. Accessed May 15, 2013. http://www.wired.co.uk/magazine/archive/2013/04/start/senseg-wants-to-bring-your-screens-to-life.
76. McCloud, *Reinventing*, 229.
77. Pilcher, Tim, and Gene Kannenberg, Jr. 2008. *Erotic Comics: A Graphic History from Tijuana Bibles to Underground Comix*. New York, NY: Abrams. 132; Pilcher, Tim. 2008. "Erotic Comics [Panel Discussion]." *Comica Festival 2008*. London.
78. von Götha, Erich. 1984. *Torrid: The Baron's Own Picture Book*. Vol. 12. Whyteleafe: Gold Star. n.p.
79. Ferguson, Frances. 1995. "Pornography: The Theory." *Critical Enquiry* 21 (3): 670–695. 682. For more on the history and significance of erotica in comics history, see particularly Tim Pilcher's and Gene Kannenberg Jr.'s *Erotic Comics* and *Erotic Comics 2*. Pilcher, Tim, and Gene Kannenberg, Jr. 2009. *Erotic Comics 2: A Graphic History from the Liberated '70s to the Internet*. New York, NY: Abrams.
80. It is worth pointing out that MacKinnon also argues this production of masturbation is problematic because it tends toward stimulating violence as well, although this latter argument in particular has been challenged by some (Ferguson, 'Pornography', 688).
81. Montagu, *Touching*, 312. Shelton, James D. 2010. "Masturbation: Breaking the Silence." *International Perspectives on Sexual and Reproductive Health* 36 (3): 157–158. 157.
82. Classen, *Book*, 3.
83. Yawn, Brother, and Grant Morrison. 2002. "Interview with an Umpire." *Barbelith*. Accessed June 14, 2011. http://www.barbelith.com/old/interviews/interview_1.shtml. 9.
84. Callahan, Timothy. 2007 (2008). *Grant Morrison: The Early Years*. Edwardsville, IL: Sequart Research and Literacy Organization. 236.
85. Yawn and Morrison, 'Interview', 9.
86. Wolk, *Reading*, 259.
87. Will Eisner Studios & U.S. Army. 1969. *The M16A1 Rifle: Operation and Preventative Maintenance*. U.S. Army.
88. Sabin, *Adult*, 8, 261.
89. Dant, 'Pragmatics', 22.
90. Rée, *I See*, 19.

5 Smell and Taste, or, The Scent of Nostalgia and the Flavour of Advertising

5.0 SUBTLE SIGNIFICANCES

The chemical senses of smell and taste have rarely been discussed in comics scholarship. Smell (as an actual sense) does receive brief mentions from both Roger Sabin (who as we know emphasises the smells of 'dust, glue and paper' as important and irreplaceable aspects of printed comics) and Mel Gibson (who cites the scent of paper as a significant element in readers' memories of comics).[1] The notion of a symbolism of smells (or at least the mechanisms by which one might be conveyed) is also picked up on briefly by Scott McCloud in *Understanding Comics*, as is the significance of taste, but it is generally fair to say that there is something of a dearth of scholarship on the chemical senses as they relate to comics.[2] This is not to say that these senses do not play roles in the creation and reading of comics. Indeed, as we will discover from the wide range of examples presented in this chapter, the chemical senses often play significant if subtle roles in the ways in which comics are perceived by readers, and they can contribute substantially to the amount and type of information that those readers receive. Nor has the impact of smell in particular gone unnoticed by creators and readers, who have at times been known to espouse the 'sweet, delicious scent of comic books' as one reason to love comics.[3] Taste, though less obvious in terms of overt reader appreciation, also plays a role in the composition of a number of comics. While it would certainly be difficult to argue that smell and taste are of truly equal significance in the medium to its visual, auditory, or tactile aspects, they do warrant some attention here because of the ways in which they connect readers to the objects with which they are interacting and affect the ways they think about them.

Over the course of this chapter I will provide an indication of the various ways in which comics engage readers' senses of smell and taste both intentionally and unintentionally. To do so I will follow a similar model to that employed in my writing on the sense of hearing in chapter 3, which took as its structuring mechanism the sources of sounds. In this chapter I will similarly consider the smells and tastes of, in, with and around comics (I have yet to encounter any examples of smells or tastes *as* comics, but that is not to say that they could not exist). In structuring the chapter in this way, I mean to imply some similarities between smell and taste and the sense of hearing. All three of these senses are strongly connected to time, but where hearing has a tendency to enforce duration in a work, we will see that smell and taste subvert duration and linearity. They deny us the possibility for a clear, logical path forward by pulling us backwards into our memories and personal experiences. In some instances, comics creators use olfactory and gustatory elements very effectively to challenge or intervene in our memories, an idea we will discuss in relation to Alan Moore and colleagues' *1963*. Like sounds, the smells and tastes involved in comics can come from a variety of sources, and in some cases creators implicate the reader very strongly in the production of this multisensory experience. Recipes, adverts and even scratch and sniff systems all involve the reader in producing, in *performing*, the comic to a greater degree than we might otherwise expect, and all emphasise that the reader is more than a passive receiver of information. Before we go on to discuss the applications of smell and taste in comics more specifically, though, let us first consider their natures as biological processes.

5.1 A BRIEF INTRODUCTION TO THE CHEMICAL SENSES

If sight and hearing are powerful but insubstantial means for experiencing the world and touch connects us to the reality of the world's substance very directly, smell and taste would seem to sit somewhere in the middle. Although they tend to be grouped within the category of the contact senses, smell in particular presents something of a challenge to that classification because it resists the definite notion of contact between an object and the sense organ that it stimulates.[4] Because we are generally distant from the object we smell, it seems difficult to agree that we are truly in contact with it. Thus, Jonathan Rée, for example, is only willing to go as far as saying that smell 'probably' falls into this grouping.[5] The reason that he does end up on this side of the fence is likely due to the physiological processes involved in the sense of smell. In order to smell something, the object must either be or contain what is called a volatile (i.e., easily vaporisable) substance. When we breathe in, the volatile molecules emitted by the object are drawn into the nasal passageways and land on a mucous membrane called the olfactory epithelia, which contains olfactory sensory neurons that allow us to detect smells.[6] If the volatile molecules are water and lipid (fat) soluble, they will pass through the watery film and lipid layer that covers the olfactory receptors and come into contact with the neurons themselves; if they are not, we will not smell them (hence we cannot smell pure water).[7] Given that the volatile molecules mentioned here are (initially at least) part of the objects we smell, it can be argued that smell does indeed bring us into direct contact with them, even if those molecules are apart from the objects' main bodies when we encounter them. We have around 20 million olfactory receptors, which break down into 300–400 different types. Although this is a significant number, more than for any other sense except sight (cf. 640,000 touch receptors, see section 4.1), it is worth noting that we are relatively impoverished when compared to other species. Bloodhounds have around 200 million scent receptors to our 20 million, while mice have approximately 1,000 different types of receptor to our 300–400.[8] It is generally believed that there are 10,000 or more possible complex odours, although this number has not been experimentally proven.[9] While attempts have been made to identify a set of primary odours from which all others are derived (e.g., Henning's smell prism model, which identifies putrid, ethereal, fragrant, spicy, burned and resinous), none have so far proven satisfactory in the way that we tend to identify four primary tastes (see below).[10]

Although taste and smell can be divided in humans to a greater degree than some animals, it is important to note that they are not wholly separable; rather they are 'anatomically distinct but functionally united mechanisms'.[11] It should therefore come as little surprise that the physical processes involved in the two senses bear some similarities to each other. Where smell is reliant upon volatile molecules, taste involves the interaction between chemicals present in objects and the body's taste receptors, which are located in the mouth. The tongue is the primary location of these receptors, but they are also present in the throat, pharynx, inside the cheeks and in the soft palate at the top of the mouth.[12] Although it is often suggested that different parts of the tongue correspond to different types of taste, this is not true; taste buds are distributed evenly in type across the surface of the tongue and surrounding areas.[13] Humans have 9,000–10,000 taste receptors, the majority of which are contained in small elevations on the tongue called papillae.[14] It is generally accepted that there are four primary tastes: sweet, salty, sour and bitter. Additional possibilities such as umami (savouriness), metallic and alkaline have been suggested but they are somewhat contentious.[15] One final point worth mentioning is a terminological one: the distinction between taste and flavour. While these two words are often used interchangeably (e.g., "this tastes of popcorn"), they actually mean different things. The *taste* of an object derives solely from the taste receptors, while the *flavour* of it is taken from the combination of taste with smell. Some foods, therefore, may be almost tasteless but still flavoursome.

In cultural terms, smell and taste have generally been the most heavily denigrated of the five senses. Lumped (along with touch) among the 'lower' senses and classified as largely feminine in nature, they have been subjected to marginalisation along gender lines, as well as being deemed elements of uncivilised humanity, with Sigmund Freud even going so far as to suggest that 'the devaluation of olfactory stimuli' that occurred when humans began to walk upright contributed to 'the founding of the family, and so to the threshold of human civilization'.[16] While the distance senses have been deemed 'nobler, purer [and] more detached', the contact senses have largely been understood as irrational and even animalistic.[17] For this reason, the relative dearth of research and criticism into these senses and their functions within the media is somewhat understandable; rather than a particular slight it is indicative of a more general lack of work on taste and smell. Although there have been some notable works on these senses as they apply to other media, the understanding of their functions in comics is extremely limited, something I hope to begin to remedy over the remainder of this chapter. Having now outlined the biological context of the discussion and given an (admittedly brief) indication of some of the cultural concerns at play here, let us move on to discuss smell and taste in comics more specifically. We will begin our attempt to move beyond symbolic/synaesthetic understandings of smell and taste in media by considering the smells *of* comics.

5.2 THE SMELLS AND TASTES OF COMICS

While it may seem a little unusual to consider the smells and tastes of comics in any detail, there is much to be learned about both the medium and its readership by doing so. In general, the smells of comics tend to be associated with the printed form, and as Roger Sabin's remarks make clear, the transition to digital comics is viewed by some as a negation of the olfactory character of the medium. Yet it is not only the shift from printed to digital comics that is a cause for concern, with some fans and critics lamenting the modernisation of production methods and the changing materials of comics' composition as well. In one article dedicated to the smells of comics, writer Bill Reed asserts: 'I miss the smell of the old comics [. . .]. The new ones, what with their slick pages and fancy printing, have become too artificial for me'.[18] These sentiments are echoed in readers' comments on Reed's article and this, along with Mel Gibson's determination that the smells of comics are important factors in readers' memories of the medium, suggests that smells serve to link readers to past experiences of comics quite strongly. This notion is borne out by the biological processes involved in smell, because the sense is very strongly linked to the centres of memory within the brain itself. As Rachel S. Herz explains: '[O]nly three synapses are needed to connect to the hippocampus, which is necessary for associative learning and various forms of memory'.[19] More than this though, the sense of smell is also strongly linked to the emotional cores of the brain: '[O]nly two synapses separate the olfactory bulb from the amygdala, which is critical for the expression and experience of emotion'.[20] It should therefore come as little surprise that the smells of comics tend to be discussed in terms of nostalgia, an emotionally charged form of remembering, rather than through the more detached epistemological approach that might be taken. Readers tend not to use their noses to determine the age or material composition of a comic in a scientific sense, there is no taxonomy of comics' bouquets, but there would seem to be a general longing for a past that is (at least somewhat) accessible through their sense of smell. It was perhaps Marcel Proust who most powerfully communicated the power of smells and tastes in drawing forth the past when he wrote:

> [. . .] when from a long-distant past nothing subsists, after the people are dead, after the things are broken and scattered, still, alone, more fragile, but with more vitality, more unsubstantial, more persistent, more faithful, the smell and taste of things remain poised a long time, like souls, ready to remind us, waiting and hoping for their moment, amid the ruins of all the rest; and bear unfalteringly, in the tiny and almost impalpable drop of their essence, the vast structure of recollection.[21]

Gilles Deleuze has observed of Proust's writing that the sensual signs within it do not refer to themselves (indeed they would not be signs if they did), 'but as the sign of an *altogether different* object that we must try to decipher'.[22] Drawing on the writing of Bill Reed cited above we can see that the same is true of the sensual qualities of comics, in particular smells. Thierry Groensteen has argued quite forcefully that comics are specifically linked to childhood, asserting: 'Comics have a privileged relationship with childhood because it is in childhood that each of us discovered them and learnt to love them'.[23] While this type of generalisation is somewhat problematic, it is a truism that comics have for many years been associated, rightly or wrongly, with children and childhood, and it is quite possible that the formative experiences and the smells children encounter when reading comics contribute to their viewpoint on them in later life. Thus, when confronted with the smell of an old comic in adulthood, those readers who read comics as a child will find within it 'the vast structure of recollection'; the smell refers them back to their own pasts. Specifically, as Deleuze notes on Proust, to the sensuality and the materiality, of their pasts: 'It is not only [the signs'] origin, it is their explanation, their development that remains material'.[24]

It is not difficult to see that this type of response to comics is relatively easy to manipulate. This is something that has already begun to develop, with publishers such as Prion Books offering modern-day facsimile editions of publications such as *Jackie* (1964–1993), which conform to the publication formats of the original series. As Mel Gibson has observed, this is indicative not only of the ways in which the publication format can serve to establish and modulate a relationship between reader and text, for example along class lines, but also that publishers are acutely aware of the importance of format.[25] The Prion website emphasises this awareness in statements such as: '[D]elving into the facsimile pages of [*The Best of Jackie*], is like being given a ticket to travel back in time'; or, '"All Your Favourites" is another treasure trove of hilarious nostalgic gems, reproduced in facsimile form true to the original, to pore over and enjoy'; and '[A]fter the huge success of "The Best of Jackie", this is the follow-up title, "The Best of Jackie Annual"—more great material, reproduced in facsimile form true to the original'.[26] It is worth noting that not all of Prion's output *is* issued in such a manner, and in some cases the artwork has been modified substantially to ensure that it appeals to readers. *Against All Odds,* for example, a collection of stories from *War Picture Library* (1958–1984), is described on the company website as featuring artwork that is 'reproduced 25 per cent bigger than the originals so you can feel every bullet hit, every crashing wave and every nerve-shattering explosion'.[27] It would therefore be unwise to assume that a nostalgia-charged return to a familiar format is desirable per se, but it is evidently of interest to some markets, and in this case it is sufficiently valuable (and sufficiently visible) that the publishers have decided to take advantage of it.

Although Mel Gibson's research is relatively specific in its focus on *Jackie,* this is not the only example of a nostalgic element of comics being brought into play by a publisher through a manipulation of the physical format and/or a comment upon it. In some cases, this manipulation does include explicit mention of the sense of smell, and the ways in which the material composition of the object affects its olfactory character. In the third issue of Alan Moore and colleagues' *1963,* the olfactory elements of comics are brought to the fore in the 'Al's Amphitheater!!!' feature (a satirical play on Stan Lee's 'Soapbox' in the Marvel Comics of the 1960s to which *1963* pays homage/parodies). 'Affable Al' writes of the comic's 'RETRO-format' (which stands for '*R*eally *E*asy *T*o *R*eproduce *O*ld-format'):

> If you hold the comic book you are reading up to your nose and inhale slowly, you will discern the most distinctive difference of all between RETRO and ANY OTHER FORMAT!! That's RIGHT, revellers! With the miracle of our professionally patented AROMARAMA process, contemporary comic collectors can at last enjoy the laser-accurate HOLOGRAPHICALLY REPRODUCED odor of yesteryear!![28]

While Moore's tongue is clearly firmly in his cheek here, like everything within the *1963* series these remarks do draw upon the history and culture of the comics industry and its fan base for their inspiration. As Mel Gibson and Bill Reed make evident, smell *is* important to some readers. It should therefore come as little surprise that Moore's column in *1963* is mentioned in comments on Reed's article, with one writer, Kyle, stating that it prompted him to smell the comic, an action that 'brought back fond memories' of his youth.[29] Another writer, Wayne, noted that the effect of the article had been longer lasting on him and that since reading it he had been 'acutely tuned into' the smell of old comics.[30]

What is interesting about this type of response is not just the fact that readers appreciate particular smells that are associated with particular types of comics, but that publishers and creators are also aware of them, and in some instances seek to use them in very particular ways. In this case, the power of smell contributes to what we might call a manufactured nostalgia that permeates *1963*; the series gestures backwards to an earlier form of comics storytelling, and in so doing subverts and implicitly critiques the "grim and gritty" mode of superheroes that Moore helped to develop through works such as *Watchmen*. But as the mention of smell here emphasises, Moore's project in *1963* is not solely narrative but holistic; the series seeks to emphasise that the stories told in the comics of 1963 were different to those of 1993, but also that the *experiences* of reading comics, the *performances* they engendered, were substantively different as well. As one reviewer noted, *1963* is 'not only a recreation of a 1960s story, but a complete 1960s comic', and this includes the smell.[31] As the comic ages and deteriorates, the physical breakdown will proceed in similar fashion to the comics of the 1960s, and this olfactory element will become more prominent still.

The effect of working with formats in these ways is that readers are not simply *reminded* of the comics of the past, they are *immersed* in the experience of reading/performing them. Writing on new media, Lister and colleagues describe aspects of immersion in the following way:

> Instead of a text-based experience aimed at finding and connecting bits of information, the goals of the immersed user will include the visual and sensory pleasures of spatial exploration.[32]

Although the *Jackie* reprints and *1963* are some way from the completely immersive virtual-reality environments described here, it is clear that through a conscious employment of particular formats they do serve to immerse their readers in the reading experience to some degree. Smell is strongly implicated here because of the sheer power of its connections to memory. We have already noted the writing of Marcel Proust in this area (see above), and Walter Benjamin has also remarked on this aspect of smell, writing that '[a] scent may drown entire years in the remembered odor it evokes'.[33] Thus, the odours to which the reader is exposed while reading *Jackie* and perhaps to a greater extent *1963* serve to bridge the gap between original instances of reading in the past, and the present moment of reading, whether this was at the time of these publications' original issue or later. Crucially, as those remarks from Proust and Benjamin cited above emphasise, this type of experience can go beyond a simple feeling of remembering, because smell's strong links to both memory and emotion can give the impression that one is actually reliving the past. The power of smell is such that one can "re-feel" the emotions (s)he originally experienced when (s)he encountered a particular odour. The validity of these emotional responses is further emphasised by the particularity of odour. Because we cannot mentally draw forth a smell from our memory or olfactory imagination as easily as we might take an image or a sound from our visual or auditory imaginations, we must necessarily encounter smells 'in the present, [our odor memory must be stimulated] by the same odor or by a similar odor easily confused with it'.[34] Therefore it tends to be the case that olfactory memories of comics are coupled with a physical encounter with that comic (or an object composed of near-identical materials). Thus, we might argue, the use of format in the *Jackie* reprints and *1963* serves to return readers to a past context of performance (in the case of *Jackie*) or insert them into one (in the case of *1963*).

At the same time, though, a gap between past and present is maintained by the very newness of the product, and the references *backwards* either within the comics themselves or within the marketing material that surrounds them. Of the two, it is perhaps the *Jackie* reprints that most overtly signal their historical positioning through titles such as *The Best of Jackie,* which indicates the completion of the original magazine sequence and emphasises that this new volume is a revisiting of older material. *1963,* by contrast, persistently attempts to present itself as a comic of the 1960s in terms of writing style, narrative structures and physical format, but it does also display an awareness of "future" developments such as specialised comics retailers, and acknowledges its own time period precisely by trumpeting its status as a 'RETRO' publication. What this means is that while both series faithfully recreate earlier formats, the material within them subverts the notion that one is literally returning to the original experience of reading, and the reader is always held slightly apart from the material in an intellectual sense. The reader is not drawn into the past; material from the past is pulled into the present day. This maintenance of a distance between past and present would seem to be a valuable asset for the publishers of the *Jackie* reprints in particular, who, while emphasising the fidelity of the books to the original publication formats in the quotations presented above, also seem to acknowledge that much of the pleasure and meaning that readers derive from the volumes is likely to come from the contrasts between their experiences reading *Jackie* as children and their situations in the present day. Yet as the website entries for two of the *Jackie* annuals emphasise, there are a number of reasons why readers might take pleasure in the reprints. Consider this extract from an entry on one of the books:

> [*The Best of "Jackie" Annual* features e]verything a young girl growing up in the seventies would want in an annual, and everything a woman in her thirties and forties would want to laugh at now.[35]

While this description makes the book sound like little more than a pastiche (in the sense that Fredric Jameson uses the term, i.e., a parody divested of its political implications), a very similarly worded description of another of the reprints implies an alternative reading/response[36]:

> [*The Biggest "Jackie" Annual Ever!* features e]verything a young girl growing up in the seventies would want in an annual, and everything that will bring back fond memories for a woman in her thirties and forties.[37]

This statement is preceded by a lengthy discussion not only of what is in the book itself, but also how it might be employed to develop a closer relationship between adults and children:

> Now is your change [sic] to relive all of those golden Jackie moments and show the youngsters in your life what life was like when you were growing up.[38]

In part of course, this statement gestures towards the notion of immersion that I discussed earlier, but it also suggests that the experiences generated by that immersion are now opened up to critique and reevaluation by the distancing effects of time. Mentions of MTV and other post-*Jackie* developments further contribute to the sense that these books are intended to facilitate a recontextualisation and reexamination of the reader's childhood. They are an invitation to readers to develop better understandings of themselves, or, in the case of the previous description, to look back mirthfully on the naivety of youth.[39]

This type of approach is also evident in *1963,* which employs relatively subtle techniques to indicate important contradictions and issues that did exist during the 1960s, but were perhaps not widely known or reported on, or were downplayed by publishers to avoid public relations problems. To explicate this element of the comic more fully, it is worth quoting a long extract from the letters page of issue one, along with the editor's response, and the letter that follows it (all letters and responses were written by Alan Moore; they are not from or to real readers):

> Dear Al and the Gang,
>
> I am a great fan of all your comic books, and since I one day hope to be a comic artist worthy to sit at the feet of the great Roarin' Rick Veitch, I sent away for a duplicated amateur magazine about comics that I saw advertised. The magazine was called The Comics Gazette, and since it featured an interview with the Roarin' One himself, how could I pass it up? Well, I read the interview, and I have to admit that I'm kind of troubled by some of the things that Rick said, especially about everybody in the Sixty Three sweatshop having to sign contracts that make Affable Al the sole owner of any characters they create, or that their descendants create. I admit that there was a lot of stuff in the interview that I maybe didn't understand, like for example what does "Work For Hire" mean? All the same, this thing about contracts doesn't seem fair, although I know that The Affable One would never do anything mean, and I wondered if you could maybe explain it to me. But don't worry . . . whatever the explanation, you can bet that I'll Be Sure To See It's Sixty-Three!!
>
> Ralph J. Hutty, 58 Genesee St.
> Englewood, N.J.
>
> Ralph, we'd bet our bottom dollar on it . . . especially when we reveal that Roarin' Rick's rib-tickling rant was just another example of the screwy, scatter-brained sense of silliness that's all a part of slaving in the sensational Sixty-Three sweatshop! The Roarin' One was indulging in some good-natured joshing by ribbing Affable Al about the perennial pesky pranks that our lovable leader persistently pulls around the office,

> like handing out wacky gag contracts for everyone to sign! As for the magnificently mysterious motto "Work For Hire", let the serried ranks of Sixty Three-dom hereby receive notice that "hire" is the nickname of Handsome HIRAM GLICK, our swingin' septuagenarian Voucher Clerk! Y'See, whenever one of our prodigious pencillers or inimitable inkers finishes a job, he has to fill out a voucher for Hiram to process, which is, of course, making additional "Work for Hire", even though the cheery old codger never utters a word of complaint. Anyway, Ralph, much as we'd love to delve even further into this tantalizing topic, there are even more pressing issues that we have to find room for, such as the ones mentioned in our next letter:
>
> Dear Al and Rick,
>
> In MYSTERY INC. #17, on page 5 in the last panel, King Zero's leg is blue instead of white. Also, on page eighteen you have Crystalman saying "We have to stop him reaching the the Devolvo Ray", with the word "the" repeated twice. Is there a reason for this or did you just make a mistake?
>
> Owen Bevels, 139 Bridge St.
> Daly City, Calif.[40]

What we see here is Alan Moore engaging with some of the more controversial aspects of the American comics industry in the manner of Stan Lee. During his time at Marvel, Lee was involved in the creation of a number of iconic characters including Spider-Man and the Incredible Hulk, in association with Steve Ditko and Jack Kirby respectively. Problematically, issues have subsequently arisen regarding who was responsible for the creation of these characters and why, with Lee arguing for example that he is 'generous' to give Ditko the title of '"cocreator"', asserting: '[. . .] I'm the guy who dreamed up the title, the concept, and the characters'.[41] The notion of work for hire is similarly problematic; it refers to the practice within Marvel (and other companies, although it is Marvel's titles that *1963* most clearly references) of paying writers and artists by the page for their work, without giving them any rights to remuneration beyond the initial hire fee they are paid for creating the page in the first place. Any characters or designs that a writer creates are owned by the company, not the individual. Dissatisfaction with these types of terms has caused much upheaval within the industry, and was a contributing factor in the formation of Image Comics, the company that published *1963*.[42] What is interesting about the relatively lengthy discussion of the subject in the *1963* letters column is that it indicates a point of slippage between the familiar, friendly atmosphere that Stan Lee endeavoured to generate in the Marvel comics of the 1960s and the more ambiguous morality surrounding the production of those comics.[43] Just as the descriptions of *Jackie* as something to laugh at or to look back fondly upon invite readers to reevaluate their own impressions of the magazine series and think about it relative to their current understanding, so too does *1963* ask its readers to think more rigorously about their stance on the practices of the comics industry. Here, the real power of smell as an immersive technology and a connective tissue becomes clear. While the smells of *1963* may have brought back 'fond memories' for some readers, these memories are resituated by the text; they become considerably more complex.[44] It is unclear whether those memories can truly be cherished as happy recollections of days gone by, or whether they must be critiqued as an indication of naivety on the part of readers who have allowed what are arguably reprehensible practices to persist even up to the present day. By working with format in this way, Moore and colleagues develop *1963* as not just a parody of the comics of the 1960s, but as an intervention into the readers' memories and a demand that those memories be rethought.

Although these types of formal interventions are relatively rare in comics, they are worth making note of because they are indicative of the ways in which even ostensibly minor senses can contribute substantially to the reader's perceptions, and the meaning of a work. Many of the concerns and processes outlined here are evident in all facsimile editions, but some of them apply to reprints and republications as well. Understanding the ways in which the scent of a comic changes as it undergoes republication and reformatting, for example, may help us to understand how readers interpret that comic over the longer term.

Smells also represent important focal points for some creators, even in the more limited capacity of producing a desirable object. Just as the tactile qualities of a comic's cover and its pages are significant weapons in the fight against online piracy (see section 4.3), the scents of a comic can provide a reason for remaining with a printed object rather than making a transition to digital, and there is evidence to suggest that creators do in some instances seek to select materials for their works that will have the right odour. The UK small press anthology *Solipsistic Pop* provides an excellent example of such attention to detail. Writing on the publication's website in November 2009, the book's editor and publisher Tom Humberstone remarked:

> On the day Solipsistic Pop launched [. . .] people were walking up to offer their support and feedback for the book. The most popular phrase being:
>
> "*You got the smell right!*"
>
> This was heartening to hear. Believe it or not, I'd gone to a lot of trouble to make sure the book had that *just printed* aroma. It was part of the reason the anthology existed.[45]

For Humberstone, it is not enough to simply produce a comic as a physical object without thinking about why he is doing so: there must be a reason for creating a printed comic rather than, for example, a digital one (a sentiment which has met with support from those who have commented on Humberstone's article).[46] In thinking so carefully about the physical characteristics of comics as objects, it is natural that Humberstone came to consider the smell of the printed page to be a critical element of the work because this is something that is not currently accessible in the digital environment. Indeed, it is proving somewhat difficult to develop smell-based technologies that are feasible for the digital era. While haptic feedback devices of the type employed in *Scott Pilgrim's Precious Little App* (see section 4.3) are relatively widespread, systems for the dissemination of smells have had no such success in the digital arena. Perhaps the most promising piece of technology to have been developed so far is a device called, somewhat dubiously, the iSmell, developed by the company DigiScents at the beginning of the 21st century. The idea was that the iSmell would take digital recipe codes from websites and then use chemicals inside the device to synthesise aromas that would be emitted from a grill on its front. Though an interesting concept it was ultimately unsuccessful, and in 2006 it was listed by *PC World* Magazine as one of the 25 worst tech products of all time.[47] Until technology develops further, it seems that smell will remain an aspect of printed comics that cannot be replicated in digital ones (although electronic devices do produce olfactory phenomena of their own). Moreover, as digital formats become the norm and it becomes increasingly important to demonstrate *why* a comic should be published in a printed form, it is likely that smell will gain in prominence as an aspect of the comic's identity.

One element of the medium that has not received so much development is the taste of comics. In general the notion of eating comics has been treated as a humorous idea, with interpretations of this idea ranging from vulgar sexual comedy (Robert Crumb's *Cunt Comics* (1968) bore the cover line '"The Only Comic You Can Eat"') to knowing references to the American comic book collector's market (DC Comics' *Legion of Superheroes* #49 (1993) boasted '"the world's 1st edible cover"' as a 'special "enhancement"', though it also included a caveat asserting that the cover was only actually edible if the reader possessed the same superpower as Matter Eater Lad, a character 'with the ability to eat and digest anything').[48] This is not to say that taste is entirely absent from comics, but comics that can be tasted are both rare and relatively difficult to study. The reasons for this difficulty stem from the very nature of the sense of taste, which tends to be engaged when we *consume* something in the sense of eating or drinking it. This also brings into play other definitions of that term, given that the consumption of food or drink tends to lead to its destruction, its using up. To taste a comic is, in all probability, to destroy it, and this can make understanding the effects of comics' gustatory elements quite a challenge. Yet comics that can be consumed in this way do present a number of interesting possibilities for both their creators and their eaters, and to understand these possibilities more fully we can now turn to an example. In 2008, J.B. Winter put together an edible comic entitled *Imaginary Food:*

An Edible Twenty Four Hour Comic using food decorator pens on quesadillas. The comic was produced as part of the annual comics-production event, 24 Hour Comics Day, and it was served to other creators participating in the event. The initial artwork took the form of a story told over twenty-three images (and a title page), each of which was presented on an individual tortilla. The tortillas were then laid on top of each other and filled to give twelve double-sided "leaves", each bearing two images. Following cooking, these leaves were each cut into six sections, which were then divided up among the various creators working on comics for the event.[49]

In this example we see a strong emphasis upon the notion of comic-as-experience. The comic is not simply an artefact that persists over time as we assume a paper object does, it is something to be consumed and through that consumption, performed. In this regard we can draw some comparisons between Winter's work and Grant Morrison's 'wankathon' concept (see section 4.3.1.1), in that both involve the performance of a particular action at a particular time. In Morrison's case, this time period is determined by the nature of the ritual, that is, the ritualistic act of masturbation could only be undertaken at the particular time Morrison specified or it was no longer part of that particular ritual, while in Winter's the performance time was dictated by the nature of the performance itself. While the consumption of the comic was not necessarily specific to a particular time period, it was limited to a single occurrence. Once it had been consumed, it was gone. More than that, though, the explicitly edible nature of the comic (something that was not just indicated by the materials of composition but also by the title of the work) means that that act of consumption is inherent within it. The comic was not complete until it had been eaten. In this way, the act of eating, and the accompanying gustatory sensations, are incorporated into the comic itself. The destruction of the comic is part of the process of reading it (although this term is perhaps stretched beyond reasonable limits by edible comics). Furthermore, unlike the printed comic, which can be collected and preserved without being read, the relatively high speed with which food items degrade (through rotting etc.) means that there would be almost no way to preserve such an object without substantially modifying it through a process such as freezing (see section 4.2.4 for more on temperature).

These qualities have two major effects on the understanding of these comics. Firstly, they serve to push the notion of *performing* comics by emphasising the spatial and temporal specificity of the act of consuming comics. While visual, auditory, tactile and olfactory qualities can certainly pin down a work to an environment more or less specifically, a comic that can (or must) be eaten is limited to a single instance. One cannot "re-eat" an edible comic and thereby resituate it in a different material and temporal context in the same way one can reread a nonedible one. This is not to say that edible comics could not be mass produced. It is not difficult to imagine a line of comics printed on rice paper that could be eaten after reading. But the critical difference between a comic that is consumed in the gustatory sense and one that is consumed in a visual sense is that the former do not persist in the way that the latter do. For this reason they challenge quite strongly those elemental and knowingly incomplete definitions discussed in sections 1.1.1 and 1.1.2; they deny the persistence of the material support that is required to facilitate '[j]uxtaposed pictorial images' or 'sequential art' and point us firmly in the direction of broader and, I would argue, more satisfactory social definitions. They do, however, pose problems for scholarship for this very reason, and if we are to incorporate such comics into the field of comics scholarship/Comics Studies it becomes necessary to move further into the realm of performance research more fully, drawing on understandings of areas such as site-specific performances to build our knowledge base. This is a long-term project, and not one that we have space to undertake here, but in outlining the importance of multisensory aspects of comics it is important to mark up not only the techniques that we currently employ but also those we would do well to develop.

5.3 SMELLS AND TASTES IN COMICS

These problems are somewhat lessened, but not wholly eliminated, in the category of smells and tastes *in* comics. In this category we can place those smells and tastes that are incorporated into the body of the comic itself but do not derive from the materials of composition per se. They tend to be generated using chemicals that are designed to smell (or, theoretically, taste) a particular way, and could therefore be classed as artificial or synthetic. The most common form of this phenomenon is the scented page, which, though not hugely widespread, has been used in a number of comics to varying effect. In early American printings of Fumi Yoshinaga's series *Antique Bakery* by Digital Manga Publishing (1999–2002), whose storyline revolves around the staff of a bakery, the covers were impregnated with different smells relating to the foods cooked at the bakery. The reader scratched a section of the cover to release the smell, in a similar fashion to the scratch and sniff cards used in John Waters' 1981 film *Polyester* and the 1986 videogame *Leather Goddesses of Phobos,* although unlike those examples the covers of *Antique Bakery* were physically integrated rather than separable components of the form. As comic shop owner Christopher Butcher remarked in an article on the series, the effect of these smells was to draw the reader more comprehensively into the diegesis:

> Each volume would have a new scratch-and-sniff, strawberries, chocolate, all meant to entice you into the baking world within. No manga publisher had done something that clever, to that point. It was pretty cool, and got people talking.[50]

A similar technology was also intended for use in an issue of Boom! Studios' *Zombie Tales,* although I have yet to discover what smell was used.[51] It is a fair assumption, given the nature of the title, that it was not a pleasant one, but it likely served a similar purpose to those presented in *Antique Bakery*, serving to immerse the reader within a particular diegetic environment and suggest something of the physical atmosphere that was present within it.

Scratch and sniff technology has the potential to generate very powerful reading experiences. While the natural smells of the comic that I described in section 5.2 certainly contribute to a long-term relationship between the comic and its reader, and may seem to draw that reader into the past/pull the past into the present, they are rarely specifically modulated to do so. Alan Moore's comments in *1963* may suggest a certain "targeting" of the smell, but this is only making clever use of an existing smell; it is improbable that the smell itself was chosen for its meanings (although the paper stock that was selected may have been chosen partly for its aroma). Similarly, even in works where the materials of composition are unusually relevant to the narrative of the storyline, as is the case in the two Plastic Man books discussed in section 4.2.2, the smell is more likely to be an incidental element of the book's design than a primary consideration. Although both *Jack Cole and Plastic Man* and *Plastic Man: On the Lam!* have covers that emit plastic aromas, it is probable that this is more by coincidence than design. It seems somewhat unlikely that DC Comics began with the smells and worked from there, and any meanings that these smells may infuse into a work are therefore largely uncontrolled.

Scratch and sniff technology, by contrast, *does* offer the possibility for a measure of control because it enables creators to choose which smells their works possess, and to insert those smells into the narrative itself if they so choose. While the application of the system in *Antique Bakery* was fairly broad and basic (each volume had just one smell on the book's cover), it is certainly possible to imagine a book with multiple smells on different pages (Avon catalogues have featured such collections of smells for years), or a detachable scratch and sniff card that corresponded to various points in the narrative (although this would perhaps tip over into the category of smells *with* comics, see below). When coupled with the book's visual content, this would allow for the possibility of a semiotics of smell, something that has been marked up as problematic by thinker Laura U. Marks, who writes:

> Visual and sound images call up, to different degrees, a shared cultural symbolic. And this is what narrative filmmakers depend on: that viewer/listeners will have a common understanding of visual and sonic signs, so that we can experience a common story. Smell, however, provokes individual stories, calling upon a semiotics that is resolutely specific.[52]

While Marks' comments are certainly correct in regard to visually depicted smells or actual smells that are not paired with a specific visual representation (as was the case with the smells in *1963*, which drew upon generic, rather than specific, memories), the multimodal nature of communication in comics means that there is the possibility for a more complex semiotics of smell to develop, although there are technical restrictions on this.[53] Smells do not stop and start cleanly, for example, so it is necessary that a collection of odours either be chosen to blend well together or be spaced far enough apart that they do not interfere with each other, although scratch and sniff is perhaps less susceptible to these problems than other media-related smell-production technologies have been in the past.[54] Yet one might, through the association of a particular smell to a particular visual cue, begin to develop a system whereby smells are able to signify in a relatively specific way. Fairly complex systems of "scent language" would not be particularly difficult to develop because once a codified system had been established through a scent/sight connection (and this would theoretically be achievable over the course of a single page) it should be possible to deploy scents in isolation in such a way that they would still cue the reader's understanding. Such a technique would be comparable to the use of sounds to add information to a comic's narrative that I discussed in section 3.2.3.

Yet as Christopher Butcher's comments above indicate, scratch and sniff technology in comics is still something of a novelty and it does not feature in many. Furthermore, although controlled, manufactured smells of the types employed in scratch and sniff offer a means by which creators can communicate specific ideas to the readership, they do not last a particularly long time. Even a scratch and sniff card of the type used in *Polyester* does not long retain the odours with which it has been impregnated, and this can be something of a problem if the smell is made a critical aspect of the work. If the reader *must* smell something to understand its meaning within the narrative, then this meaning will be lost as soon as the smell fades. Furthermore, as I mentioned above (see section 5.2), the integration of smells into digital narratives is proving difficult because technologies such as the iSmell have floundered; a further barrier to the integration of odours into narratives, particularly given the progressive moves being made towards digital publishing. Finally, financial and technological barriers mean that systems such as scratch and sniff are inaccessible for many. This is not to say, however, that smells and tastes in the broader sense are all so difficult to incorporate into comics, and as we move now to consider smells and tastes *with* comics, we will see that in actuality these very powerful senses can be accessed both easily and cheaply.

5.4 SMELLS AND TASTES WITH COMICS

In using the term 'smells and tastes with comics' I am referring to those sensory stimuli that are packaged with a comic but not physically integrated into the body of the work, in the same way that the CDs and records discussed in section 3.2.3 were physically separable from the comics' body. Examples would include detachable scratch and sniff devices, and foodstuffs packaged with comics. It is also worth marking up the fact that while the 'in' comics category tends to be skewed in favour of smells (to the point that I have not been able to locate a single example of what could convincingly be called a 'taste in comics', which would presumably require lickable pages), the 'with' category is more taste-oriented (although there is at least one example of smells with comics).[55] The reason for this is likely to be similar to that mentioned in section 5.2, namely that to taste something tends to mean destroying it. Packaging a tasted object *with* a comic but not making it a part of that comic allows for a dually effective mode of presentation, in that the comic's edible content can be consumed fully without the entirety of the comic being destroyed (as it would be if it were an edible comic). By contrast, although smells may fade over time they can be experienced in a relatively nondamaging way by the reader, so it does make sense to incorporate them into the body of the comic itself in the manner described above.

The only example of smells with comics that I have so far come across comes from the first issue of Marvel Comics' *The Ren & Stimpy Show,* which came packaged with one of two varieties of 'air fouler'. As the name suggests, this device was intended to produce an undesirable odour when it was scratched, 'reportedly smelling either of wet Chihuahua or kitty litter box [depending on the version]'.[56] While this may seem to be a relatively minor application of scratch and sniff technology, it is interesting to note because it draws quite heavily upon both biological and sociocultural elements of the sense of smell to effect a response. Specifically, in labelling the device an air *fouler,* Marvel Comics situated it in a position of opposition not only to the conventional air *freshener* but also to normal atmospheric conditions. This is a device intended to generate a particularly undesirable odour, to disrupt the atmosphere in a negative way. In the sense of smell we find a particularly potent means for doing this because of the strong links between smell sensation and emotion. While these biological connections may enable the development of the nostalgia that I discussed in section 5.2, they also facilitate strong revulsion when smells are unpleasant. Interestingly, although there are certain transcultural taboos surrounding smells (for example those produced through flatulence), it is generally believed that most smell preferences are learned.[57] Thus, it is through the marking up of particular smells as pleasant or unpleasant that we come to develop these categorisations in our own thoughts. We decide what we like based on what we are told (though the term 'decide' is of course a vast oversimplification of the psychological and biological processes through which preferences develop). In this example, Marvel Comics contributes to this process of situation in two ways, firstly by marking the odour up as unpleasant, and secondly by providing no clear indication of what it is likely to be. In actuality, if the smells of wet Chihuahua or kitty litter box are correct, they would correspond to the identities of the comics' lead characters (Ren and Stimpy are a dog and a cat, respectively), but this is more or less irrelevant given that they are simply identified as foul, that is, unpleasant.

Here then, we find a very clear example of how smells can be used not only to generate a pleasant immersion within a narrative of the type found in *Antique Bakery* but more negative reactions as well, and we also begin to identify another aspect of smell and taste that emphasises their position as contact senses. Just as I described touch as both the most and the least intimate of the senses, given that on the one hand it requires direct physical contact between two bodies while on the other it resolutely refuses the penetration of one body by the other (see section 4.1), so too are smell and taste divided fairly starkly into pleasant and unpleasant. While desirable smells may help to draw readers into the narrative by stimulating the recall of happy memories and generating positive emotions, undesirable ones can serve to distance them and hold them apart from the text. Like tactile sensations, smells and tastes can make readers more aware of comics' corporeality and drive them to move closer to it or to get away from it. Critically, the learned nature of preferences (again, with some possible exceptions) means that the pleasantness or unpleasantness of smells is entirely subjective, and determined by the personal history of the reader, who is again drawn into the act of producing or *performing* the comic rather than passively receiving a message from an author. Here we are again reminded of the notion of the 'contract' between author and reader that Will Eisner spoke of (see section 1.4), and of an expanded notion of Scott McCloud's concept of closure (the idea that the reader mentally constructs what happens in the spaces between a comic's panels). Yet it is perhaps David Mack who best marks up the issues at play here when he says:

> For me, comics are a collaboration between the reader and the creator. For me, the artwork and the story are not on the physical page. The physical page is just an artefact. It is a navigational device. It is the equivalent of a road map. And it is as different from the actual art and story as a road map is from the actual geography it is suggesting. By the nature of sequential art, the reader's mind is filling in what happens between the images that I present. The readers are bringing their own past experience and perspective. The artwork, the story, happens inside the readers' mind when they read the book.[58]

In smell and taste, the senses which are most powerful in terms of emotionality, and which require us to take in something of the substance of the object, comics creators are offered some very effective ways of working to affect readers. Yet accessing those effects means relinquishing control over the work to an even greater degree than Mack acknowledges here. In this sense, smells and tastes are almost the opposite of sounds (see section 3.2.2), in that where sounds can instruct readers to perform a work in a particular way and at a particular speed, and thereby afford the creator a high level of control, smells and tastes subvert notions of duration, and detach readers from the text itself by plunging them into memory, nostalgia, and emotional responses that are very difficult to cue or direct. While a basic semiotics of the type described in section 5.3 may be viable, it would be very difficult to effect such a system on a wide scale because smell is too personal a sense to be completely codified.

The same is true of taste which, like smells, tend to be involved only relatively generically with comics. Either the tastes employed are the tastes of the compositing materials, which will not necessarily correspond to the narrative (the story told in *Imaginary Food: An Edible Twenty Four Hour Comic* relates to food and eating in general but not to quesadillas specifically), or they are attached to the comic, and here again there may be relatively little correspondence between them and the comic's narrative itself. The most common means by which tastes are incorporated into comics is as part of the paratext; confectionary items, for example, regularly feature as free gifts in children's comics. Yet although such items may be packaged in such a way as to make them relatively congruent with the narratives of the comic, the level of meaning we are capable of gleaning from them is unlikely to be much greater than that which the filmgoer derives from the popcorn (s)he eats at the cinema; the food is usually generic rather than specific to a particular storyline or character. Nevertheless, where a comic is regularly packaged with the same type of food, as is the case with the *Bazooka Joe* comic strips that were packaged with Bazooka bubble-gum from the 1950s until 2012, it is probable that a more specific type of association is able to develop as readers come to treat the taste of the food in a similar fashion to the scent or feel of the paper; something that helps to form the comic's identity in their minds and affect their memories of it in later life.[59] Alternatively it would be possible for a food to be associated quite strongly with a narrative or a character simply by having the attached food being eaten by a character in that narrative. As Emile Peynaud has observed in relation to wine and wine tasting, nongustatory elements of the act of consumption such as the physical context in which something is consumed or the expectation one has of what a taste will or should be like can influence perception, and connections between comics and the foodstuffs with which they are packaged may very well serve to modulate the tastes the reader/eater experiences. Again, the connection between character and reader through the contact senses can serve to develop affinity, and may aid immersion (a similar effect was evident in the vibration systems employed in *Scott Pilgrim*; see section 4.3), or, as with the *Bazooka Joe* series, help encourage readers to buy more of the product the comic is associated with (in this case bubble-gum).[60] Thus while it can be seen that there are clear economic imperatives for attaching edible items to comics (a child required by economic limitations to choose between a comic and sweets is more likely to pick the comic if it comes *with* sweets), there are certainly good creative reasons for doing so as well.

Yet in dealing with such items we are again confronted with the problem of longevity that plagues edible comics and scratch and sniff systems. An attached item to smell or taste lasts only a very short time. As a promotional object to stimulate a purchase this is of little import; if the object is intended only to draw a reader into buying a particular comic, this objective is completed as soon as the purchase is made. But where smells and tastes *are* used more creatively, perhaps even playing significant roles in the narrative of the comic, it is important to think about ways in which those roles can be fulfilled if the edible elements of the comic are consumed.

5.4.1 Producible Smells and Tastes

While the relatively high-tech systems discussed above can be very effective, it is much simpler and cheaper to incorporate actual smells and tastes into a comic-reading experience by providing readers with the ability to produce them by themselves. Although this is clearly not always possible or would not always be effective, it can be a very powerful way of communicating information to the reader. Perhaps the most obvious means by which tastes and smells can be included in comics is through the presentation of recipes in the books themselves.[61] This is the route taken in Julian Hanshaw's *The Art of Phở*, in which the narrative revolves around a Vietnamese noodle soup called phở and a character called Little Blue, whose job is cooking and selling it and other foods. The book includes numerous recipes in comics form, which demonstrate how phở and other dishes should be prepared and served.[62] In one instance, the book also instructs readers on 'How To Drink Cà Phê'.[63] In this way, the work provides a means by which readers are able to go beyond the printed images upon the page and access the smells, textures and tastes that are represented by those images. Readers are thereby immersed far more comprehensively within the narrative environment; they are able to engage with it in a multisensory fashion and the comic gives them more than a purely visual understanding might indicate. There are obvious parallels here with the examples of specific directed touch that I discussed in section 4.3.1.2, but this type of performance perhaps differs from instruction books because while *The Art of Phở* does encourage its readers to move outside the body of the work, what they produce by doing so does relate back to the text. Where the primary focus of the instruction books put out by Will Eisner Studios and others was to enable individuals to construct or maintain something external to the comic, and the comic was therefore a supplement to (or perhaps at most a part of) the object; in *The Art of Phở*, the cooking and consumption of the dishes is a part of the text. Though they are not essential to the understanding of the text, they are an enrichment of it, an expansion of it, rather than a subordination of it to a different goal (in this sense they are comparable to the notion of producible sounds discussed in section 3.2.3.1). The act of cooking the food, and the senses of taste, touch and smell are therefore foregrounded in this example. This is not to say that all works featuring recipes integrate them so fully into the body of the text. The first issue of the Danish small press anthology *Penneveninder* features a recipe for cucumber cakes that does not relate at all to the rest of the book, but nevertheless injects the possibility for a multisensory aspect into the piece.[64] Such simple but potentially effective modes of communication are likely to be the more common means of integrating recipes, but the more elaborate form used in *The Art of Phở* is not so difficult to use as to be prohibitive should a creator wish to engage with it.[65] Furthermore, it is worth pointing out that unlike the majority of the integration systems I have discussed here, this mode of interaction is not denied to the producer of digital comics, given that it is as easy to present recipes on the computer screen as it is on the printed page.

Perhaps the most common means by which smells and tastes are incorporated into comics, however, is through advertising. I have already mentioned *Bazooka Joe,* and given that comics are a medium of communication, it is unsurprising that a number of food producers have turned to them as a means of advertising their products. In addition to conventional adverts of the kind seen in magazines and on billboards and so forth, we can also observe a number of adverts that are themselves comics, situated within other comics. To give one example, Marvel Comics' *The Incredible Hulk*, Vol. 1 #329 (1987), includes a comic strip advert for Brachs' Gum Dingers that features the licensed characters Gumby and Pokey.[66] The strip features a narrative that incorporates the food products into a storyline and suggests a fairly fantastical use for them as flight aids, although the fantasy element here is relatively congruent with other appearances of Gumby.[67] While it could be argued that the primary connection here is between a comic and a product, rather than a comic and a taste or a smell per se, there is a clear suggestion on the part of the advertisers that the reader should go out and purchase a particular food item. Further, note the attempt to situate the reader within a context of continued consumption through the use of known, familiar characters; Gumby was the title character of a stop-motion animation series that ran from 1955 to 1989, and the ad is printed in another long-running title with a well-known title character, *The Incredible Hulk*. Readers are also encouraged to purchase a 'Gumby and Pokey Fun Kit', and to follow the continued adventures of Gumby and Pokey; the title of this piece reads 'Gum Dinger Adventures continue . . .' and a caption box in the last panel states that the story is 'To Be Continued . . .' Similar techniques (albeit without licensed characters) were also used in a series of adverts for Mars' 3 Musketeers chocolate bar in the early 1990s. While such advertising techniques may be so common as to go almost unnoticed by the majority of readers, they do represent an important aspect of the ways in which comics come to be associated with particular food products. We must also remember that the creators of such comics are by definition comics artists too, even if the comics they produce are arguably more commercially than artistically oriented (even Art Spiegelman, one of the foremost comics creators in the history of the medium, worked for Topps Chewing Gum Co. between 1966 and 1989).[68] That a comic is produced for commercial reasons does not render it unworthy of study. Given the powerful relationships between smell and taste and emotion and memory, it is worth considering the roles played by comics in advertising and vice versa, particularly since it can provide clues as to why and how advertising is so powerful. If, as thinkers such as Thierry Groensteen and Mel Gibson suggest, we approach comics with an emotional openness and/or a nostalgically charged interest, it is perhaps the case that advertising's ability to influence is increased, and this is certainly something that is worthy of further research.

5.5 SMELLS AND TASTES AROUND COMICS

One final category that we should consider, albeit relatively briefly, is comprised of those smells and tastes that readers experience while reading comics, but which are not naturally connected to those comics (i.e., they do not necessarily draw from a direct link between the page and the environment of consumption). Such smells and tastes are roughly analogous to the sounds around comics that I discussed in section 3.4, and like them they may fall into the category of environmental interference or 'noise' as it is described by Randy Duncan and Matthew J. Smith.[69] Interestingly, just as some readers are keen to determine and discuss the music they listen to while reading comics, so too are there those who think consciously about the products they eat while reading. In a 2011 issue of Marvel/Panini Comics' *The Mighty World of Marvel*, one reader, Steve Cook, framed his comments within a discussion of the food he chose to eat while reading the comic.[70]

While such elements of the reading experience are unlikely to be as important to readers as music and other sounds are (this is the only letter I have so far come across that mentions the food eaten around comics), they clearly do play something of a role, and again we call to mind the linked concepts of memory and emotion; both of which have strong ties to smell and taste, and both of which likely inform reading experiences and readers' memories of the media with which they are confronted. If we are to understand comics and readers' experiences of them more holistically, it is essential that these factors be taken into account more comprehensively. It is also worth considering the distinctions between formats in this regard—it could intuitively be argued that one is more likely to read "the funnies" in a newspaper while eating breakfast than to consume a bowl of spaghetti Bolognese while reading a thick, heavy graphic novel, although further research would need to be conducted to determine whether this intuition is borne out in reality. Although it is difficult to see how such variable conditions could be dealt with on a large scale, there may be ways of integrating them and it is certainly something to think about in the longer term.

5.6 CONCLUSION

In drawing the first chapter of this book to a close, I restated the core question that lies at the heart of the mechanical project in comics scholarship: How do comics work? In coming to consider all five of the senses, I argued, rather than privileging sight to the exclusion of hearing, touch, smell and taste, we might be able to develop a more satisfactory answer to that question. Over the course of chapters 2–5, I have sought to present a selection of elements of comics, some common, some more unusual, that in the first instance challenge the idea that comics *are* a purely visual medium, and in the second emphasise that the nonvisual elements are both foundational and active in the production of meaning within the medium. By this I mean that while the audible, tactile, olfactory and gustatory elements of comics are generally taken to be passive and inessential components of the medium that are easily modified or eliminated without harming the visual text, this assumption is at the very least inaccurate. Smell and taste are perhaps the senses that make the strongest arguments for this position, because they are so fundamentally linked to the reader's sense of personal identity and memories. These senses generate strong memories for readers, and they evoke particular contexts of consumption, tying the act of reading to moments in time, moments of performance. Thus while they are to some extent supplements to a visual text (just as sounds and tactile qualities are) they are also the elements that readers remember, and which can most quickly immerse people in their own pasts, 'bear[ing] unfalteringly, in the tiny and almost impalpable drop of their essence, the vast structure of recollection'.[71]

As we have seen in this and the preceding chapters, the olfactory and gustatory components of comics are not alone in holding a powerful sway over readers. While the ocularcentric mode of comics scholarship implies a disembodied interaction between ideas; ideas transmitted from the comic to the reader, what the various aspects of comics outlined here emphasise is that reading comics is in fact a very overtly physical *experience* that takes place in multiple sensory modalities simultaneously. Although I have separated the five senses into individual chapters here for ease of communication, it is important to remember that the various processes are not so clearly distinguishable at the moment of experience as might be suggested by this separation. Multiple factors are in play at the same time. Comics is not a monosensory medium, it is a multisensory one, and it is reliant not upon passive readers but upon active *performers* for the communication of its meanings. This interdependence, and the complexity of the medium, are worth remembering as we move now to consider a case study, which will take in a number of the sensory elements I have discussed in chapters 2–5, and indicate the numerous ways in which a study of even a single creator's works can be developed using multisensory analysis. In so doing, I also aim to test and refine the multisensory approach, taking the initial catalogue of sensory components discussed here and applying them more comprehensively to a set of works in order to understand what multisensory analysis can bring to a reading, and how it might be modified through application.

NOTES

1. Sabin, Roger. 2000. "The Crisis in Modern American and British Comics, and the Possibilities of the Internet as a Solution." In *Comics and Culture: Analytical and Theoretical Approaches to Reading Comics*, edited by Anne Magnussen and Hans-Christian Christiansen, 43–57. Copenhagen, Denmark: Museum Tusculanum Press and University of Copenhagen. 52; Gibson, Mel. 2008. "What You Read and Where You Read It, How You Get It, How You Keep It: Children, Comics and Historical Cultural Practice." *Popular Narrative Media* 1 (2): 151–167. 151–152.
2. McCloud, Scott. 1993. *Understanding Comics: The Invisible Art*. New York, NY: HarperPerennial. 88–89, 128–129.
3. Reed, Bill. 2007. "365 Reasons to Love Comics #342 [The Smell]." *Comic Book Resources*. December 8. Accessed July 25, 2011. http://goodcomics.comicbookresources.com/2007/12/08/365-reasons-to-love-comics-342/.
4. Rée, Jonathan. 1999. *I See a Voice: Language, Deafness and the Senses—A Philosophical History*. London: Harper Collins. 34.
5. Ibid.
6. Herz, Rachel S. 2006. "I Know What I Like: Understanding Odor Preferences." In *The Smell Culture Reader*, edited by Jim Drobnick, 190–203. Oxford: Berg. 190–191.
7. Schiffman, Harvey Richard. 1996. *Sensation and Perception: An Integrated Approach*. 4th ed. New York, NY: Wiley. 470.
8. All statistics here from: Herz, 'I Know', 190–191.
9. Bartoshuk, Linda M., and B. Valerie Duffy. 2005 (2007). "Chemical Senses: Taste and Smell." In *The Taste Culture Reader: Experiencing Food and Drink*, edited by Carolyn Korsmeyer, 25–33. Oxford: Berg. 26.
10. Schiffman, *Sensation*, 471.
11. Ibid., 450.
12. Ibid., 452.
13. Bartoshuk and Duffy, 'Chemical', 27.
14. Schiffman, *Sensation*, 452.
15. Bartoshuk and Duffy, 'Chemical', 25.
16. Classen, Constance. 2005. "The Witch's Senses: Sensory Ideologies and Transgressive Femininities from the Renaissance to Modernity." In *Empire of the Senses: The Sensual Culture Reader*, edited by David Howes, 70–84. Oxford: Berg. 70; Freud, Sigmund. 1930 (2004). *Civilization and Its Discontents*. Translated by David McLintock. London: Penguin Books. 46.
17. Rée, *I See*, 34.
18. Reed, *365*, n.p.
19. Herz, 'I Know', 191.
20. Ibid., 190–191.
21. Proust, Marcel. 2006. *Remembrance of Things Past*. Translated by C.K. Scott Moncrieff and Stephen Hudson. 2 vols. Ware, Hertfordshire, UK: Wordsworth Editions. Vol. 1, 63.
22. Saussure, Ferdinand de. 1983 (2005). *Course in General Linguistics*. Translated by Roy Harris. London: Gerald Duckworth. 65–70; Deleuze, Gilles.

2008. *Proust and Signs: The Complete Text*. Translated by Richard Howard. London: Continuum. 8.

23. Groensteen, Thierry. 2009. "Why Are Comics Still in Search of Cultural Legitimization?" In *A Comics Studies Reader*, edited by Jeet Heer and Kent Worcester, 3–11. Jackson, MS: University Press of Mississippi. 11.
24. Deleuze, *Proust*, 9.
25. Gibson, Mel. 2003. "'You Can't Read Them, They're For Boys!' British Girls, American Superhero Comics and Identity." *International Journal of Comic Art* 5 (1): 305–324. 312.
26. Carlton Publishing Group. n.d. "The Best of Jackie." *Carlton Publishing Group Website*. Accessed July 25, 2011. http://www.carltonbooks.co.uk/display.asp?K=9781853758010&sf1=title%5Findex&st1=jackie&y=0&sort=sort%5Fdate%2Fd&x=0&m=1&dc=6; Carlton Publishing Group. n.d. "'Jackie' Annual All Your Favourites." *Carlton Publishing Group Website*. Accessed July 25, 2011. http://www.carltonbooks.co.uk/display.asp?K=9781853756269&sf1=title%5Findex&st1=jackie&y=0&sort=sort%5Fdate%2Fd&x=0&m=3&dc=6; Carlton Publishing Group. n.d. "The Best of 'Jackie' Annual." *Carlton Publishing Group Website*. Accessed July 25, 2011. http://www.carltonbooks.co.uk/display.asp?K=9781853756085&sf1=title%5Findex&st1=jackie&y=0&sort=sort%5Fdate%2Fd&x=0&m=5&dc=6; Gibson, Mel. 2011. "'I Do Have the Annuals but Somehow They Are Just Not the Same as the Weeklies Printed on That Dreadfully Poor Quality Paper': British Girls' Comics, Publication Formats and Perceptions of Class." *Materiality and Virtuality: A Conference on Comics*. Leeds.
27. Carlton Publishing Group. n.d. "Against All Odds 12 of the Best 'War Picture Library' Comic Books Ever!" *Carlton Publishing Group Website*. Accessed July 25, 2011. http://www.carltonbooks.co.uk/display.asp?ISB=9781853756610&.
28. Moore, Alan, Rick Veitch, and Steve Bissette. 1993. *1963*. 6 vols. Fullerton, CA: Image Comics. (3): 14.
29. Reed, *365*, n.p.
30. Ibid.
31. Burgas, Greg. 2007. "Comics You Should Own Flashback—1963." *Comic Book Resources*. August 26. Accessed July 25, 2011. http://goodcomics.comicbookresources.com/2007/08/26/comics-you-should-own-flashback-1963/.
32. Lister, Martin, Jon Dovey, Seth Giddings, Iain Grant, and Kieran Kelly. 2003. *New Media: A Critical Introduction*. Abingdon, UK: Routledge. 21.
33. Benjamin, Walter. 2003. "On Some Motifs in Baudelaire." In *Walter Benjamin: Selected Writings*. Vol. 4, *1938–1940*, by Walter Benjamin, edited by Howard Eiland and Michael W. Jennings, translated by Edmund Jephcott, 313–355. Cambridge, MA: Harvard University Press. 335.
34. Looby, Christopher. 2006. "'The Roots of the Orchis, the Iuli of Chesnuts': The Odor of Male Solitude." In *The Smell Culture Reader*, edited by Jim Drobnick, 289–304. Oxford: Berg. 290.
35. Carlton Publishing Group, 'Best of "Jackie" Annual', n.p.
36. Jameson, Fredric. 1991. *Postmodernism, or, The Cultural Logic of Late Capitalism*. London: Verso. 17.
37. Carlton Publishing Group. n.d. "The Biggest 'Jackie' Annual Ever! The Best Thing for Girls—Next to Boys." *Carlton Publishing Group Website*. Accessed July 26, 2011. http://www.carltonbooks.co.uk/display.asp?K=9781853756672&sf1=title%5Findex&st1=jackie&sort=sort%5Fdate%2Fd&m=2&dc=6.

38. Ibid.
39. For more on the ways in which readers and critics have understood the messages conveyed in *Jackie*, see the seminal work: Barker, Martin. 1989. *Comics: Ideology, Power and the Critics*. Manchester, UK: Manchester University Press.
40. Moore, Veitch and Bissette, *1963* #1, 26.
41. Lee, Stan, and George Mair. 2002. *Excelsior! The Amazing Life of Stan Lee*. London: Boxtree. 172. For more on Lee's interpretation of his role in the co-creation of Spider-Man and his relationships with Steve Ditko and Jack Kirby, see: Lee and Mair, *Excelsior!*, 129–132, 170–174.
42. Conroy, Mike. 2002. *500 Great Comicbook Action Heroes*. London: Chrysalis Impact. 158–159.
43. Lee and Mair, *Excelsior!*, 148–156.
44. Reed, *365*, n.p.
45. Humberstone, Tom. 2009. *Getting the Smell Right*. November 29. Accessed July 25, 2011. http://solipsisticpop.com/2009/11/29/getting-the-smell-right/. Italics in original.
46. Joe. 2009. "Solipsistic Pop—I Love the Smell of Comics in the Morning . . ." *Forbidden Planet International*. November 30. Accessed June 25, 2011. http://forbiddenplanet.co.uk/blog/2009/solipsistic-pop-i-love-the-smell-of-comics-in-the-morning/.
47. Tynan, Dan. 2006. *The 25 Worst Tech Products of All Time: Numbers 21 to 25*. May 26. Accessed May 10, 2010. http://www.pcworld.com/article/125772–6/the_25_worst_tech_products_of_all_time.html. For more on the iSmell, see: Marks, Laura U. 2002. *Touch: Sensuous Theory and Multisensory Media*. Minneapolis, MN: University of Minnesota Press. See also: Paterson, Mark W.D. 2006. "Digital Scratch and Virtual Sniff: Simulating Scents." In *The Smell Culture Reader*, edited by Jim Drobnick, 358–367. Oxford: Berg.
48. Skinn, Dez. 2004. *Comix: The Underground Revolution*. Brighton: Quality Communications. 60; Rosenkranz, Patrick. 2008. *Rebel Visions: The Underground Comix Revolution 1963–1975*. Seattle, WA: Fantagraphics Books. 133; Pustz, Matthew J. 1999. *Comic Book Culture: Fanboys and True Believers*. Jackson, MS: University Press of Mississippi. 154.
49. Winter, J.B. 2008. *Edible 24 Hour Comic*. November 1. Accessed August 23, 2011. http://www.jbwinter.com/2008/10/edible-24-hour-comic.html.
50. Butcher, Christopher. 2010. *Manga Milestones 2000–2009: 10 Manga That Changed Comics* #7. January 11. Accessed May 10, 2010. http://comics212.net/2010/01/11/manga-milestones-2000–2009–10-manga-that-changed-comics-7/.
51. Paterson, 'Digital Scratch', 361.
52. Marks, *Touch*, 118–119.
53. It is worth pointing out that Marks does not dismiss smell as a conveyor of meaning altogether; she has written elsewhere on the possibility of using the sense to develop an 'immanent epistemology' (see: Marks, Laura U. 2008. "Thinking Multisensory Culture." *Paragraph* (Edinburgh University Press) 31 (2): 123–137).
54. Paterson, 'Digital Scratch', 360.
55. *Raw Purple* (1977) had a small white spot on its cover, around which text reads: 'THIS SPOT is impregnated with d-Lysergic Acid Diethylamide 25. Licking it will make you dance, sing and see weird colours.' My thanks to Roger Sabin for providing me with a scan of this cover; it is the only comic I have so far encountered that encourages its readers to lick it.

56. Atomic Avenue Inc. n.d. *Ren & Stimpy Show.* Accessed August 25, 2011. http://www.atomicavenue.com/atomic/titledetail.aspx?TitleID=4731.
57. Largey, Gale, and Rod Watson. 2006. "The Sociology of Odors." In *The Smell Culture Reader*, edited by Jim Drobnick, 29–40. Oxford: Berg. 31–32; Herz, 'I Know', 190.
58. Mack, David. 2005. "The Whole-Brained Approach." In *The Education of a Comics Artist: Visual Narrative in Cartoons, Graphic Novels, and Beyond*, edited by Michael Dooley and Steven Heller, 86–90. New York, NY: Allworth Press. 89.
59. For an excellent overview of the history of *Bazooka Joe*, see: Stewart, Bhob. 1988. "Bubbling Over." *Blab!*, September: 21–35. My thanks go to Hugo Frey for recommending this article to me.
60. Stewart, 'Bubbling', 23.
61. Although I do not have space to discuss it here, the Japanese genre of *gurume manga* (also known as gourmet manga) revolves around food and the contexts of its consumption, and often includes recipes.
62. Hanshaw, Julian. 2010. *The Art of Phở*. London: Jonathan Cape. n.p.
63. Ibid.
64. Penneveninders. 2010. *Penneveninder.* Vol. 1. *Coretoon.dk*. 37.
65. For more examples of recipes in comics form, see Saveur.com's 'Recipe Comix' series, accessible at: http://www.saveur.com/comix.
66. *The Incredible Hulk: The Complete Collection.* 2007. Graphic Imaging Technology and Marvel. *Incredible Hulk* vol. 1, #329, n.p.
67. See, for example: Hersh, Mike, Mel Smith, Shepherd Hendrix, Lance Borde, and Ken Hooper. 2008. *Gumby [Free Comic Book Day 2008] Coloring Comic Book Special #1*. Walnut Creek, CA: Wildcard Ink.
68. Witek, Joseph, ed. 2007. *Art Spiegelman: Conversations*. Jackson, MS: University Press of Mississippi. x–xi, xvii–xviii, xx.
69. Duncan, Randy, and Matthew J. Smith. 2009. *The Power of Comics: History, Form and Culture.* New York, NY: Continuum. 12.
70. Cook, Steve. 2011. "Untitled Letter." *The Mighty World of Marvel* Volume 4 #22, June 8: 75.
71. Proust, *Remembrance*, Vol. 1, 63.

6 Multisensory Aspects of the Comics of Alan Moore

6.0 MULTIMODAL MOORE

In previous chapters of this book I have referred to the works of numerous creators and drawn on a wide range of examples to demonstrate specific and limited modes of nonvisual, and to a lesser extent visual, expression in the medium of comics. While this approach has allowed me to outline a variety of elements of the medium, it has also been somewhat partial, and strictly speaking it has not moved beyond the monosensory limitations that I criticised in chapter 1 (although the senses under discussion have changed). In this chapter I will take the elements identified in chapters 2–5 and apply them more holistically to a particular set of works in order to demonstrate their usefulness in developing our understanding of said works. Selecting a corpus of works to focus on for such a case study is not necessarily an easy task. On the one hand, the categories I have discussed in the book are widely applicable, so in theory it should be possible to interrogate any comic in the light of them. On the other, there are few individual works that will demonstrate all or most of the various techniques I have discussed; for that reason it can be expected that the model I propose here be taken more as a supplement to existing approaches than a replacement for them. While the various sensory elements I have brought to bear on individual examples of comics do seriously weaken, if not dispel, the notion that comics are a solely or primarily visual medium, it would be erroneous to suggest that most or all comics employ all the reader's senses to their fullest potential all the time. Nevertheless, there are a number of creators whose works do make very definite use of the reader's senses in particular ways, and who have strived to engage with the senses in a sustained fashion over the course of their careers. Some such creators, such as Art Spiegelman and Chris Ware, have already been discussed in the preceding chapters. Alan Moore has also featured previously in the book (see sections 2.3 and 5.2), but it is his work that I would like to focus on in more detail in this chapter. While this may seem like a strange choice given that Moore's work in the medium has largely been undertaken from the position of a writer and he has rarely gone beyond this role, there are a number of very good reasons to think that his works are suitable for discussion here.

The first and perhaps most basic reason is that Moore's works are often hailed as major texts for the medium. While we must of course be wary of hyperbole, claims that Moore is 'an authentic genius for the twenty first century', 'one of the most influential writers to engage with the [comics] form' and 'a figure who transcends his *oeuvre*' are not entirely without foundation.[1] He has written a huge number of works in various genres and for numerous publishers, and his influence on the field is undeniable. For good or ill this influence extends beyond the visual content of comics, the words and pictures that ostensibly comprise the narrative elements of the form, and into the fields of publishing and production on a larger scale as well. Along with Art Spiegelman, Moore is often credited with the creation of the 'graphic novel' as a publishing category as a result of his work on *Watchmen,* although like Spiegelman he is not particularly fond of the term or the debates around terminology that have arisen from it.[2] Nevertheless, the breadth of Moore's influence makes his works extremely promising as subjects for analysis because they allow us to consider a wide range of elements, from the deployment of words and images upon the page to the publication format and cultural contexts of production and consumption in which those works sit. Moore's works also present interesting examples of texts that have been adapted and/or extended in various ways. In some cases, his pieces have been adapted or extended into other media such as film or music; in others his works have themselves been adaptations. In the contemporary environment, where the boundaries between media are becoming increasingly blurred by the progress of technology, Moore's multimodal works can provide us with useful insights into the various possibilities for communication that arise from a mixing of forms. We have already seen how he makes use of FocusMotion in *Watchmen* (see section 2.3) and through a simple but effective use of text draws smell into the reading experience in *1963* (section 5.2), and over the remainder of this chapter I would like to extend these discussions by considering some of what might be called his major works, with reference to a selection of other pieces as well (though I make no claims to producing an exhaustive survey of his extensive bibliography).[3]

6.1 MASTER OF MATERIALITY

Of all Moore's works it is perhaps *V for Vendetta* that makes the most explicit allusions to the senses, which are presented throughout the narrative as sources of both pleasure and power. Set in a fascist-governed UK in 1997, the narrative deals with the actions of an anarchist freedom fighter/terrorist (depending on one's perspective) known only as 'V', and follows his path of resistance to the government as he carries out a vendetta against various individuals who imprisoned him in a concentration camp in Larkhill, Wiltshire, sometime prior to the start of the story. The story also presents V's relationship with a young woman, Evey Hammond, who is rescued by V at the start of the book and goes on to assume the 'V' role following the original's death towards the end of the narrative. Featuring artwork by David Lloyd, *V for Vendetta* represents Moore's 'first attempt at a continuing series' (along with *Marvelman*), and has been credited with '[establishing] many of the 'rules' for the adult comics boom of the mid-Eighties'.[4] It has been published in a variety of formats since its launch as part of the black-and-white UK-based anthology *Warrior* in 1982. In addition to the printed series, a music album, with lyrics by Moore and musical arrangements by David J, was released. Initially a twelve-inch vinyl record in 1984, like the book the album has been reissued in various form(at)s. Some of the tracks were also included on David J's record 'On Glass', and the whole album is now available as a digital download.

Throughout the text, the senses are employed as mechanisms of both control and pleasure. The former aspect is emphasised through the ubiquity of CCTV cameras throughout the urban environments in which V operates, the latter through references to various art forms, particularly music, throughout the text. Upon Evey's first visit to V's underground headquarters—the shadow gallery—music serves to indicate the relative sensual freedom V enjoys: 'The music is beautiful!' Evey remarks to V, going on to indicate the degree of control the state has over all aspects of the media: 'All I've ever *heard* is the military stuff they play on the radio'.[5] The music she hears is subsequently identified as 'Dancing in the Streets' by Martha and the Vandellas, an appropriate choice for V given the piece's role as a protest song in the 1967 Detroit riots, a reference that is unlikely to have escaped Moore's attention, and suggests a gesturing outwards into a real and realisable world outside the text.[6] Sounds around comics (see section 3.4) are here politicised and utilised in a subtle but significant way.

'Dancing in the Streets' is not the only piece of music referenced directly within *V for Vendetta*. A second notable preexisting piece employed in the narrative is Tchaikovsky's *1812 Overture*, which is featured in the prologue to the third act of the story, 'The Land of Do-As-You-Please'. In the book, V conducts a series of bombings in two senses of the word, both causing them to happen and using them as musical instruments in a performance of the overture, parts of whose score is depicted upon the pages of the book itself. Maggie Gray has argued that this sequence encapsulates the idea that 'V's form of resistance is ultimately a cultural one', asserting:

> V's struggle is [. . .] predicated on culture as a revolutionary force, a means of achieving the mental, ideological and metaphysical liberation necessary for people to achieve social and economic liberation from authoritarianism [. . .] As an anarchist, V's aim is not to lead mass

> resistance to fascism but to facilitate self-emancipation through destructive and negating interventions.[7]

The function of V then, is not to act as a messianic figure who brings or leads a revolution, but rather to inspire individuals to act independently to attain their own freedom, which, Gray suggests, may have broader repercussions because it 'implies a resolution external to the comic'.[8] Indeed by presenting artworks that do exist in the real world, Moore and Lloyd empower readers to engage with the cultural forms that have affected and influenced V as a character, and thereby engage directly with the cultural resistance that character embodies. If there is 'only an idea' within V's cloak, it is an idea that readers are able to encounter outside the text by reading the books V reads, listening to the music V listens to and so on.[9] In this way the text makes a strongly ideological use of the sounds around comics to expand the remit of the work, pushing the reader to perform it by playing the music it features rather than simply experiencing it as passive visual input. The musical pieces cited within the text (I have not covered all of them here) may well serve as a kind of sound track to the comic, but they go beyond a generic accompaniment to the reading and serve as an extension of the text itself into acoustic space, at the same time as drawing the musical works into the body of the text. The specific pieces included within the text not only map out a truly audible soundscape for the comic, they also prompt the reader to value sensory pleasures by presenting particular objects that the reader can access but that are denied to most of the characters in the book (V and Evey being notable exceptions to this general rule).

The idea that readers should go further in their engagement with the text and literally *perform* the music within it is taken still further in 'This Vicious Cabaret', the prelude to the series' second act, which bears the same title.[10] In this five-page sequence, the reader is required to rotate the book 90° clockwise in order to continue the narrative, which incorporates a written score for voice above and below the panels. This score includes all the information necessary to sing the piece (treble clef, time signature, notation etc.), and its validity as a performable piece of music is further attested to by a small copyright notice on the first page of the sequence that reads 'Music © V Songs, 1983'.[11] The lyrics for the song are presented as part of the score, but also in the speech balloons and caption boxes attributed to V throughout. Moore has described this mode of presentation as 'stylistic experimentation', indicating that it was undertaken in this instance to determine whether '[it was] possible to do one episode as a song, with music'.[12] As one might expect, this tune was one of the pieces included on the *V for Vendetta* album, although the recorded version does vary from that presented in the book; where the book presents only music for the vocal performance the recorded version also incorporates instrumentation: piano, strings and percussion instruments. The presence of the score in 'This Vicious Cabaret' brings a number of elements into play that connect the visual material in *V for Vendetta* with the environment in which it is consumed, and the reader who consumes (and perhaps performs) it, and these are worth considering here.

The first point of note about the sequence is the way in which it is presented on the page. As mentioned above, the five-page section (which I will hereafter refer to as the prelude to distinguish it from the various other meanings of the phrase 'This Vicious Cabaret') requires the reader to rotate the book 90° in order to continue reading.[13] This has the effect of modifying the book's shape in the reader's hands (and the way it feels) considerably, shifting the layout from a pair of vertically oriented pages opened into a landscape-format spread to a pair of horizontally oriented pages in a portrait-format spread. The reader no longer progresses by taking hold of the right-hand page and pulling it to the left, instead moving the bottom page upwards and laying it on the top. Though this mode of structuring is fairly simple from a technical point of view, it fundamentally reorganises the flow of information upon the page and modifies the way in which we encounter the text. Writing on the conventional layout of books, Gérard Genette has argued: 'The right hand, or *recto*, page is the side that generally has the advantage, perceptually speaking, at least in our system of writing'.[14] Similarly, Thierry Groensteen has remarked of comics specifically: 'The pages on the left and the pages on the right are not equivalent with regard to the utilization of sites'; he follows Jean-Claude Raillon in emphasising the value of the bottom right-hand corner of the right-hand page in offering the opportunity to build narrative tension prior to the reader's turning of the page.[15] In presenting the prelude in the alternate orientation, Moore and Lloyd subvert the reader's expectations regarding the way in which both books in general and comics in particular present information. At the same time it confounds the reader's expectations that page motion occurs in a left-to-right direction; expectations that have been upheld by the previously conventional orientation of the material within the book. The wide horizontal panels and the presence of staves in a single visual sequence that runs across and down the whole spread rather than breaking at the spine and resetting also requires a different mode of FocusMotion and further disrupts the conventional mode of reading that has been employed up to this point. The combined effect of these modifications is to emphasise the physicality of the work to readers and to demand a different mode of interaction from them. From the very moment they turn the page onto the opening of the prelude, readers are informed that they are now required to work differently with the text.

This sense of working differently with *V for Vendetta* is further emphasised by the notation upon the pages, which of course suggests the possibility that the work might be performed (i.e., sung), and since the only part presented on the page is the vocal, the act of performing the text is made easier for the reader as there is no instrumentation required. Particularly interesting here is the way in which the creators invite the reader to participate in the production of the narrative and its ideas in a physical sense, which differs from, but is nonetheless related to, the idea of V as a user of culture as a form of resistance. While the intertextuality described above enables the reader to engage with the material forms of culture that V employs throughout the text, the prelude to 'This Vicious Cabaret', and in particular the song itself, enables readers to not only encounter V but to *become* V. As Annalisa Di Liddo has marked up, the notion that the role of V is unstable and transferrable is presented within the text itself: '[. . .] Evey makes it clear for the reader that V must remain an idea, an emblem of otherness that becomes victorious when it defies those who try to annihilate it [. . .]'.[16] What is of critical importance here though is that this idea is not bound by any specific bodily markers, so it is not only Evey who could take on the role. Jordana Greenblatt writes: 'In Moore's text, not only does V represent an iconic embodiment of the possibility for human agency stripped of concrete markers of race, gender, and sexuality, but this form of subjectivity, framed as integrity, is transferable and attainable by anyone [. . .]'.[17] Anyone, we must infer, including the reader, whose attainment of the role is brought to the fore by the inclusion of the notation in the narrative. By enabling the reader to sing the song aloud, Moore and Lloyd emphasise that V's voice is coterminus with that reader's; the voice of resistance is the voice of the individual.

The visual elements of the page layout also contribute to this notion because there are two versions of the lyrics running throughout the prelude, which do not marry up precisely with each other. The first is the version "spoken" by the character of V, which is conveyed through a combination of speech balloons and caption boxes in the panels. The second is the version attached to the staves, which runs at a slightly different pace through the page; at times the lyrics on the stave are ahead of those in the panels, on other occasions they are behind. This slippage suggests a fragmentation between the diegesis and the reader's real-world environment. Where the panels represent a particular performance of the song that is limited to a specific time and place, the staves offer a guide for readers to produce their own performance, which may very well differ radically from the printed version. If the speech balloon 'is a symbol representing the idea or the notion that characters are speaking' and its tail '[shows] which character is the "I" in the balloon's "I'm speaking"', the functional stave is a gesture outwards to the reader that instructs: *You* speak.[18] In this regard it is only a partial unit; it is incomplete without the reader's performance, and it is incapable of preserving that performance in the way that the visual performance is preserved in the images that occupy the panels. In this way, audible (rather than visual) sound becomes essential to the project undertaken by Moore and Lloyd in *V for Vendetta*.

This relationship, and the importance of the reader's participation in the production of the work, may suggest that the official audio version of the song recorded by David J is somewhat problematic. Certainly it does serve to tie down the text to a particular audio form and thereby denies the reader agency that is prompted by the scored version on the pages of the book. The fact that the audio track runs for 03:23 also suggests a temporal specificity to the piece that is not, strictly speaking, found in the book (although there are time signatures in the score). Yet there are some reasons to think that this third version of the song is largely unproblematic for the text as well, because like the two printed versions of the song there are discrepancies between the printed versions and the audio one. In addition to some (admittedly very slight) lyrical differences, the audio version features more elaborate instrumentation than either of the printed versions indicates. Where the score includes only the vocal part and the panelled version shows V playing a grand piano in addition to speaking or singing the lyrics, the audio version includes string and percussion instruments; echo effects are also included at some points in the spoken lyrics. For this reason the audio version cannot be classed as an audible performance of the comic any more than the panels are just illustrations of the score. While all three versions present roughly the same words, there are variations between them that have the effect of multiplying the presence of 'This Vicious Cabaret'. The audio version is not the song as it *should* be performed, it is one version of the song in the audible mode, just as the panels are one version of the song in the visual mode. Importantly though, through their publication/recording both the visual and the audible interpretations of the song *are* fixed as existing performances of it that are embedded within a particular context. As Theodor Adorno observed of the phonograph record in an article originally published in German in 1934:

> There is no doubt that, as music is removed by the phonograph record from the realm of live production and from the imperative of artistic activity and becomes petrified, it absorbs into itself, in this process of petrification, the very life that would otherwise vanish. The dead art rescues the ephemeral and perishing art as the only one alive. Therein may lie the phonograph record's most profound justification, which cannot be impugned by an aesthetic objection to its reification. For this justification reestablishes [sic] by the very means of reification an age-old, submerged and yet warranted relationship: that between music and writing.[19]

Adorno goes on to argue that the changes that written notation has wrought upon live music may well be reversed by the (then newfound) ability to record music; we should not be surprised, he asserts, if 'music, previously conveyed by writing, suddenly itself turns into writing'.[20] If the audio version of 'This Vicious Cabaret' is one interpretation, one performance, of the notation upon the page that is petrified by recording, the visual version surely constitutes another; this is music turning into writing (in the broadest sense of the term 'writing'). These petrified versions persist; they are temporally fixed performances of 'This Vicious Cabaret' that sit within a particular historical context. In this sense they occupy the same position as the original V character within the narrative, who despite claiming, 'There's no flesh or blood within this cloak to kill. There's only an idea. Ideas are bulletproof', is subsequently proven to be human, and historically limited, after all.[21] This is not in and of itself problematic, however, because the V idea persists as a producible concept; a mantle for Evey to take up. It is important to note, though, that the Evey version of V (V2) is not the same as the original, unnamed version (V1); Evey draws upon the earlier historical figure to create a new interpretation of an existing idea, just as the reader of the book, in singing 'This Vicious Cabaret' aloud, is capable of producing an individual version of the song, one that may follow the words of the original but is presented in its own unique voice with all the implications that brings.

* * *

V for Vendetta does not represent Moore's only foray into the representation of sounds in comics, though to my knowledge it is the only one that draws the reader so concertedly into the production of the sound itself. Around the turn of the millennium, Eddie Campbell adapted two of Moore's performance pieces, *The Birth Caul* (performed in 1995; adaptation published in 1999) and *Snakes and Ladders* (performed in 1999; adaptation published in 2001) into the comics format. These two publications were subsequently collected in *A Disease of Language* in 2005, which is the version I refer to here. Each of the pieces was originally created for the stage, and included scripts that were read aloud by Moore and some additional performance elements: *Snakes and Ladders*, for example, featured a dancer. Audio content from *The Birth Caul* had also been released on CD by the time Campbell's version was published, but in the case of *Snakes and Ladders* the comics version preceded the CD. In both comics there is a strong sense that the intention is for the published versions to act not so much as adaptations of the performances but as records of them. The opening pages of *The Birth Caul* include the following introductory note:

> A shamanism of childhood. **The Birth Caul** was staged at the Old County Court in Newcastle-upon-Tyne on 18 November 1995, the first and sole performance of a new work by Alan Moore, reading to music written especially for the event by David J and Tim Perkins . . .[22]

A similar detail is included in *Snakes and Ladders:*

> Snakes & Ladders
>
> A Diversion for Wet Afternoons
>
> Containing a Faithful Record of the Oratory of Mr. Alan Moore, given upon the occasion of the 10th of April, A.D. 1999, at Red Lion Square, embellished with Multifarious Illustrations by Mr. Edward Campbell, with an assistance, including the Designs for the Pamphlet, by Mr. Michael Evans.[23]

In both these descriptions we find indications that the published versions seek to record something of the performances as whole events and to enable the reader to *navigate* them, not only to adapt the audio content. As Eddie Campbell has acknowledged, this idea underpinned his work on the books: '[. . .] part of my original thinking in illustrating *The Birth Caul* was that such a visual map would be very useful to a thorough understanding of the piece'.[24] Yet in creating such a map, Campbell does not simply provide a means for understanding the piece, he generates an alternative mode of performance that (to return to a term from Theodor Adorno) petrifies the temporal elements and unfolds them spatially upon the pages of the book. Marc Singer describes this process thus: '[Campbell's] art transforms a singular and ephemeral event into a permanent, mass-produced visual text that can freely move backwards and forwards in time without recourse to words'.[25] This certainly seems to tally with existing comics theory: Scott McCloud has suggested that the use of space to represent time is the foundation of comics as a medium; 'Space equals time', he asserted in a discussion with Robert Harvey in *The Comics Journal* in 1995.[26] Problematically, as Adorno has written elsewhere: 'Time, by its very nature, cannot be forced into identity with space; [. . .] anything organized via temporal organization [sic] is not simultaneous, but successive'.[27] Yet it is important to remember, as I stressed in section 2.1, that while the *text* may be static the reader's interaction with the *work* is necessarily temporal, and that interaction involves a modification of the work over time.

The ways in which this modification occurs can range from simple actions such as turning the pages of a book to less conventional modes of interaction prompted by more complex organisational principles. The 90° rotation in *V for Vendetta* is one very simple example of such a principle, and in *Snakes and Ladders* Eddie Campbell draws upon the recurrent snake motif to deploy another such system. While the majority of the book does follow a fairly standard page layout with a relatively common FocusMotion required for navigating it, on one page (see Figure 6.1), Campbell coils the text round the page in a spiral formation that ends at an image of a snake's head. Though it would be possible to read the text without moving the book, the easiest way to engage with it is to rotate the book as it is read. Assuming one does this to the conclusion of the text, the book is upside down by the time it has been read. Aside from the title page (which features an image of the board game with the same name as the book), this is the first time a snake appears in the book, and its function here can be understood as roughly analogous to that of the snake in the board game. The text, which deals with the presence of the snake image in various creation myths, serves to establish a context for the subsequent performance: 'Planets cool about the fresh-lit suns, last minute touches to the scenery before the play commences', reads the opening line of the text.[28] The reader is then invited to engage with the text and the work

Figure 6.1 Coiling text in Alan Moore and Eddie Campbell's *Snakes and Ladders*. Image used with the kind permission of the publisher.

simultaneously, turning the book first by 90° to read the text running down the length of the page, then a further 90° and so on. Intriguingly, because the text is arranged in a spiral, the physical length of the text in any one orientation decreases as the passage is read, meaning that a consistent reading speed will require an increasing speed of rotation (manual interaction) as the reading progresses. The reader falls increasingly quickly into the dense collection of text and images upon the page, and in this way (s)he is prepared for the recurring snake motif that is threaded throughout the work: coiling about the body of a dancer, slithering over a game board, suggested by a spiral staircase or DNA's double helix. In using the spiral layout on this page then, Campbell physically embeds the snake concept in the body of the work: the tactile experience of the rotation, the book's covers sliding over the reader's fingers and the sense that the text is gliding past the reader's eyes gives the snake a physical presence in the text that goes beyond the visual. The 'auditory signals' of the performance that 'have available to them only the linearity of time' and 'form a chain' are converted not only into static visual elements, but also tactile values that are temporally limited and truly sequential.[29] Despite being manifested spatially, *Snakes and Ladders* organises its material as a sequence of sensory experiences that is deployed temporally. Time is not, therefore, 'forced into identity with space', rather it is interwoven with space as a distinct but coexistent mode of expression (note that this is also distinct from the idea that 'space equals time' as Scott McCloud presents it).[30]

* * *

The complexities of time and space and the problems of expressing them and their properties also come to the fore in Moore's other works, which frequently serve to demonstrate Moore's ability to work with what is an ostensibly simple format and push it further than it has gone before. This is particularly evident in *Promethea,* a meditation on magic that stemmed from Moore's own journey into magical practices and has been described by Eddie Campbell as '[leading] directly' from the work undertaken in *Snakes and Ladders.*[31] The series' narrative concerns a New York college student named Sophie Bangs, who discovers the existence of, and eventually becomes, the mystical heroine Promethea. The book also integrates a lengthy treatise on the nature and structures of magic, drawing particularly heavily on Tarot and the Kaballah. Moore is immensely proud of the work, asserting in Gary Spencer Millidge's *Alan Moore: Storyteller*:

> I was still committed to progress, which I think was evidenced by [. . .] some of the incredibly experimental things we did in *Promethea,* which I think pushed the capacities, the capabilities, of a flimsy comic book about as far as I have ever personally pushed them. Some of the things we did on *Promethea* were so smugly clever that I'm still basking in the radiance three or four years later.[32]

While we do not have space here to cover the full range of 'smugly clever' techniques employed by Moore and artist J.H. Williams III plus coworkers on the thirty-two-issue series, there are a couple of examples that are worth picking up on here.

The first thing to note about the series is that just as in *V for Vendetta* and *Snakes and Ladders*, the orientation of the page is brought into play as a conveyor of meaning. The entirety of issue 11, for example, was printed at a 90° angle from the previous issues of the series, which required it to be read in landscape orientation, echoing *V for Vendetta*'s 'This Vicious Cabaret'. The cover bore a 1950s sci-fi movie poster-style image with a tagline reading 'Presented in wide-screen format exclusively by America's Best Comics' and the narrative within featured a storyline that is not wholly dissimilar to *The Blob* (dir. Irvin S. Yeaworth, Jr., 1958).[33] The interior panels follow up on the tagline's promise, stretched, as they are, across the full width of the page. As was the case in *V for Vendetta,* Moore here plays with the conventions of comics and subverts the traditional reading format, again requiring readers to move the pages from bottom to top, rather than right to left, in order to progress through the narrative.

In issue 15 the page's orientation is again brought into play in one of the series' most critically lauded technical feats: a double-page spread featuring a Möbius strip, with two different versions of Promethea (Sophie and Barbara) walking along it.[34] At various points the characters see and hear themselves at different moments in time, and the page's dialogue (which changes orientation according to the characters' positions, encouraging the reader to turn the page numerous times as (s)he reads) is structured in such a way that the sequence could go on infinitely. On one (horizontal) half of the page, the sun is in the sky, on the other the moon is. As the reader rotates the page 180° a number of times over the course of the reading these two change position, and the notions of top and bottom are thereby destabilised. This is a page that has no top or bottom, and it exposes the subjectivity of those terms by asking the reader to move the comic in such a way as to travel from day to night and back again with the characters. The twist in the Möbius strip is situated at the centre of the image, forming a visual axis for the physical rotation of the book. Just as the spiralling text in *Snakes and Ladders* served to visually stimulate the generation of a tactile experience, and thereby embedded a particular feeling in the book itself, the visual construction of the page here promotes a particular mode of tactile interaction. This emphasises that the book is not just an object to be leafed through monodirectionally; it can be interacted with in a variety of different ways. Two issues later, *Promethea* featured another double-page spread with a similar motif, albeit one that was deployed more subtly: a circular design that could be read in either direction and, like the Möbius strip, could theoretically continue indefinitely.[35] In both instances there is a strong sense that materiality matters to Moore and his colleagues; that the material form of the published comic is important. Stronger than this though is the sense that the conventions of reading are just that: socially constructed conventions applied to material objects. In *Promethea,* Moore makes this idea explicit by subverting those conventions and encouraging the reader to interact with the object in different tactile and visual ways to the more traditional top left to bottom right, front to back reading order. The comic becomes something to interact with in a very physical sense, not merely a 'transparent' vessel for the transmission of ideas.[36]

This idea permeates the series and arguably reaches its apotheosis in the final issue, which, despite being sold in the conventional comic book size and shape, takes full advantage of the physical properties of the object to create something that far exceeds what had been done with the medium before. In this issue the pages were arranged such that the work would read normally, but if the staples were removed and the pages were taken apart they could be reassembled into a very large double-sided poster that gave new meaning to the content on each of the "pages", since this content would be arranged in different ways to its original publication layout.[37] The two resultant posters (one from each side of the pages) were also sold separately, and incorporated as fold-out images in the collected editions of the series.[38] What is particularly interesting about all of these examples is the way in which they work entirely within the limits of an existing format but do things that are, if not new, certainly contrary to the traditional modes of FocusMotion and object manipulation employed within the comic book industry, and indeed publishing as a whole. The notion that we read by moving our eyes from the top left-hand corner of the *verso* page to the bottom right-hand corner of the *recto* is challenged by these sequences in *Promethea,* but without going outside what is conventional in terms of the objects themselves. Moore and those who worked with him challenge readers to see (and feel) things they have always known in new ways, and in this way they enunciate Moore's view of magic: 'Magic isn't some unfathomable and archaic new territory so much as it's something which you've been dealing with all your life in various forms, but have simply never chosen to see in those terms'.[39] This idea is also threaded throughout the narrative of *Promethea,* most noticeably in the concept of apocalypse.

The apocalypse features early in the series, presented to the Sophie version of Promethea in issue 5 by the Margaret version:

Margaret: [. . .] Jack Faust told you that Promethea was intended to end the *world.* / In a *way*, he was right. / Promethea makes people more *aware* of [the] vast immaterial realm [of ideas]. Maybe tempts them to *explore* it. / Imagine if too many people followed where she led? / It would be like the great *Devonian* leap, from *sea* to *land.* / Humanity slithering up the beach, from *one* element into *another.* / From *matter* . . . to *mind.* / We have many names for this event. We call it "the rapture." We call it "the opening of the 32nd path." / We call it the awakening, or the revelation, or the apocalypse. / But "end of the world" will do.

Sophie: Uhh, but . . . the end of the *world*. That's a *bad* thing, right?
Margaret: Is it?[40]

Over the course of the narrative, as Sophie grows more knowledgeable about the various magical realms and more powerful in her role as Promethea, she comes to accept that her role is indeed to herald the apocalypse; an act in which she is opposed by a number of the other characters in Moore's ABC publishing line. The apocalypse does nevertheless occur in issues 30–31 of the series, which the reader experiences through a direct address from Promethea: 'I'm the idea of the human *imagination* . . . / . . . which, when you think about it, is the only thing we can really be certain *isn't* imaginary'.[41] The character then goes on to elaborate a number of broad, universal concepts to the reader or, perhaps, a diegetic stand-in for the reader. Following this sequence the narrative environment that had been in place for the previous thirty issues reappears, but is changed by the revelation that world has just undergone. As Sophie emphasises, however, not everything has changed: 'Everybody *had* the revelation, but not everybody *understood* it, or took any *notice* of it'.[42] In this regard the narrative of *Promethea* echoes the material manipulations presented above. As Björn Quiring indicates, however, this relentless and comprehensive approach to the series' thematic concerns do present something of a challenge to some readers:

> If *Promethea* doesn't rank with Moore's most successful works, it's mainly due to the fact that an important dialectical ingredient is missing in it: The comic reads like an illustrated treatise most of the time, because the main protagonists are largely busy proclaiming the same kabbalistic wisdom that is also borne out by all aspects of the comic itself. The result is a pretty univocal, redundantly masterful affair.[43]

Nevertheless, it is clear that in both its narrative and the physical interactions it requires of readers, *Promethea* seeks to challenge conventional thinking on ingrained social norms; Sophie's idea that apocalypse is necessarily catastrophic is challenged, as are the notions that books must be read in a particular way, and that fiction and imagination are inherently less real than material forms. Yet in all cases these challenges are made without appeals to anomalous publication formats. For the entirety of its publication *Promethea* worked with the conventional comic book format, but through its narrative and complex visual and material communication systems, it pushed the limits of that form to their utmost and demanded that readers rethink the way they engage with comics in intellectual and physical terms alike.

***

One final work worth mentioning in this section is *The League of Extraordinary Gentlemen,* which is still in (sporadic) publication at the time of this writing. One of Moore's most high-concept publications, with pencilling by Kevin O'Neill, the series essentially presents a team-up of various preexisting fictional characters to combat preexisting fictional menaces. While each of the volumes of the series is interesting in its own ways, it is perhaps *The Black Dossier* (not strictly a sourcebook, not strictly a comic book, to paraphrase Alan Moore) that offers the most fruitful territory for exploration here.[44] The book, described by Moore as 'something fairly new [. . .] certainly unlike anything that I'd worked on before [. . .]' offered 'possibilities for us to include all sorts of things'.[45] These 'things' included a huge variety of formats within the text, including comic strips, illustrated prose, and cutaway drawings of Captain Nemo's Nautilus submarine. This work also incorporated a small 'Tijuana bible' section in the centre, and push-out glasses for viewing the 3D climax of the narrative. A vinyl record was also intended for inclusion but was only published later and with a very limited distribution.

In some ways *The Black Dossier* can be seen as a culmination of or reflection on the various means Moore has employed in working with materiality over the course of his career as a comic book writer. The idea of including a record goes back at least as far as the LP released with *V for Vendetta* and indicates a persistent interest in the nature of sound and its potential as a communicative system within comics proper. In this instance, the record is integrated into the narrative more tightly than the audio version of 'This Vicious Cabaret' was incorporated into *V for Vendetta;* it is mentioned by the characters in the book and probably serves to elaborate parts of the history of the League as the other documents presented in the text do (the narrative of *The Black Dossier* involves two of its members, Mina Murray and Allan Quartermain, attempting to escape from England to 'The Blazing World' with the eponymous dossier, which details the history of the various incarnations of their organisation). Unfortunately at the time of this writing I have not been able to access a copy of the record so cannot speak on its contents. The Tijuana bible, printed on a rough paper stock that implies the low production values of early, illicit pornographic pamphlets, is perhaps a nod towards Moore's knowledge of the histories of comics and pornography (see *Lost Girls* and *25,000 Years of Erotic Freedom*). Yet it is in the later sections of the work, presented in 3D, that the complexity of Moore and the others' vision becomes clearest, and the repercussions of his work on *Promethea* become most evident.

Although I have described the later sections of the book, which deal with Mina and Allan's arrival in the Blazing World, as 3D, this is not the whole story. Although the last pages of the book are indeed rendered in red/blue 3D format by noted 3D artist Ray Zone, there are a few sequences that make use of other techniques as well. In one, Allan and Mina enter a room with a series of portals on the wall. These are rendered in red/blue, but in such a fashion that they appear to be scribbles if the reader looks at them with both eyes open. If (s)he closes her/his left eye, though, images become clearly distinguishable; these have been rendered in red ink only and are covered with other images in green ink. Closing the left eye makes the red ink visible because the green lens allows only the red ink's colour to be perceived. Closing the right eye makes a different set of images visible. The same technique is also used later in the sequence to portray a character with two forms in the same space upon the page. Here, the ideas first outlined in *Promethea* around the notion of seeing things differently is taken to its logical extreme; images are not juxtaposed across the page in the x/y axis or even in the z axis, rather, they are juxtaposed within the same space. Space itself is multiplied through the manipulation of the reader's body in relation to very specific properties in the work. This multiplication is taken still further by the presence of multiple reading tracks upon the page: while one section of the narrative reads left to right, there is also a second narrative track running from right to left (with dialogue similarly reversed), requiring another reading of the same space upon the page. As in *Promethea,* the reader is required to avoid succumbing to conventions of reading, and to treat the comic as a spatial entity, but here a very explicit attempt is made to both subvert two-dimensional space (by juxtaposing multiple images within the same spaces) and to extend the work outwards along the z-axis into the third dimension (something we have already seen, albeit in a very different form, in our discussion of *Keep Our Secrets* in section 4.2.4). Again we find a demand from the text to rethink our approaches not only to how we read comics and how they communicate information, but also to epistemology in a broader sense: We are asked to think about how we know we should read in a particular way, and what the alternatives to this might be.

6.2 THE PROBLEM OF AUTHORSHIP

While some creators are noted for their attention to elements of materiality, such as book design and graphic design (Chris Ware being a particularly obvious example), Moore is rarely counted among this group and his grasp of the *physical* properties of comics (as opposed to their literary potential) is often overlooked.[46] Yet what I hope to have demonstrated over the course of this chapter so far is that Moore's understanding of the medium goes some way beyond an ability to distill the *visual* properties of the form down to a very effective mode of conveyance, and incorporates a number of other aspects as well. While this occasionally means, as was the case with *The League of Extraordinary Gentlemen: The Black Dossier*, integrating specific and unusual physical items (Tijuana bible, vinyl record, 3D glasses etc.) into the corporeality of the comic, this is not Moore's only means for approaching materiality. More often, Moore works within the limitations of what is a largely conventionalised format to present information and meaning in unusual ways. *Promethea* did not require a new type of publication, the entire series was presented in the standard comic book form of the era, but it does nonetheless employ the physicality of the comic book in meaningful ways. It tests the limits of that form and challenges the reader to engage with it in new ways without making demands on the publishers to make fundamental changes. Yet it is important not to fall into the trap of assuming authorial intent is limited to the actions of the commonly credited creators of comics (i.e., writer, penciller and sometimes inker, colourist, letterer and editor); we must remember the roles of publishers, printers and others in determining the material forms that comics take as well. Outside the field of completely artisanal self-publishing there are no works that are produced solely by their authors, and the various links in the chain will ultimately affect the composition of the end product. Even the production of a simple photocopied fanzine will require certain choices to be made regarding paper stock and fastening mechanisms, and these are of course historically contingent since paper and fastenings are evolving technologies. While it is certainly not practical to consider every element of a single comic's physical makeup, a broader range of foci is to be encouraged.

In some cases, broadening our perspectives in this way can reveal a distinction or contrast between the intentions of one author and the result of those intentions, something that is quite clear if we consider one final example of Moore's works: *Watchmen*. Originally published as a twelve-issue series 1986–1987, a collected edition of *Watchmen* was released in paperback in 1987. This was followed by a limited edition hardback released in association with Graphitti Designs in 1988. At the time this mode of publication was still relatively new for comics (attested to by the fact that in this case the paperback collection was issued before the hardback, the inverse of what is now the industry standard), though the success of the so-called 'big 3' (*Watchmen*, *Batman: The Dark Knight Returns* (Frank Miller) and *Maus* (Art Spiegelman)) meant it quickly became the norm to reissue comics in the graphic novel format whether they were suited to it or not.[47] While the original hardback version of *Watchmen* quickly went out of print, the paperback has remained in print since its original publication in 1986, and was relatively untouched until the twentieth anniversary of the original series prompted DC to publish a slipcased, dust-jacketed hardback edition with an attached bookmark as part of its Absolute Editions line, which featured recoloured artwork and a selection of prepublication documents. This new printing formed the basis for subsequent editions of the trade paperback.

While these reprintings certainly added prestige to *Watchmen* as an object, they did not necessarily tally with the authors' intentions. In an interview for *The Comics Journal* that was published while the single-issue serialisation of *Watchmen* was still ongoing, penciller Dave Gibbons outlined his approach to the creation of the artwork:

> What we wanted to do with *Watchmen* was make the story the paramount thing, and it seemed to me that, if the pictures were more or less

> all the same size, you'd get the same effect that you'd get in the theatre or at the cinema or even watching TV. Because the frame or the proscenium arch is always the same, you usually block it out. You don't notice it, and you get sucked into the picture that much more quickly.[48]

For readers too this idea of a direct contact between them and the text is something of a concern. Writing in a 1969 essay entitled 'Phenomenology of Reading', Georges Poulet clearly enunciated this position, asserting that the act of reading involves a striving on the part of the reader to divest the book of its very materiality:

> Books are objects. On a table, on bookshelves, in store windows, they wait for someone to come and deliver them from their materiality, from their immobility.[49]

He later elaborated:

> A book is not shut in by its contours, is not walled-up as in a fortress. It asks nothing better than to exist outside itself, or to let you exist in it. In short, the extraordinary fact in the case of a book is the falling away of the barriers between you and it. You are inside it; it is inside you; there is no longer either outside or inside.[50]

In the comic book version of *Watchmen,* the attempt at creating a transparent work that enables a contact between reader and text that is as direct as possible comes across quite strongly, and not only in Gibbons' artwork. Perhaps the most remarkable element of these comics as objects is the omission of intrusive adverts that would disrupt the narrative, a startling move on the part of DC Comics at the time, but one that serves to greatly smooth the reading experience. Yet as we move through the various other formats we encounter a *hardening* effect in the work, both metaphorically and physically; the square-bound format, unusual for comics at the time of the collected edition's publication, stands out precisely because of its strangeness. By the time we arrive at the Absolute Edition, published in a format reserved for only a relative few comics, we find a book that is literally 'walled-up as in a fortress': its thick pages ensconced within a solid slipcase, wrapped in a dust jacket and sandwiched between hard book covers, its weight at approximately 2,523 g (the combined weight of the original comic books is approximately 696 g).[51] This is *Watchmen* as a fetish, its text contained and presented in very specific material forms that take advantage of the various ways in which the object's prestige can be emphasised (see sections 2.2, 3.2.1, 4.0, 4.2.1 and 4.2.3).

This is not to say, however, that the shift to the Absolute format is necessarily a bad thing. In fact, the increased awareness of the book's presence and the ways in which it restricts the reading experience may well make it more difficult to access, requiring more thought on the part of the reader. This edition is too heavy to hold in the hands for any substantial amount of time, and perhaps too large and uncomfortable to be placed on the lap, suggesting a desk-based reading and a greater amount of concentration be warranted in its consumption. While we must of course remember Walter Benjamin's cautions on the dangers of concentration, the reader is in this case held apart from the text by its very hardness; (s)he is able to read it carefully without '[entering] into the work'.[52] Though this does somewhat negate Gibbons and colleagues' intentions regarding the reader '[getting] sucked into the picture', it also provides the facility for a critical engagement with the nuances of the text.[53] In *Watchmen*, then, we have a prime example of a work whose physical composition contrasts directly with the authorial intent, renegotiating the reader's relationship with that text by modifying materiality. At the same time, it could be argued that this cycle of republication and modification draws into question *who* the authors of *Watchmen* really are. While we must of course give credit to Moore and Gibbons and their coworkers, the act of republishing it does fundamentally alter the nature of the text in a number of meaningful ways, and conditions the reader's response to it, although these elements were not decided by the authors. For this reason, it is important to assert that while the techniques described in section 6.1 are indicative of the intelligence with which Moore uses the material forms of his comics, he is not always in control of these forms. Comics is an inherently collaborative medium, and this notion of collaboration is complicated still further when the material elements of comics are taken into account through, for example, a multisensory reading.

6.3 CONCLUSION

The comics of Alan Moore are a particularly useful corpus to examine through multisensory analysis because they clearly encapsulate what could be described as the two types of attention to materiality that have run throughout this book. On the one hand, there are creators (and I am using this term very widely) who opt to employ specific physical forms to communicate ideas using all the senses, or a select few, in very particular ways. The use of 3D glasses, a plastic cover material, and a facsimile edition of a comic are just a few examples of this approach. While this mode can lead to very effective communication systems (as seen in many of the examples described in this and other chapters of this book), it can also age badly and/or be seen as a gimmick or an inessential supplement if it is not used to its full potential. On the other hand there are those creators who do not seek to modify the material format of the comic, but nonetheless do a great deal with an existing, standardised format such as a newspaper supplement or serialised comic book. Again, Alan Moore's works demonstrate this type of presentation very effectively, but other examples of systems such as page rotation and performable music can be found elsewhere in this book. Neither approach is inherently superior, and what Moore's works demonstrate is that when they are used carefully and thoughtfully, either can produce works that transcend the limitations of a theoretical ideal perspective notion of vision and engage the reader in a complex, multisensory fashion.

In considering Moore's works in this chapter I have sought to emphasise that materiality matters, and that understanding materiality is about more than a conceptual notion of format (although that is an important element of multisensory analysis). Rather, we must strive to understand how comics affect readers in physical ways; how we can and do interact with the physical forms the medium takes. As works such as Moore's indicate, comics creators are well aware that the medium has far more communicative modes available to it than visual content in isolation, and the various comments from readers that I have drawn upon in previous chapters indicate that they too acknowledge that the pleasure and interest that lies in comics comes only partly from the medium's visual qualities. If the aim of the mechanical project is to understand how comics work, then it must surely address the medium's multisensory qualities as well.

NOTES

1. Millidge, Gary Spencer. 2011. *Alan Moore: Storyteller.* Lewes, UK: ILEX. 9; Starr, Mike, and Nathan Wiseman-Trowse. 2011. "The Magus in Marks and Spencer." *Studies in Comics* 2 (1): 3–5. 4.
2. Juno, Andrea. 2007. "Art Spiegelman." In *Art Spiegelman: Conversations*, edited by Joseph Witek, 163–190. Jackson, MS: University Press of Mississippi. 185; Murray, Chris. 2011. "Interview with The Magus." *Studies in Comics* 2 (1): 7–19. 18–19.
3. For more substantial introductions to Moore's oeuvre, see Millidge, *Alan*, and: Khoury, George. 2008. *The Extraordinary Works of Alan Moore: Indispensable Edition.* Raleigh, NC: TwoMorrows.
4. Moore, Alan, and David Lloyd. 1990. *V for Vendetta.* New York, NY: DC Comics. 6; Kibble-White, Graham. 2005. *The Ultimate Book of British Comics.* London: Allison and Busby. 276.
5. Moore and Lloyd, *V for Vendetta*, 18. Emphasis in original.
6. Lynskey, Dorian. 2011. *Protest Music Isn't Dead—It's Just Taken New Forms.* February 28. Accessed January 13, 2012. http://www.nme.com/blog/index.php?blog=146&title=today_s_protest_songs&more=1&c=1&tb=1&pb=1.
7. Gray, Maggie. 2010. "'A Fistful of Dead Roses . . .' Comics as Cultural Resistance: Alan Moore and David Lloyd's V for Vendetta." Edited by Joan Ormrod and David Huxley. *Journal of Comics and Graphic Novels* (Routledge) 1 (1): 31–49. 43.
8. Ibid.
9. Moore and Lloyd, *V for Vendetta*, 236.
10. Ibid., 89–93.
11. Ibid., 89.
12. Millidge, *Alan*, 89.
13. See section 2.5 for more on the implications and applications of page orientation.

14. Genette, Gérard. 1987 (1998). *Paratexts: Thresholds of Interpretation*. Translated by Jane E. Lewin. Cambridge, UK: Cambridge University Press. 33.
15. Groensteen, Thierry. 2007. *The System of Comics*. Translated by Bart Beaty and Nick Nguyen. Jackson, MS: University Press of Mississippi. 35.
16. Di Liddo, Annalisa. 2009. *Alan Moore: Comics as Performance, Fiction as Scalpel*. Jackson, MS: University Press of Mississippi. 115.
17. Greenblatt, Jordana. 2009. "I for Integrity: (Inter)Subjectivities and Sidekicks in Alan Moore's *V for Vendetta* and Frank Miller's *Batman: The Dark Knight Returns*." *ImageTexT: Interdisciplinary Comics Studies* 4 (3). Accessed January 18, 2012. http://www.english.ufl.edu/imagetext/archives/v4_3/greenblatt/.
18. Khordoc, Catherine. 2001. "The Comic Book's Soundtrack: Visual Sound Effects in Asterix." In *The Language of Comics: Word and Image*, edited by Robin Varnum and Christina T. Gibbons, 156–173. Jackson, MS: University Press of Mississippi. 161.
19. Adorno, Theodor W. 1990. "The Form of the Phonograph Record." *October* 55: 56–61. 59.
20. Ibid.
21. Moore and Lloyd, *V for Vendetta*, 236, 237–262.
22. Moore, Alan, and Eddie Campbell. 2005. *A Disease of Language*. London: Knockabout—Palmano Bennett. n.p.
23. Ibid.
24. Ibid.
25. Singer, Marc. 2004. "Unwrapping the Birth Caul: Word, Performance, and Image in the Comics Text." Edited by John A. Lent. *International Journal of Comic Art* 6 (1): 236–249. 243.
26. Harvey, Robert C. 1995. "Round and Round with Scott McCloud." *The Comics Journal* (179): 52–81. 64.
27. Adorno, Thefodor W. 1995. "On Some Relationships between Music and Painting." *The Musical Quarterly* 79 (1): 66–79. 69.
28. Moore and Campbell, *Disease*, n.p.
29. Saussure, Ferdinand de. 1983 (2005). *Course in General Linguistics*. Translated by Roy Harris. London: Gerald Duckworth. 70. See section 3.3 for more on this notion as it relates to comics.
30. Adorno, 'On Some', 69; Harvey, 'Round', 64.
31. Moore and Campbell, *Disease*, n.p.
32. Millidge, *Alan*, 237.
33. Moore, Alan, J.H. Williams III, and Mick Gray. 2001. *Promethea Book Two*. La Jolla, CA: WildStorm Productions. n.p.
34. Moore, Alan, J.H. Williams III, Mick Gray, and Jeromy Cox. 2002. *Promethea Book Three*. La Jolla, CA: WildStorm Productions. n.p.
35. Ibid.
36. Hatfield, Charles, and Jared Gardner. 2011. *Charles & Jared Talk Comics and Narrative Theory*. April 19. Accessed January 27, 2012. http://thepanelists.org/2011/04/charles-jared-talk-comics-and-narrative-theory/.
37. This technique was also used by Dave Sim in *Cerebus* #20; for more on this see: Wilkins, Peter. 2012. *#59: Disorient/Reorient: Cerebus #20*. March 6. Accessed March 17, 2012. http://www.graphixia.cssgn.org/2012/03/06/59-disorientreorient-cerebus-20/.
38. Millidge, *Alan*, 236.
39. Moore and Campbell, *Disease*, n.p.

40. Moore, Alan, J.H. Williams III, Mick Gray, and Charles Vess. 2000. *Promethea Book One*. La Jolla, CA: WildStorm Productions. n.p.
41. Moore, Alan, J.H. Williams III, Mick Gray, Jose Villarrubia, and Jeromy Cox. 2005. *Promethea Book Five*. La Jolla, CA: America's Best Comics. n.p.
42. Ibid.
43. Quiring, Björn. 2010. "'A Fiction That We Must Inhabit'—Sense Production in Urban Spaces According to Alan Moore and Eddie Campbell's 'From Hell.'" In *Comics and the City: Urban Space in Print, Picture and Sequence*, edited by Jörn Ahrens and Arno Meteling, 199–213. New York, NY: Continuum International. 202.
44. Nevins, Jess. 2008. *Impossible Territories: The Unofficial Companion to* The League of Extraordinary Gentlemen: The Black Dossier. Austin, TX: MonkeyBrain Books. 177–178.
45. Ibid., 178.
46. See: Kannenberg, Gene, Jr. 2001. "The Comics of Chris Ware: Text, Image and Visual Narrative Strategies." In *The Language of Comics: Word and Image*, edited by Robin Varnum and Christina T. Gibbons, 174–197. Jackson, MS: University Press of Mississippi. 190–196; Bredehoft, Thomas A. 2006. "Comics Architecture, Multidimensionality, and Time: Chris Ware's Jimmy Corrigan: The Smartest Kid on Earth." *MFS Modern Fiction Studies* (Johns Hopkins University Press) 52 (4): 869–890.; Kuhlman, Martha B. 2010. "In the Comics Workshop: Chris Ware and the Oubapo." In *The Comics of Chris Ware: Drawing Is a Way of Thinking*, edited by David M. Ball and Martha B. Kuhlman, 78–89. Jackson, MS: University Press of Mississippi. 80, 88; Raeburn, Daniel. 2004. *Chris Ware*. New Haven, CT: Yale University Press. 11, 16–17.
47. Sabin, Roger. 1993. *Adult Comics: An Introduction*. London: Routledge. 246.
48. Stewart, Bhob. 1987. "Dave Gibbons: Pebbles in a Landscape." *The Comics Journal* (116): 97–103. 100.
49. Poulet, Georges. 1969. "Phenomenology of Reading." *New Literary History* 1 (1): 53–68. 53.
50. Ibid., 54.
51. Ibid.
52. Benjamin, Walter. 2003. "The Work of Art in the Age of Its Technological Reproducibility (Second Version)." In *Walter Benjamin: Selected Writings*. Vol. 3, *1935–1938*, by Walter Benjamin, edited by Howard Eiland and Michael W. Jennings, translated by Edmund Jephcott and Harry Zohn, 101–133. Cambridge, MA: Harvard University Press. 119. Benjamin writes:

    > A person who concentrates before a work of art is absorbed by it; he enters into the work, just as, according to legend, a Chinese painter entered his completed painting while beholding it. By contrast, the distracted masses absorb the work of art into themselves. Their waves lap around it; they encompass it with their tide. This is most obvious with regard to buildings. Architecture has always offered the prototype of an artwork that is received in a state of distraction and through the collective.

53. Stewart, 'Dave', 100.

Conclusion

The central premise of this book can be concisely stated as: Comics is not just a visual medium. In making this argument over the six chapters of the book, I have sought not to attack existing scholarship on the medium but to expand it. As I argued in my introduction, the field of comics scholarship and the discipline of Comics Studies, both more stable and more formalised than they have ever been before, must now look to determine their identities and their purposes. This does not only mean asking, 'Why study comics?' but also, 'What are we studying?' Rather than getting trapped in a closed loop of definitions that endlessly refine common knowledge on the medium, what I asserted in chapter 1 was that we might more usefully consider *how we define,* the processes of definition, not just the definition in and of itself. While the arguments for comics as a series of images are for the large part valid, and may well gesture towards what is unique about the medium, we never actually encounter those unique elements in reality because we are bound to observe them on the page or the computer screen. Resultantly, no definition that emphasises what is unique will be able to account for the entirety of the medium, or to provide a comprehensive overview of its elements. I would argue that we might therefore profit from considering the common, the generic, the mundane elements of comics, how they are determined by creators, and how they affect readers. It is not the ontologically unique that is our object of study, but rather the unique *combinations* of generic elements in particular places and times.

These mundane components have, for the large part, constituted the foci of chapters 2–5. While elements such as format, gloss, hardness, temperature and the sounds and smells of comics are not unique to the medium per se, they are nonetheless relevant to Comics Studies because they are *present* in comics. The fact that they are also present in prose books and in some cases films, video games and other media does not excuse us from studying the ways they work in "our" medium. On the contrary, it compels us to do so in order that we might better understand the similarities and differences between communication systems in an increasingly mediated world. What I have attempted to provide here is a starting point, a catalogue, of the multisensory elements of comics. I do not claim it is comprehensive, and

I very much hope that it will be expanded upon by future scholars, but it does offer a selection of relevant elements that are already in use by comics creators and have already demonstrated the possibilities for communicating meaning in ways that go beyond the visual. As I indicated in chapter 2, however, this should not be taken as a wholesale critique of visuality or the visual emphasis but rather a complication of it; an argument that the *physicality* of sight and seeing is meaningful in its own way. Comics are not *only* visual, but this is not the same as saying that comics are *not* visual.

I have suggested that *performance* might be one means for better understanding the ways in which comics are consumed. In making this suggestion, I am striving to emphasise that it is not only the text that matters, but the *work,* the text as it is manifested physically, and the context (both spatial and temporal) in which it is read, along with the reader. Just as a performance of Wagner's *Ring* cycle at the Bayreuther Festspielhaus would differ from one at the Royal Albert Hall, or a showing of a film in an IMAX cinema would be different to the same film watched on a smartphone, so too does a reading of the first instalment of *V for Vendetta* in *Warrior* magazine in a school playground in 1982 vary from a reading of the same comic in its Absolute format in a university library in 2014. While there are of course other terms we might use to describe an awareness of the environment in which readings take place and the (often very active) ways they engage the reader, *performance* is one that does reasonably accurately match up to the types of elements we are describing. Of course, as I noted in section 2.0 and elsewhere, accounting for every factor of a reading and attempting to conceptualise comics as *events*—unique moments in space and time—is not practical. Nevertheless, consideration of some or all of the factors I have outlined in this book does offer a means by which we might look to expand the remit of our understanding and further develop our answers to the question, 'How do comics work?'

This expanded understanding is what I sought to both employ and develop through my consideration of the works of Alan Moore in my case study in chapter 6. As I showed there, an acknowledgement of the sensory qualities of comics can bring much to a reading of the visual text, echoing or enlarging upon the themes and ideas contained therein. Although my selection of Moore as a subject for the case study was in some senses arbitrary (in that I aimed to show that the sensory approach can be applied to any and all comics, it is not restricted to a few pioneers or fringe examples), it has also demonstrated that Moore's works have, if anything, been underestimated in the past. If Moore is indeed 'a magician' whose works comprise a 'complex and tricky oeuvre', it is not only in his work as a writer that he has accomplished these feats.[1] Moore's great works are not solely great works of words and pictures or of sequential art, they are great works of *comics* that expand the limits of what comics are and what they can be through an appeal to the reader's senses, and the intellect that those senses inform. Of course he is a purveyor of ideas, but these ideas are manifested physically within Moore's works, not only in terms of visual/linguistic abstraction. Moore and his collaborators do not only represent music and motion, they employ them in communicating. This is emphasised by a multisensory analysis of his works.

Yet my examination of Moore's comics has also indicated how closer consideration of the works of a single author or a single work might further build on the multisensory approach I have applied here. To give but one example, I would suggest that the principle of 'petrification' that I discussed with reference to the *V for Vendetta* record in section 6.1 might constitute another area to consider in building multisensory analysis beyond the catalogue provided here. While I have not had space to fully elaborate an expanded model of multisensory analysis, I would expect that if the approach were to be applied on a case-study basis in future, further categories for understanding would be uncovered.

In closing, it remains only for me to note how much work there is still to be done in the field of multisensory approaches to comics. While I have remained fairly closely focused on existing comics and for the large part utilised already published research in my writing here, the possibilities of the field and the ways in which comics are taking advantage of new technologies are vast. Giving consideration to the innovative ways in which creators engage such technologies is important. The development of sociological approaches to comics and engagement with readers and producers using social research methods will likely constitute a significant element of this consideration, as will a more sustained engagement with the growing field of sensory history and sensory theory more broadly.[2] Yet there is a second major field that bears some consideration too, specifically, the hidden readers whose existence is exposed by a number of the techniques and technologies presented here.

Consider the production of an 'Audio Edition' of Marvel's *Daredevil* #1 in 2011. The press release for this comic read:

> Since his inception in 1964, Daredevil has stood out as a unique figure in comic books: A blind man able to leap through the air and battle evil thanks to a special radar enhancing his other senses. The Man Without Fear has been a Marvel stalwart for nearly 50 years as well as a representative of the visually-impaired in popular fiction, but up to this point, those deprived of sight themselves have had to rely on friends reading them copies of DAREDEVIL in order to experience Matt Murdock's adventures.
>
> About a month ago, Marvel Senior Editor Steve Wacker came up with the idea to record an audio edition of DAREDEVIL #1 so that the visually-impaired could enjoy the dawn of a new era for DD, his friends and his enemies. Additionally, this special project provides those who can see with a new take on what's already being hailed as one of the best comics of 2011.

> DAREDEVIL writer Mark Waid provides full panel descriptions directly from his script on this audio edition, while Marvel editors Tom Brennan, Ellie Pyle and Jordan D. White lent their voices to Daredevil/ Matt Murdock, Kirsten McDuffie and Foggy Nelson, with White and Wacker also providing additional vocals. Marvel.com Video Editor Todd Wahnish recorded the piece, Marvel.com Associate Editor Ben Morse directed and Jordan White edited the final recording.
>
> Enjoy the audio edition of DAREDEVIL #1, and if you've got a friend who'se [sic] visually-impaired, please share this with them.[3]

While this audio comic is interesting enough in and of itself, what is particularly notable about it is the way in which it demonstrates Marvel's desire to engage a new audience: comics readers who cannot see. The idea that comics is a visual medium implicitly rejects the existence of this audience, but what I hope to have demonstrated in discussing works such as Ben Katchor and David Isay's audio cartoons (see section 3.3) is that there already exist ways in which it can be engaged quite directly. Further research into how blind and visually impaired readers can and do engage with comics is likely to prove fruitful in the longer term as well, and it is my hope that the research presented in this book is able to contribute to that project.

These two areas of study may well be time-consuming enough, but I doubt they exhaust the potential of approaching comics using all the senses, rather than just one. The possibilities for research into multisensory elements of comics are numerous; to unlock them one need only know where to look, or listen, or touch, or smell, or taste.

NOTES

1. Di Liddo, Annalisa. 2009. *Alan Moore: Comics as Performance, Fiction as Scalpel.* Jackson, MS: University Press of Mississippi. Cover (comment by Jeet Heer).
2. For more on the growth of sensory theory in general, see Introduction. For good introductions to some of the additional complications an engagement with sensory history specifically would bring to the fore, see: Smith, Mark M. 2007. "Producing Sense, Consuming Sense, Making Sense: Perils and Prospects for Sensory History." *Journal of Social History* 40 (4): 841–858. See also: Knapp, James A. 2003. "'Ocular Proof': Archival Revelations and Aesthetic Response." *Poetics Today* (Duke University Press) 24 (4): 695–727.
3. Marvel Entertainment LLC. 2011. "Daredevil #1 Audio Edition [News Article]." *Marvel.com.* August 23. Accessed September 25, 2011. http://marvel.com/news/story/16485/daredevil_1_audio_edition.

References

Abbot, Edwin A. 2008 (1884). "Flatland: A Romance of Many Dimensions (Illustrated)." Vers. EPUB. *Project Gutenberg*. March 10. Accessed June 27, 2010. http://www.gutenberg.org/ebooks/201.epub.noimages.

Adorno, Theodor W. 1990. "The Form of the Phonograph Record." *October* 55: 56–61.

———. 1995. "On Some Relationships between Music and Painting." *The Musical Quarterly* 79 (1): 66–79.

Alexander, Jessica D., and Lynne C. Nygaard. 2008. "Reading Voices and Hearing Text: Talker Specific Auditory Imagination in Reading." *Journal of Experimental Psychology: Human Perception and Performance* 34 (2): 446–459.

Anonymous. 1984. "WHOOPEE! (and Wow!)." London: IPC Magazine, October 27.

Anonymous. 2010. "News in Brief: Right-Handed People Choose the Best Cinema Seats for Themselves without Knowing It." *Focus*, March: 19.

Atomic Avenue Inc. n.d. *Ren & Stimpy Show*. Accessed August 25, 2011. http://www.atomicavenue.com/atomic/titledetail.aspx?TitleID=4731.

Audium. n.d. *What Is Audium?* Accessed December 14, 2010. http://www.audium.org/omhpp.cgi?src=what_is_audium.hpp.

Baetens, Jan. 2001. "Revealing Traces: A New Theory of Graphic Enunciation." In *The Language of Comics: Word and Image*, edited by Robin Varnum and Christina T. Gibbons, 145–155. Jackson, MS: University Press of Mississippi.

———. 2011. "Abstraction in Comics." Edited by Jared Gardner and David Herman. *SubStance* 40 (1 (#124)): 94–113.

———. 2011. "From Black & White to Colour and Back: What Does It Mean (Not) to Use Colour." *College Literature* 38 (3): 111–128.

Baker, Kyle. 2004. *Plastic Man: On the Lam!* New York, NY: DC Comics.

———. 2006. *Plastic Man: Rubber Bandits*. New York, NY: DC Comics.

Barker, Keith, ed. 1993. *Graphic Account: The Selection and Promotion of Graphic Novels in Libraries for Young People*. Newcastle-under-Lyme: Youth Libraries Group.

Barker, Martin. 1989. *Comics: Ideology, Power and the Critics*. Manchester: Manchester University Press.

———. 1992. *A Haunt of Fears: The Strange History of the British Horror Comics Campaign*. Jackson, MS: University Press of Mississippi.

———. 2002. "Kicked into the Gutters: Or, 'My Dad Doesn't Read Comics, He Studies Them.'" Edited by John A. Lent. *International Journal of Comic Art* 4 (1): 64–77.

Barthes, Roland. 1977. *Image, Music, Text*. Edited by Steven Heath. London: Fontana Press.

———. 2000. *Mythologies*. Translated by Annette Lavers. London: Vintage.

Bartoshuk, Linda M., and B. Valerie Duffy. 2005 (2007). "Chemical Senses: Taste and Smell." In *The Taste Culture Reader: Experiencing Food and Drink*, edited by Carolyn Korsmeyer, 25–33. Oxford: Berg.

BBC. 2010. *Turner Prize: Susan Philipsz Wins with Lowlands Away*. December 7. Accessed December 14, 2010. http://bbc.co.uk/news/entertainment-arts-11928557.

Beaty, Bart. 2007. *Unpopular Culture: Transforming the European Comic Book in the 1990s*. Toronto, Canada: University of Toronto Press.

———. 2009. "Comics Off the Page: Towards a Theory of Performance in the Comics World." *International Bande Dessinée Society Sixth Bi-Annual Conference*. London.

———. 2010. "Review: The Power of Comics: History, Form and Culture, Randy Duncan and Matthew J. Smith (2009)." Edited by Julia Round and Chris Murray. *Studies in Comics* (Intellect Ltd.) 1 (1): 179–181.

———. 2012. *Comics versus Art*. Toronto, Canada: University of Toronto Press.

Beeck, Nathalie op de. 2006. "Found Objects (Jem Cohen, Ben Katchor, Walter Benjamin)." *MFS Modern Fiction Studies* (Johns Hopkins University Press) 52 (4): 807–830.

Benjamin, Walter. 2003. "On Some Motifs in Baudelaire." In *Walter Benjamin: Selected Writings*. Vol. 4, *1938–1940*, by Walter Benjamin, edited by Howard Eiland and Michael W. Jennings, translated by Edmund Jephcott, 313–355. Cambridge, MA: Harvard University Press.

———. 2003. "The Work of Art in the Age of Its Technological Reproducibility (Second Version)." In *Walter Benjamin: Selected Writings*. Vol. 3, *1935–1938*, by Walter Benjamin, edited by Howard Eiland and Michael W. Jennings, translated by Edmund Jephcott and Harry Zohn, 101–133. Cambridge, MA: Harvard University Press.

———. 2005. "A State Monopoly on Pornography." In *Walter Benjamin: Selected Writings*. Vol. 2, Part 1, *1927–1930*, by Walter Benjamin, edited by Michael W. Jennings, Howard Eiland and Gary Smith, translated by Rodney Livingstone, 72–74. Cambridge, MA: The Belknap Press of Harvard University Press.

Berlatsky, Eric L. 2010. "Review of Annalisa Di Liddo's Alan Moore: Comics as Performance, Fiction as Scalpel." *ImageText* 5 (4). Accessed September 22, 2011. http://www.english.ufl.edu/imagetext/archives/v5_4/berlatsky/.

Beronä, David A. 2008. *Wordless Books: The Original Graphic Novels*. New York, NY: Abrams.

Blackbeard, Bill. 1974–1975. "Mislabeled Books." *Funnyworld* (16): 40–41.

———. 2003. "The Four Color Paper Trail: A Look Back." Edited by John A. Lent. *International Journal of Comic Art* 5 (2): 205–215.

Blanchard, Louis Gabriel. 1672 (2008). "Conference on the Merits of Colour." In *Art in Theory 1648–1815: An Anthology of Changing Ideas*, edited by Charles Harrison, Paul Wood and Jason Gaiger, 177–182. Oxford: Blackwell.

Bolinger, Dwight, ed. 1972. *Intonation: Selected Readings*. Harmondsworth: Penguin.

Bottorf, Michael Rhode Ray, Jr. 2001. "The Grand Comics Database (GCD): An Evolving Research Tool." Edited by John A. Lent. *International Journal of Comic Art* 3 (1): 263–274.

Bredehoft, Thomas A. 2006. "Comics Architecture, Multidimensionality, and Time: Chris Ware's Jimmy Corrigan: The Smartest Kid on Earth." *MFS Modern Fiction Studies* (Johns Hopkins University Press) 52 (4): 869–890.

Brienza, Casey. 2010. "Naturalizing Foreign Comics: How Book Publishing Companies Made Manga American." *Graphic Novels and Comics: An International Conference*. Manchester.

———. 2010. "Producing Comics Culture: A Sociological Approach to the Study of Comics." Edited by David Huxley and Joan Ormrod. *Journal of Graphic Novels and Comics* 1 (2): 105–119.

Bruno, Giuliana. 2002 (2007). *Atlas of Emotion: Journeys in Art, Architecture and Film*. New York, NY: Verso.

Bull, Michael, and Les Back, eds. 2003 (2005). *The Auditory Culture Reader*. Oxford: Berg.

Burgas, Greg. 2007. "Comics You Should Own Flashback—1963." *Comic Book Resources*. August 26. Accessed July 25, 2011. http://goodcomics.comicbookresources.com/2007/08/26/comics-you-should-own-flashback-1963/.

Butcher, Christopher. 2010. *Manga Milestones 2000–2009: 10 Manga That Changed Comics* #7. January 11. Accessed May 10, 2010. http://comics212.net/2010/01/11/manga-milestones-2000–2009–10-manga-that-changed-comics-7/.

Callahan, Timothy. 2007 (2008). *Grant Morrison: The Early Years*. Edwardsville, IL: Sequart Research and Literacy Organization.

Campbell, Dean. 2007. "Untitled Letter." *Astonishing Spider-Man* Volume 2 #6, July 11: 75.

Carlton Publishing Group. n.d. "Against All Odds 12 of the Best 'War Picture Library' Comic Books Ever!" *Carlton Publishing Group Website*. Accessed July 25, 2011. http://www.carltonbooks.co.uk/display.asp?ISB=9781853756610&.

———. n.d. "The Best of Jackie." *Carlton Publishing Group Website*. Accessed July 25, 2011. http://www.carltonbooks.co.uk/display.asp?K=9781853758010&sf1=title%5Findex&st1=jackie&y=0&sort=sort%5Fdate%2Fd&x=0&m=1&dc=6.

———. n.d. "The Best of 'Jackie' Annual." *Carlton Publishing Group Website*. Accessed July 25, 2011. http://www.carltonbooks.co.uk/display.asp?K=9781853756085&sf1=title%5Findex&st1=jackie&y=0&sort=sort%5Fdate%2Fd&x=0&m=5&dc=6.

———. n.d. "The Biggest 'Jackie' Annual Ever! The Best Thing for Girls—Next to Boys." *Carlton Publishing Group Website*. Accessed July 26, 2011. http://www.carltonbooks.co.uk/display.asp?K=9781853756672&sf1=title%5Findex&st1=jackie&sort=sort%5Fdate%2Fd&m=2&dc=6.

———. n.d. "'Jackie' Annual All Your Favourites." *Carlton Publishing Group Website*. Accessed July 25, 2011. http://www.carltonbooks.co.uk/display.asp?K=9781853756269&sf1=title%5Findex&st1=jackie&y=0&sort=sort%5Fdate%2Fd&x=0&m=3&dc=6.

Carrier, David. 2000. *The Aesthetics of Comics*. University Park, PA: Pennsylvania State University Press.

Casterman. n.d. *1968–2008 . . . N'effacez pas nos traces!* Accessed May 10, 2010. http://bd.casterman.com/albums_detail.cfm?id=11764.

CGC. n.d. *CGC Signature Series*. Accessed July 5, 2012. http://www.cgccomics.com/grading/SignatureSeries.asp.

———. n.d. *Grading*. Accessed July 5, 2012. http://www.cgccomics.com/grading/grading.asp.

Chion, Michel. 2008. "Sound Film—Worthy of the Name." In *Visual Sense: A Cultural Reader*, edited by Elizabeth Edwards and Kaushik Bhaumik, 249–254. Oxford: Berg.

Chute, Hillary L. 2006. "Decoding Comics." *Modern Fiction Studies* (Johns Hopkins University Press) 52 (4): 1014–1027.

———. 2007. "Temporality and Seriality in Spiegelman's *In The Shadow of No Towers*." *American Periodicals: A Journal of History, Criticism, and Bibliography* (Ohio State University Press) 17 (2): 228–244.

———. 2010. *Graphic Women: Life Narrative and Contemporary Comics*. New York, NY: Columbia University Press.

Cioffi, Frank L. 2001. "Disturbing Comics: The Disjunction of Word and Image in the Comics of Andrzej Mleczko, Ben Katchor, Robert Crumb, and Art Spiegelman." In *The Language of Comics: Word and Image*, edited by Robin Varnum and Christina T. Gibbons, 97–122. Jackson, MS: University Press of Mississippi.

Classen, Constance, ed. 2005. *The Book of Touch*. Oxford: Berg.

———. 2005. "The Witch's Senses: Sensory Ideologies and Transgressive Femininities from the Renaissance to Modernity." In *Empire of the Senses: The Sensual Culture Reader*, edited by David Howes, 70–84. Oxford: Berg.

Cohn, Neil. 2005. "Un-Defining 'Comics': Separating the Cultural from the Structural in Comics." Edited by John A. Lent. *International Journal of Comic Art* 7 (2): 236–248.

Conroy, Mike. 2002. *500 Great Comicbook Action Heroes*. London: Chrysalis Impact.

Cook, Steve. 2011. "Untitled Letter." *The Mighty World of Marvel* Volume 4 #22, June 8: 75.

Cooley, Heidi Rae. 2004. "It's All about the Fit: The Hand, the Mobile Screenic Device and Tactile Vision." *Journal of Visual Culture* 3 (2): 133–155.

Couch, Chris. 2000. "The Publication Formats of Comics, Graphic Novels and Tankobon." *Image and Narrative: Online Magazine of the Visual Narrative* 1 (1). Accessed December 14, 2009. http://www.imageandnarrative.be/inarchive/narratology/chriscouch.htm.

Covey, Suzanne. 2006. "Beyond the Balloon: Sound Effects and Background Text in Lynn Johnson's For Better or For Worse." *ImageText: Interdisciplinary Comics Studies* 2 (2). Accessed January 18, 2012. http://www.english.ufl.edu/imagetext/archives/v2_2/covey/.

Crane, Jordan. 2012. *Keep Our Secrets*. San Francisco, CA: McSweeny's, McMullens.

Dant, Tim. 1996. "Fetishism and the Social Value of Objects." *Sociological Review* 44 (3): 495–516. Accessed May 15, 2013 at http://eprints.lancs.ac.uk/33407/1/Fetishism_eprint.pdf; all page numbers refer to this version.

———. 2007. "The 'Pragmatics' of Material Interaction." *Journal of Consumer Culture* 8 (1): 11–33.

Deleuze, Gilles. 2008. *Proust and Signs: The Complete Text*. Translated by Richard Howard. London: Continuum.

Di Liddo, Annalisa. 2009. *Alan Moore: Comics as Performance, Fiction as Scalpel*. Jackson, MS: University Press of Mississippi.

Dines, Gail. 1995. "Toward a Critical Sociological Analysis of Cartoons." *Humor* 8 (3): 237–255.

Drobnick, Jim, ed. 2006. *The Smell Culture Reader*. Oxford: Berg.

Duncan, Randy, and Matthew J. Smith. 2009. *The Power of Comics: History, Form and Culture*. New York, NY: Continuum.

Ecke, Jochen. 2010. "Spatializing the Movie Screen: How Mainstream Cinema Is Catching Up on the Formal Potentialities of the Comic Book Page." In *Comics as a Nexus of Cultures: Essays on the Interplay of Media, Disciplines and International Perspectives*, edited by Mark Berninger, Jochen Ecke and Gideon Haberkorn, 7–20. Jefferson, NC: McFarland.

Eco, Umberto. 1972. "The Myth of Superman." *Diacritics* (Johns Hopkins University Press) 2 (1): 14–22.

———. 1987. "A Reading of Steve Canyon." In *Comic Iconoclasm Exhibition Catalogue*, edited by Sheena Wagstaff, translated by Bruce Merry, 20–25. London: Institute of Contemporary Arts.

———. 1994. *Apocalypse Postponed*. Edited by Robert Lumley. Bloomington, IN: Indiana University Press and British Film Institute.

EduComics. n.d. *Edu Comics Project*. Accessed December 13, 2010. http://www.educomics.org/.

Edwards, Elizabeth, and Kaushik Bhaumik. 2008. *Visual Sense: A Cultural Reader*. Oxford: Berg.

Einstein, Albert. 2004. *Relativity: The Special and General Theory*. Translated by Robert W. Lawson. London: The Folio Society.

Eisner, Will. 2006. *Comics and Sequential Art*. Paramus, NJ: Poorhouse Press.

———. 2006. *Graphic Storytelling and Visual Narrative*. Paramus, NJ: Poorhouse Press.

Elsaesser, Thomas, and Malte Hagener. 2010. *Film Theory: An Introduction through the Senses*. New York, NY: Routledge.

Ferguson, Frances. 1995. "Pornography: The Theory." *Critical Enquiry* 21 (3): 670–695.

Fischer, Craig, and Charles Hatfield. 2011. "Teeth, Sticks, and Bricks: Calligraphy, Graphic Focalization and Narrative Braiding in Eddie Campbell's Alec." Edited by Jared Gardner and David Herman. *SubStance* 40 (1 (#124)): 70–93.

Fisher, Adam. 2010. "Untitled Letter." *The Mighty World of Marvel* Volume 4 #12, September 1: 75.

Forceville, Charles. 2004. "Visual Representations of the Idealized Cognitive Model of Anger in the Asterix Album *La Zizanie*." *Journal of Pragmatics*: 69–88.

Fraction, Matt, and Salvador Larroca. 2010. "Invincible Iron Man #2." *Marvel Legends #51*, November 17: 3–25.

Frahm, Ole. 2000. "Weird Signs. Comics as Means of Parody." In *Comics and Culture: Analytical and Theoretical Approaches to Reading Comics*, edited by Anne Magnussen and Hans-Christian Christiansen, translated by Michael Hein, 177–191. Copenhagen: Museum Tusculanum Press and University of Copenhagen.

Fresnault-Deruelle, Pierre. 1989 (1990). "Semiotic Approaches to Figurative Narration." In *The Semiotic Web*, 587–603. Berlin: Mouton de Gruyter.

Freud, Sigmund. 1930 (2004). *Civilization and Its Discontents*. Translated by David McLintock. London: Penguin Books.

Gaiman, Neil et al. 2006–2008 (reprints material originally published 1988–2000). *The Absolute Sandman*. 4 vols. New York, NY: Vertigo.

Gardner, Jared. 2012. *Projections: Comics and the History of Twenty-First Century Storytelling*. Stanford, CA: Stanford University Press.

Gelles, David. 2011. "Action Heroes' Digital Challenge." *Financial Times*, November 8: 14.

Genette, Gérard. 1987 (1998). *Paratexts: Thresholds of Interpretation*. Translated by Jane E. Lewin. Cambridge: Cambridge University Press.

Gerber, Ernst W. 1991. *The Photo-Journal Guide to Marvel Comics*. 2 vols. Minden, NV: Gerber.

Gibbons, Dave, Chip Kidd, and Mike Essl. 2008. *Watching the Watchmen*. London: Titan Books.

Gibson, Mel. 1993. "Too Graphic? Graphic Novels in a Dual Use Library." In *Graphic Account: The Selection and Promotion of Graphic Novels in Libraries for Young People*, edited by Keith Barker, 24–27. London: Youth Libraries Group.

———. 2003. "'You Can't Read Them, They're For Boys!' British Girls, American Superhero Comics and Identity." *International Journal of Comic Art* 5 (1): 305–324.

———. 2008. "What You Read and Where You Read It, How You Get It, How You Keep It: Children, Comics and Historical Cultural Practice." *Popular Narrative Media* 1 (2): 151–167.

———. 2011. "'I Do Have the Annuals but Somehow They Are Just Not the Same as the Weeklies Printed on That Dreadfully Poor Quality Paper': British Girls'

Comics, Publication Formats and Perceptions of Class." *Materiality and Virtuality: A Conference on Comics*. Leeds.

Gifford, Denis. 1984. *The International Book of Comics*. London: Deans International Publishing.

Golden Records. n.d. *Golden Book & Record Sets Advert*. Accessed December 13, 2010. http://www.neatstuffsite.com/npics/300–1110–204b.jpg.

Gombrich, E.H. 1960 (1988). *Art and Illusion: A Study in the Psychology of Pictorial Representation*. Oxford: Phaidon Press.

Gordon, Ian. 1998. *Comic Strips and Consumer Culture: 1890–1945*. Washington, DC: Smithsonian Institution Press.

Grange, Dominique, and Jacques Tardi. 2008. *1968–2008 . . . N'effacez pas nos traces!* Tournai, Belgium: Casterman.

Gray, Maggie. 2010. "'A Fistful of Dead Roses . . .' Comics as Cultural Resistance: Alan Moore and David Lloyd's *V for Vendetta*." Edited by Joan Ormrod and David Huxley. *Journal of Comics and Graphic Novels* (Routledge) 1 (1): 31–49.

Gray, Scott, ed. 2010. *The Mighty World of Marvel* Volume 4 #12. Tunbridge Wells: Panini.

Greenblatt, Jordana. 2009. "I for Integrity: (Inter)Subjectivities and Sidekicks in Alan Moore's *V for Vendetta* and Frank Miller's *Batman: The Dark Knight Returns*." *ImageTexT: Interdisciplinary Comics Studies* 4 (3). Accessed January 18, 2012. http://www.english.ufl.edu/imagetext/archives/v4_3/greenblatt/.

Groensteen, Thierry. 2000. "Töpffer, the Originator of the Modern Comic Strip." In *Forging a New Medium: The Comic Strip in the 19th Century*, 107–114. Brussels: VUB University Press.

———. 2007. *The System of Comics*. Translated by Bart Beaty and Nick Nguyen. Jackson, MS: University Press of Mississippi.

———. 2008. "A Few Words about The System of Comics and More . . ." Edited by Laurence Grove, Mark McKinney and Ann Miller. *European Comic Art* 1 (1): 87–93.

———. 2009. "Why Are Comics Still in Search of Cultural Legitimization?" In *A Comics Studies Reader*, edited by Jeet Heer and Kent Worcester, 3–11. Jackson, MS: University Press of Mississippi.

———. 2012. "The Current State of French Comics Theory." *Scandinavian Journal of Comic Art* 1 (1): 111–122.

Gross, Richard D. 1992 (1999). *Psychology: The Science of Mind and Behaviour*. London: Hodder and Stoughton Educational.

Hague, Ian. 2012. "Adapting *Watchmen*" In *Framing Film: Cinema and the Visual Arts*, edited by Steven Allen and Laura Hubner, 37–55. Bristol: Intellect.

———. 2012. *The Nimble Scholar: An Interview with Chris Murray*. March 20. Accessed March 20, 2012. http://comicsforum.org/2012/03/20/the-nimble-scholar-an-interview-with-chris-murray-by-ian-hague/.

Hajdu, David. 2008. *The Ten Cent Plague: The Great Comic Book Scare and How It Changed America*. New York, NY: Farrar, Straus & Giroux.

Hall, Thomas, and Daniel Bradford. n.d. "Robot 13 #1." Compiled by Robot Comics. *Blacklist.com*.

Hansen, William F. 2002. *Ariadne's Thread: A Guide to International Tales Found in Classical Literature*. Ithaca, NY: Cornell University Press.

Hanshaw, Julian. 2010. *The Art of Phở*. London: Jonathan Cape.

Harvey, Robert C. 1995. "Round and Round with Scott McCloud." *The Comics Journal* (179): 52–81.

Hatfield, Charles. 2005. *Alternative Comics: An Emerging Literature*. Jackson, MS: University Press of Mississippi.

———. 2009. *The State of Comics Studies, and What to Do about It*. September 9. Accessed September 18, 2009. http://www.thoughtballoonists.com/2009/09/the-state-of-comics-studies.html.

———. 2010. "Indiscipline, or, The Condition of Comics Studies." *Transatlantica* 1–15.

———, and Jared Gardner. 2011. *Charles & Jared Talk Comics and Narrative Theory.* April 19. Accessed January 27, 2012. http://thepanelists.org/2011/04/charles-jared-talk-comics-and-narrative-theory/.

Havelock, Eric A. 1963. *Preface to Plato.* Cambridge, MA: The Belknap Press of Harvard University Press.

Hegarty, Paul. 2007. *Noise/Music: A History.* New York, NY: Continuum International.

Hergé. 1995. "The Adventures of Tintin: The Castafiore Emerald." In *The Adventures of Tintin Volume 7*, by Hergé, 1–64. London: Methuen Children's Books.

———. 2003. "The Adventures of Tintin: Land of Black Gold." In *The Adventures of Tintin Volume 5*, by Hergé, 3–64. London: Egmont Books.

Hernandez, Gilbert. 2008. *Beyond Palomar: A Love and Rockets Book.* London: Titan Books.

Hersh, Mike, Mel Smith, Shepherd Hendrix, Lance Borde, and Ken Hooper. 2008. *Gumby [Free Comic Book Day 2008] Coloring Comic Book Special #1.* Walnut Creek, CA: Wildcard Ink.

Herz, Rachel S. 2006. "I Know What I Like: Understanding Odor Preferences." In *The Smell Culture Reader*, edited by Jim Drobnick, 190–203. Oxford: Berg.

Hooke, Robert. 2005. "Micrographia: Some Physiological Descriptions of Minute Bodies Made by Magnifying Glasses with Observations and Inquiries Thereupon." Vers. EPUB. *Project Gutenberg.* March 29. Accessed March 5, 2012. http://www.gutenberg.org/ebooks/15491.epub.images.

Horn, Maurice. 1996. "The Upside Downs of Little Lady Lovekins and Old Man Muffaroo." In *100 Years of American Newspaper Comics: An Illustrated Encyclopedia,* edited by Maurice Horn, 384–385. New York, NY: Gramercy Books.

Horrocks, Dylan. 2001. "Inventing Comics: Scott McCloud's Definition of Comics." *The Comics Journal* (234): 29–39.

Howes, David, ed. 2009. *The Sixth Sense Reader.* Oxford: Berg.

Huges, Jake S., dir. 2009. *Watchmen: The Complete Motion Comic.* DVD.

Humberstone, Tom. 2009. *Getting the Smell Right.* November 29. Accessed July 25, 2011. http://solipsisticpop.com/2009/11/29/getting-the-smell-right/.

———, ed. 2009–2012. *Solipsistic Pop.* 4 vols. London: Solipsistic Pop Books.

Huxley, Aldous. 1932 (2004). *Brave New World.* London: Vintage.

Huxley, David. 2011. *A Dazzling Lack of Respectability: Comics and Academia in the UK: 1971–2011.* Edited by Ian Hague. July 29. Accessed October 4, 2011. http://comicsforum.org/2011/07/29/a-dazzling-lack-of-respectability-comics-and-academia-in-the-uk-1971—2011-by-david-huxley/.

Ihde, Don. 2003 (2005). "Auditory Imagination." In *The Auditory Culture Reader,* edited by Michael Bull and Les Back, 61–66. Oxford: Berg.

The Incredible Hulk: The Complete Collection. 2007. Graphic Imaging Technology and Marvel.

Isay, David. n.d. *Julius Knipl: Real Estate Photographer Audio Cartoons.* Accessed September 20, 2010. http://hearingvoices.com/webwork/isay/knipl.html.

Jameson, Fredric. 1991. *Postmodernism, or, The Cultural Logic of Late Capitalism.* London: Verso.

Jay, Martin. 1994. *Downcast Eyes: The Denigration of Vision in Twentieth Century French Thought.* Berkeley, CA: University of California Press.

Joe. 2009. "Solipsistic Pop—I Love the Smell of Comics in the Morning . . ." *Forbidden Planet International.* November 30. Accessed June 25, 2011. http://forbiddenplanet.co.uk/blog/2009/solipsistic-pop-i-love-the-smell-of-comics-in-the-morning/.

Juno, Andrea. 2007. "Art Spiegelman." In *Art Spiegelman: Conversations*, edited by Joseph Witek, 163–190. Jackson, MS: University Press of Mississippi.

Kannenberg, Gene, Jr. 2001. "The Comics of Chris Ware: Text, Image and Visual Narrative Strategies." In *The Language of Comics: Word and Image*, edited by Robin Varnum and Christina T. Gibbons, 174–197. Jackson, MS: University Press of Mississippi.

Katchor, Ben. 2000. *Julius Knipl: Real Estate Photographer: The Beauty Supply District*. New York, NY: Pantheon Books.

Kelly, Stephen. 2013. *How Helsinki-Based Startup Senseg Creates Touchscreens You Can Feel*. April 11. Accessed May 15, 2013. http://www.wired.co.uk/magazine/archive/2013/04/start/senseg-wants-to-bring-your-screens-to-life.

Khordoc, Catherine. 2001. "The Comic Book's Soundtrack: Visual Sound Effects in Asterix." In *The Language of Comics: Word and Image*, edited by Robin Varnum and Christina T. Gibbons, 156–173. Jackson, MS: University Press of Mississippi.

Khoury, George. 2008. *The Extraordinary Works of Alan Moore: Indispensable Edition*. Raleigh, NC: TwoMorrows.

Kibble-White, Graham. 2005. *The Ultimate Book of British Comics*. London: Allison and Busby.

Kidd, Chip. 2005. *Book One—Work: 1986–2006*. New York, NY: Rizzoli International.

King, Frank O. 2006. *Walt and Skeezix: 1923 & 1924*. Montreal, Canada: Drawn & Quarterly Books.

Knapp, James A. 2003. "'Ocular Proof': Archival Revelations and Aesthetic Response." *Poetics Today* (Duke University Press) 24 (4): 695–727.

Koda, Harold, and Andrew Bolton. 2008. *Superheroes: Fashion and Fantasy*. New York, NY: The Metropolitan Museum of Art and Yale University Press.

Kramer's Ergot. 2008. *Kramer's Ergot 7: About*. Accessed December 15, 2010. http://www.buenaventurapress.com/KE7/about.php.

Kraut, Robert. 2007. *Artworld Metaphysics*. Oxford: Oxford University Press.

Kuhlman, Martha B. 2010. "In the Comics Workshop: Chris Ware and the Oubapo." In *The Comics of Chris Ware: Drawing Is a Way of Thinking*, edited by David M. Ball and Martha B. Kuhlman, 78–89. Jackson, MS: University Press of Mississippi.

Kunzle, David. 1973. *The Early Comic Strip: Narrative Strips and Picture Stories in the European Broadsheet from c.1450 to 1825*. Berkeley, CA: University of California Press.

———. 2001. "The Voices of Silence: Willette, Steinlen and the Introduction of the Silent Strip in the Chat Noir, with a German Coda." In *The Language of Comics: Word and Image*, edited by Robin Varnum and Christina T. Gibbons, 3–18. Jackson, MS: University Press of Mississippi.

———. 2003. "Kunzle and the Comic Strip." Edited by John A. Lent. *International Journal of Comic Art* 5 (1): 3–7.

Labio, Catherine. 2009. "Turning to Art: Comic Books and Artists' Books." *International Bande Dessinée Society Sixth Bi-Annual Conference*. London.

Lacan, Jacques. 1966 (2002). *Ecrits: A Selection*. Translated by Bruce Fink. New York, NY: Norton.

Laine, Tarja. 2007. "'It's the Sense of Touch': Skin in the Making of Cinematic Consciousness." *Discourse* (Wayne State University Press) 29 (1): 35–48.

Largey, Gale, and Rod Watson. 2006. "The Sociology of Odors." In *The Smell Culture Reader*, edited by Jim Drobnick, 29–40. Oxford: Berg.

Le Brun, Charles. 1672 (2008). "Thoughts on M. Blanchard's Discourse on the Merits of Colour." In *Art in Theory 1648–1815: An Anthology of Changing Ideas*, edited by Charles Harrison, Paul Wood, and Jason Gaiger, 182–185. Oxford: Blackwell.

Lee, Stan, and Jack Kirby. 2010. "Fantastic Four #64: The Sentry Sinister." *Fantastic Four Adventures* Volume 2 #10, November 12: 52–72.

———, and George Mair. 2002. *Excelsior! The Amazing Life of Stan Lee*. London: Boxtree.

Lefèvre, Pascal. 1999. "Recovering Sensuality in Comic Theory." Edited by John A. Lent. *International Journal of Comic Art* 1 (1): 140–149.

———. 2000. "The Importance of Being 'Published'. A Comparative Study of Different Comics Formats." In *Comics and Culture: Analytical and Theoretical Approaches to Reading Comics*, edited by Anne Magnussen and Hans-Christian Christiansen, 91–105. Copenhagen: Museum Tusculanum Press and University of Copenhagen.

———. 2010. "Intertwining Verbal and Visual Elements in Printed Narratives for Adults." *Studies in Comics* 1 (1): 35–52.

Lent, John A. 2010. "The Winding, Pot-Holed Road of Comic Art Scholarship." Edited by Julia Round and Chris Murray. *Studies in Comics* (Intellect Ltd.) 1 (1): 7–33.

Lichtenstein, Roy. n.d. *Whaam!* Accessed December 15, 2010. http://www.tate.org.uk/collection/T/T00/T00897_9.jpg.

Liotard, Jean-Etienne. 2000 (2008). "Treatise on the Principles and Rules of Painting (Extract)." In *Art in Theory 1648–1815: An Anthology of Changing Idea*, edited by Charles Harrison, Paul Wood, and Jason Gaiger, 673–677. Oxford: Blackwell.

Lister, Martin, Jon Dovey, Seth Giddings, Iain Grant, and Kieran Kelly. 2003. *New Media: A Critical Introduction*. Abingdon: Routledge.

Lombard, Matthew, John A. Lent, Linda Greenwood, and Asli Tunç. 1999. "A Framework for Studying Comic Art." Edited by John A. Lent. *International Journal of Comic Art* 1 (1): 17–32.

Looby, Christopher. 2006. "'The Roots of the Orchis, the Iuli of Chesnuts': The Odor of Male Solitude." In *The Smell Culture Reader*, edited by Jim Drobnick, 289–304. Oxford: Berg.

Lukács, Georg. 1968 (1971). *History and Class Consciousness: Studies in Marxist Dialectics*. Translated by Rodney Livingstone. London: Merlin Press.

Lynskey, Dorian. 2011. *Protest Music Isn't Dead—It's Just Taken New Forms*. February 28. Accessed January 13, 2012. http://www.nme.com/blog/index.php?blog=146&title=today_s_protest_songs&more=1&c=1&tb=1&pb=1.

Mack, David. 2005. *Kabuki: Metamorphosis*. Berkeley, CA: Image Comics.

———. 2005. "The Whole-Brained Approach." In *The Education of a Comics Artist: Visual Narrative in Cartoons, Graphic Novels, and Beyond*, edited by Michael Dooley and Steven Heller, 86–90. New York, NY: Allworth Press.

MacLeod, Catriona. 2009. "Gazing at the Female in French-Language Comic Strips." *Women in Comics Conference*. Cambridge.

Manilla, Ben. 2008. *The Sounds of American Culture: NYC Mayor LaGuardia's Legendary Radio Readings*. MP3 (downloaded from http://www.npr.org/player/v2/mediaPlayer.html?action=1&t=1&islist=false&id=97621982&m=97621965, December 15, 2010).

Marks, Laura U. 2002. *Touch: Sensuous Theory and Multisensory Media*. Minneapolis, MN: University of Minnesota Press.

———. 2008. "Thinking Multisensory Culture." *Paragraph* (Edinburgh University Press) 31 (2): 123–137.

Martin, F. David. 1978. "On Perceiving Paintings and Sculpture." *Leonardo* (MIT Press) 11 (4): 287–292.

Martinson, Leslie H., dir. 1966 (2002). *Batman: The Movie*. DVD.

Marvel Entertainment LLC. 2011. "Daredevil #1 Audio Edition [News Article]." *Marvel.com*. August 23. Accessed September 25, 2011. http://marvel.com/news/story/16485/daredevil_1_audio_edition.

Marx, Karl. 1990. *Capital: A Critique of Political Economy*. Translated by Ben Fowkes. Vol. 1 of 2 vols. London: Penguin Books.

Mazzucchelli, David. 2009. *Asterios Polyp*. New York, NY: Pantheon Books.
McCloud, Scott. 1993. *Understanding Comics: The Invisible Art*. New York, NY: HarperPerennial.
———. 2000. *Reinventing Comics*. New York, NY: Paradox Press.
———. 2006. *Making Comics: Storytelling Secrets of Comics, Manga and Graphic Novels*. New York, NY: HarperCollins.
———. 2009. *Scott McCloud on Comics*. Online video. Produced by TED. Performed by Scott McCloud. Accessed September 25, 2011. http://www.ted.com/talks/scott_mccloud_on_comics.html.
McCormick, Barry. 1988 (1992). "Basic Acoustics." In *Constructing Deafness*, edited by Susan Gregory and Gillian M. Hartley, 84–86. London: Pinter Publishers in association with the Open University.
Men Without Fear: Creating Daredevil. 2003. DVD. Produced by Eric Young.
Meskin, Aaron. 2007. "Defining Comics?" *The Journal of Aesthetics and Art Criticism* 65 (4): 369–379.
Miller, Ann. 2007. *Reading Bande Dessinée*. Bristol: Intellect Books.
Millidge, Gary Spencer. 2009. *Comic Book Design*. Lewes: ILEX.
———. 2011. *Alan Moore: Storyteller*. Lewes: ILEX.
Montagu, Ashley. 1986. *Touching: Human Significance of the Skin*. 3rd ed. New York, NY: Harper.
Moore, Alan, and Eddie Campbell. 2005. *A Disease of Language*. London: Knockabout—Palmano Bennett.
———. 2006. *From Hell: Being a Melodrama in Sixteen Parts*. London: Knockabout Comics.
Moore, Alan, Melinda Gebbie, and Todd Klein. 2009. *Lost Girls*. Marietta, GA: Top Shelf Productions.
Moore, Alan, Dave Gibbons, and John Higgins. 1986–1987. *Watchmen*. Edited by Len Wein and Barbara Randall. 12 vols. New York, NY: DC Comics.
———. 1987. *Watchmen*. New York, NY: DC Comics.
———. 2005. *Absolute Watchmen*. New York, NY: DC Comics.
———. 2007. *Watchmen*. 2007 British TPB. London: Titan Books.
Moore, Alan, and David Lloyd. 1990. *V for Vendetta*. New York, NY: DC Comics.
Moore, Alan, and Kevin O'Neill. 2007. *The League of Extraordinary Gentlemen: The Black Dossier*. La Jolla, CA: WildStorm Productions.
Moore, Alan, Rick Veitch, and Steve Bissette. 1993. *1963*. 6 vols. Fullerton, CA: Image Comics.
Moore, Alan, J.H. Williams III, and Mick Gray. 2001. *Promethea Book Two*. La Jolla, CA: WildStorm Productions.
Moore, Alan, J.H. Williams III, Mick Gray, and Jeromy Cox. 2002. *Promethea Book Three*. La Jolla, CA: WildStorm Productions.
———. 2003. *Promethea Book Four*. La Jolla, CA: WildStorm Productions.
Moore, Alan, J.H. Williams III, Mick Gray, and Charles Vess. 2000. *Promethea Book One*. La Jolla, CA: WildStorm Productions.
Moore, Alan, J.H. Williams III, Mick Gray, Jose Villarrubia, and Jeromy Cox. 2005. *Promethea Book Five*. La Jolla, CA: America's Best Comics.
Morris, Robert. 1966–1967 (2007). "Notes on Sculpture." In *Art in Theory 1900–2000: An Anthology of Changing Ideas*, edited by Charles Harrison and Paul Wood, 828–835. Oxford: Blackwell.
Morrison, Grant, and Doug Mahnke. 2009. "Superman Beyond #1." *Superman Legends* #26, July/August: n.p.
———. 2009. "Superman Beyond #2 (Extract)." *Batman Legends Volume 2 #31*, August/September: n.p.
———. 2009. "Superman Beyond #2 (Extract)." *Superman Legends* #26, July/August: n.p.

Morrison, Grant, and John Van Fleet. 2007. *Batman*. No. 663. New York, NY: DC Comics.

Murray, Chris. 2011. "Interview with The Magus." *Studies in Comics* 2 (1): 7–19.

Nagel, Thomas. 1986. *The View from Nowhere*. New York, NY: Oxford University Press.

Nevins, Jess. 2008. *Impossible Territories: The Unofficial Companion to* The League of Extraordinary Gentlemen: The Black Dossier. Austin, TX: MonkeyBrain Books.

Nielsen, Jesper, and Søren Wichmann. 2000. "America's First Comics? Techniques, Contents, and Functions of Sequential Text-Image Pairing in the Classical Maya Period." In *Comics and Culture: Analytical and Theoretical Approaches to Reading Comics*, 59–77. Copenhagen: Museum Tusculanum Press and University of Copenhagen.

Noise Collector. 2005. *Sample: Guitarsolo1.wav*. July 8. Accessed November 26, 2010. http://www.freesound.org/samplesViewSingle.php?id=3649.

Nuckolls, Janis B. 1999. "The Case for Sound Symbolism." *Annual Review of Anthropology* 28: 225–252.

O'Malley, Bryan Lee. 2010. "Scott Pilgrim's Precious Little App." Compiled by Robot Media SL. London: HarperCollins.

Overstreet, Robert M., and Arnold T. Blumberg. 2006. *The Official Overstreet Comic Book Grading Guide*. 3rd ed. New York, NY: Gemstone.

Paterson, Mark W. D. 2005. "Digital Touch." In *The Book of Touch*, edited by Constance Classen, 431–436. Oxford: Berg.

———. 2006. "Digital Scratch and Virtual Sniff: Simulating Scents." In *The Smell Culture Reader*, edited by Jim Drobnick, 358–367. Oxford: Berg.

Penneveninders. 2010. *Penneveninder*. Vol. 1. *Coretoon.dk*.

Perricone, Christopher. 2006. "The Aspiration to the Condition of Touch." *Philosophy and Literature* 30 (1): 229–237.

———. 2007. "The Place of Touch in the Arts." *Journal of Aesthetic Education* (University of Illinois Press) 41 (1): 90–104.

Petersen, Robert S. 2009. "The Acoustics of Manga." In *A Comics Studies Reader*, edited by Jeet Heer and Kent Worcester, 163–171. Jackson, MS: University of Mississippi Press.

Peynaud, Emile. 2005. "Tasting Problems and Errors of Perception." In *The Taste Culture Reader: Experiencing Food and Drink*, edited by Carolyn Korsmeyer, 272–278. Oxford: Berg.

Pilcher, Tim. 2008. "Erotic Comics [Panel Discussion]." *Comica Festival 2008*. London.

Pilcher, Tim, and Gene Kannenberg, Jr. 2008. *Erotic Comics: A Graphic History from Tijuana Bibles to Underground Comix*. New York, NY: Abrams.

———. 2009. *Erotic Comics 2: A Graphic History from the Liberated '70s to the Internet*. New York, NY: Abrams.

Pollmann, Joost. 1999. "An Art of the Real: About the Adulthood of Contemporary Comics." Edited by John A. Lent. *International Journal of Comic Art* 1 (2): 107–126.

———. 2001. "Shaping Sounds in Comics." Edited by John A. Lent. *International Journal of Comic Art* 3 (1): 9–21.

Poulet, Georges. 1969. "Phenomenology of Reading." *New Literary History* 1 (1): 53–68.

Priego, Ernesto. 2010. "Floppy Things with Staples: Comics and Materiality in the Digital Age." *Graphic Novels and Comics Conference*. Manchester.

———. 2010. "On Cultural Materialism, Comics and Digital Media." *Opticon 1826*, 1–3.

———. 2011. *Interview with Roger Sabin*. December 5. Accessed March 16, 2012. http://www.comicsgrid.com/2011/12/roger-sabin-interview/.

Proof Spirit. n.d. *Cardboard Comics*. Vol. 1. Proof Spirit.

Proust, Marcel. 2006. *Remembrance of Things Past.* Translated by C.K. Scott Moncrieff and Stephen Hudson. 2 vols. Ware, Hertfordshire, UK: Wordsworth Editions.

Pustz, Matthew J. 1999. *Comic Book Culture: Fanboys and True Believers.* Jackson, MS: University Press of Mississippi.

Quiring, Björn. 2010. "'A Fiction That We Must Inhabit'—Sense Production in Urban Spaces According to Alan Moore and Eddie Campbell's 'From Hell.'" In *Comics and the City: Urban Space in Print, Picture and Sequence,* edited by Jörn Ahrens and Arno Meteling, 199–213. New York, NY: Continuum International.

Raeburn, Daniel. 2004. *Chris Ware.* New Haven, CT: Yale University Press.

Rée, Jonathan. 1999. *I See a Voice: Language, Deafness and the Senses—A Philosophical History.* London: Harper Collins.

Reed, Bill. 2007. "365 Reasons to Love Comics #342 [The Smell]." *Comic Book Resources.* December 8. Accessed July 25, 2011. http://goodcomics.comicbookresources.com/2007/12/08/365-reasons-to-love-comics-342/.

Rogers, Mark C. 2001. "Ideology in Four Colours: British Cultural Studies Do Comics." Edited by John A. Lent. *International Journal of Comic Art* 3 (1): 93–108.

Rosenkranz, Patrick. 2008. *Rebel Visions: The Underground Comix Revolution 1963–1975.* Seattle, WA: Fantagraphics Books.

Russell, Bertrand. 1997. *The ABC of Relativity.* London: Routledge.

Sabin, Roger. 1993. *Adult Comics: An Introduction.* London: Routledge.

———. 2000. "The Crisis in Modern American and British Comics, and the Possibilities of the Internet as a Solution." In *Comics and Culture: Analytical and Theoretical Approaches to Reading Comics,* edited by Anne Magnussen and Hans-Christian Christiansen, 43–57. Copenhagen: Museum Tusculanum Press and University of Copenhagen.

———. 2009. "Ally Sloper: The First Comics Superstar?" In *A Comics Studies Reader,* edited by Jeet Heer and Kent Worcester, 177–189. Jackson, MS: University Press of Mississippi.

———. 2009. "Mavericks and Zinesters: Comics Scholarship in the UK before 'Comics Scholarship.'" *Possibilities and Perspectives: A Conference on Comics.* Leeds.

Sanders, Joe Sutliff. 2011. "Valentine, Mobile Comics and Participatory Readers." *First International Conference on Comics and Graphic Novels: Sites of Visual and Textual Innovation.* Alcalá de Henares.

Saraceni, Mario. 2003. *The Language of Comics.* London: Routledge.

Saussure, Ferdinand de. 1983 (2005). *Course in General Linguistics.* Translated by Roy Harris. London: Gerald Duckworth.

Schiffman, Harvey Richard. 1996. *Sensation and Perception: An Integrated Approach.* 4th ed. New York, NY: Wiley.

Shaff, Stanley. 2002. "AUDIUM: Sound-Sculptured Space." *Leonardo* (The MIT Press) 35 (3): 248.

Shelton, James D. 2010. "Masturbation: Breaking the Silence." *International Perspectives on Sexual and Reproductive Health* 36 (3): 157–158.

Shepherd, John. 1991. *Music as Social Text.* Cambridge: Polity Press.

Siegel, Jerry, and Joe Shuster. 2006. *The Superman Chronicles.* Vol. 1. New York, NY: DC Comics.

Singer, Marc. 2004. "Unwrapping the Birth Caul: Word, Performance, and Image in the Comics Text." Edited by John A. Lent. *International Journal of Comic Art* 6 (1): 236–249.

Sjoerdsma, Al. n.d. *Audio: Golden Records: Amazing Spider-Man #1 [Review].* Accessed December 13, 2010. http://www.spiderfan.org/audio/reviews/spiderman_record_comics/golden_records_asm1.html.

Skinn, Dez. 2004. *Comix: The Underground Revolution*. Brighton: Quality Communications.
Smith, Jeff. 2010. *RASL* #8. Columbus, OH: Cartoon Books.
Smith, Mark M. 2007. "Producing Sense, Consuming Sense, Making Sense: Perils and Prospects for Sensory History." *Journal of Social History* 40 (4): 841–858.
Spiegelman, Art. 2003. *The Complete Maus*. London: Penguin Books.
———. 2004. *In the Shadow of No Towers*. New York, NY: Pantheon Books.
———. 2008. *Breakdowns: A Portrait of the Artist as a Young %@&*!* London: Penguin.
———. 2011. *MetaMaus*. London: Viking (Penguin Group).
Spiegelman, Art, and Chip Kidd. 2001. *Jack Cole and Plastic Man: Forms Stretched to their Limits!* New York, NY: Chronicle Books.
Starr, Mike, and Nathan Wiseman-Trowse. 2011. "The Magus in Marks and Spencer." *Studies in Comics* 2 (1): 3–5.
Steranko, Jim, Joe Sinnott, and Sam Rosen. 2004. "Strange Tales #166 [Excerpt]." *The Mighty World of Marvel* Volume 3 #23, December 1: 40–51.
Stewart, Bhob. 1987. "Dave Gibbons: Pebbles in a Landscape." *The Comics Journal* (116): 97–103.
———. 1988. "Bubbling Over." *Blab!*, September: 21–35.
Sunday Press Books. n.d. *What the World Is Saying about LITTLE NEMO IN SLUMBERLAND—SPLENDID SUNDAYS*. Accessed March 22, 2011. http://www.sundaypressbooks.com/testimonials.htm.
Swanson, Gunnar. 2005. "The Four Tribes of Comics: [Interview with] Scott McCloud." In *The Education of a Comics Artist*, edited by Michael Dooley and Steven Heller, 204–209. New York, NY: Allworth Press.
Talbot, Bryan. 2007. *Alice in Sunderland, or, A Night at the Empire: An Entertainment*. London: Jonathan Cape.
———. 2009. "Style and Storytelling Technique in 'The Tale of One Bad Rat'." *Possibilities and Perspectives: A Conference on Comics*. Leeds.
Taylor, Todd. 2001. "If He Catches You, You're Through: Coyotes and Visual Ethos." In *The Language of Comics: Word and Image*, edited by Robin Varnum and Christina T. Gibbons, 40–59. Jackson, MS: University Press of Mississippi.
Thompson, Michael. 1977 (2006). "An Anatomy of Rubbish." In *Arts in Society*, edited by Paul Barker, 40–46. Nottingham: Five Leaves.
Tynan, Dan. 2006. *The 25 Worst Tech Products of All Time: Numbers 21 to 25*. May 26. Accessed May 10, 2010. http://www.pcworld.com/article/125772-6/the_25_worst_tech_products_of_all_time.html.
Vance, Ashlee. 2011. *Haptics Adds New Dimensions to Touchscreens*. June 16. Accessed June 27, 2011. http://www.businessweek.com/magazine/content/11_26/b4234043549730.htm.
Varnum, Robin, and Christina T. Gibbons. 2001. *The Language of Comics: Word and Image*. Jackson, MS: University of Mississippi Press.
Vasseleu, Cathryn. 1998. *Textures of Light: Vision and Touch in Irigaray, Levinas and Merleau-Ponty*. New York, NY: Routledge.
Verhoeff, Nanna. 2009. "Theoretical Consoles: Concepts for Gadget Analysis." *Journal of Visual Culture* 8 (3): 279–298.
Versaci, Rocco. 2007. *This Book Contains Graphic Language: Comics as Literature*. New York, NY: Continuum International.
Versluys, Kristiaan. 2006. "Art Spiegelman's In the Shadow of No Towers: 9/11 and the Representation of Trauma." *MFS Modern Fiction Studies* 52 (4): 980–1003.
von Götha, Erich. 1984. *Torrid: The Baron's Own Picture Book*. Vol. 12. Whyteleafe: Gold Star.

Walton, Saige. 2009. "Baroque Mutants in the 21st Century? Rethinking Genre through the Superhero." In *The Contemporary Comic Book Superhero*, edited by Angela Ndalianis, 86–106. New York, NY: Routledge.
Ware, Chris. 2001 (2005). *Jimmy Corrigan: The Smartest Kid on Earth*. London: Jonathan Cape.
Warzecha, Jason. 2010. "Untitled Letter." *RASL* #8, July.
Watterson, Bill. 1995. *The Calvin and Hobbes Tenth Anniversary Book*. London: Warner Books.
Whitlock, Gillian. 2006. "Autographics: The Seeing 'I' of the Comics." *MFS Modern Fiction Studies* 52 (4): 965–979.
Wilkins, Peter. 2012. *#59: Disorient/Reorient: Cerebus #20*. March 6. Accessed March 17, 2012. http://www.graphixia.cssgn.org/2012/03/06/59-disorientreorient-cerebus-20/.
Will Eisner Studios & U.S. Army. 1969. *The M16A1 Rifle: Operation and Preventative Maintenance*. U.S. Army.
Williams, Mark. 2007. "Untitled Letter." *Astonishing Spider-Man* Volume 2 #9, August 22: 75.
Windsor-Smith, Barry. 2003. *Young GODS & Friends*. Seattle, WA: Fantagraphics Books.
Winter, J. B. 2008. *Edible 24 Hour Comic*. November 1. Accessed August 23, 2011. http://www.jbwinter.com/2008/10/edible-24-hour-comic.html.
Witek, Joseph. 1989. *Comic Books as History: The Narrative Art of Jack Jackson, Art Spiegelman, and Harvey Pekar*. Jackson, MS: University Press of Mississippi.
———. 1999. "Comics Criticism in the United States: A Brief Historical Survey." Edited by John A. Lent. *International Journal of Comic Art* 1 (1): 4–16.
———, ed. 2007. *Art Spiegelman: Conversations*. Jackson, MS: University Press of Mississippi.
———. 2009. "The Arrow and the Grid." In *A Comics Studies Reader*, edited by Jeet Heer and Kent Worcester, 149–156. Jackson, MS: University Press of Mississippi.
Wolk, Douglas. 2007. *Reading Comics: How Graphic Novels Work and What They Mean*. Cambridge, MA: Da Capo Press.
Woo, Benjamin. 2011. "The Android's Dungeon: Comic-Bookstores, Cultural Spaces, and the Social Practices of Audiences." Edited by David Huxley and Joan Ormrod. *Journal of Graphic Novels and Comics* 2 (2): 125–136.
Wood, Brian, and Ryan Kelly. 2008. *Local*. Portland, OR: Oni Press.
Worth, Jennifer. 2007. "Unveiling Persepolis as Embodied Performance." *Theatre Research International* 32 (2): 143–160.
Yawn, Brother, and Grant Morrison. 2002. "Interview with an Umpire." *Barbelith*. Accessed June 14, 2011. http://www.barbelith.com/old/interviews/interview_1.shtml.

Index

Printed in Great Britain
by Amazon

49150172R00123